JULIAN E. HOCHBERG

Professor of Psychology
Columbia University

second edition

Perception

PRENTICE-HALL, INC., ENGLEWOOD CLIFFS, NEW JERSEY 07632

Library of Congress Cataloging in Publication Data

HOCHBERG, JULIAN E
    Perception.

    Bibliography: p.
    Includes index.
    1. Perception. I. Title.
BF311.H58 1978   153.7   77-27274
ISBN 0-13-657106-9
ISBN 0-13-657098-4 pbk.

FOUNDATIONS OF MODERN PSYCHOLOGY SERIES
Richard S. Lazarus, Editor

© *1978, 1964 by*
Prentice-Hall, Inc., Englewood Cliffs, N.J. 07632

10 9 8 7 6 5 4 3 2

Prentice-Hall International, Inc., London
Prentice-Hall of Australia Pty. Limited, Sydney
Prentice-Hall of Canada, Ltd., Toronto
Prentice-Hall of India Private Limited, New Delhi
Prentice-Hall of Japan, Inc., Tokyo
Prentice-Hall of Southeast Asia Pte. Ltd., Singapore
Whitehall Books Limited, Wellington, New Zealand

Contents

SIX

SEVEN

Preface

to the First Edition

Perception is one of the oldest subjects of speculation and research in the study of man, with a correspondingly long history of theory and fact. I have tried to keep this brief introduction open to new approaches and possibilities, but at the same time conservative—as a science must be if it is to profit from the inquiry of previous centuries.

This dual aim requires a rather condensed treatment of this increasingly technical discipline; however, details are presented only in the context of the broader questions that make them important, and the more demanding material has been collected in plates that may be skipped without serious loss to the overall discussion. Figures in this latter category are: 39, 49, 50, 51, 52, 54, 65 and 71 (2nd edition) these aside the figures and their captions should be treated as integral parts of the text, since pictorial display has been used mainly as a substitute for (not as a supplement to) written exposition.

The reader is also urged to follow the order of the chapters, since there is a close development from one to the next as we pursue the general question of "Why things look as they do."

to the Second Edition

The first edition has been largely rewritten, and a chapter added, to accommodate the advances (and revisions) that have been made since then in our knowledge about perception and its neighboring disciplines. I have again tried, wherever possible, to discuss research findings and problems in terms of the theoretical settings which gave them purpose. My own theoretical stance is essentially a "constructivist" one, close to what I see as the core of Hebb's and of Neisser's positions, and the order of the topics reflects both that orientation and my effort to maintain an historical perspective throughout.

Julian E. Hochberg

Introduction

chapter one

A. *The Study of Perception*

We study perception in order to explain our observations of the world around us. Some of the reasons for undertaking this study are specific and practical. Some are general and theoretical, and arise out of the very old problem of how man comes to know his world.

In fact, the study of perception started long before a science of psychology existed. A great deal of the early research in this area was the work of physiologists and physicists, and many important contributions to perceptual psychology were made by men who are not usually thought of as psychologists. This is still true today because the problems of perception cut across other sciences: We cannot begin to understand human perception of the world unless we also understand something about the world as a set of physical events and about the human being as a physiological structure.

THE OBSERVATIONS TO BE EXPLAINED

It is not enough to say that the study of perception is concerned with the observations of the world: so are physics, chemistry, and all the other sciences. Moreover, as we shall see, these physical sciences are capable of completely explaining the world and everything in it—at least in principle. Why, then, do we need a separate study of *perception?* We may first become concerned about the perceptual process in the context of the following kinds of problems:

1. *When our observation turns out to be in error,* and damaging accidents occur (misjudging an aircraft landing or automobile traffic conditions) or awkward social situations develop (mistaking someone's anger for joy). Such occasions of mistaken perceptions, or *illusions* (in which there are discrepancies between the perceived world and the physical world) call for the study of the processes that are responsible for our perceptions. The general question of the trustworthiness of our "senses" has intrigued philosophers for centuries. More prosaically, many persons in technical professions (such as traffic safety engineers) are concerned with eliminating misperceptions, and at least as many are concerned with causing them— beauticians, fashion designers, and above all, artists and filmmakers.

2. *We may want to replace the real world by some specially prepared substitutes* (or *surrogates*) such as pictures, TV, or hi-fi, to which observers will respond as they would have responded to the real objects or events.

3. *We may wish to use a machine to replace a human observer.* In this case, we must first find out exactly what the machine has to do if it is to replace, say, a human plane spotter, map reader, or apple sorter. Frequently, only the end result is important: The automatic door opener at the supermarket does not have to *see* you in the same way that a doorman must in order to do his job. Sometimes, however, our real purpose in designing such a machine is to show that we understand how human perceivers, as biophysical mechanisms, operate; in that case, we must first examine the human perceptual process in great detail in order to know what it is we are trying to simulate.

4. *We may wish to discover the bodily processes upon which our perceptions depend.* For example, when we seek to understand and remedy sensory defects (such as poor vision or hearing), we must study how our sensory organs contribute to our perception of the world; when we seek to understand the effects of more central factors (such as the disturbances produced by drugs or by brain lesions), we must in addition study how the activities of the central nervous system contribute to perception.

PERCEPTION, PHYSICS, AND PSYCHOLOGY

There are vast differences between the "real," or physical, world as it is defined and measured by the instruments of physical science and the perceived world of normal, unaided observation.[1] Four kinds of differences will be important to us in this book:

1. Many physical events cannot be observed at all by the unaided sense organs: the too-large, the too-small, and the energies for which we lack sensory organs such as harmful radiation from X-rays or from nuclear fission. Physical science needs instruments to detect what our senses cannot. (We discuss these limitations in Chapter 2.) The reverse is also true. There are many properties for which no physical instruments can presently be devised such as tastiness, sexual attractiveness, and artistic quality.

2. What we perceive is never in exact correspondence with the physical situation. Some aspects are omitted, some added, some distorted. An *illusion,* such as that in Figure 1, exists when observations made with the aid of physical instruments yield different results from observations made without such instruments. In fact, most of the perceived qualities of the world (*size, color, weight,* and so on) are only very loosely related to the physical measurements to which we have given the same names. (Illusions will be discussed in Chapter 4.)

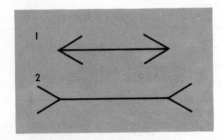

FIGURE 1. Perceived length vs. measured length. The Mueller-Lyer pattern shown here is an "illusion": Are lines 1 and 2 of equal length? As measured by some physical instrument (a ruler, for example), they are both about one inch in length. As observed without such aids, 1 appears shorter than 2.

3. Even if some event can *affect our sense organs, there is no guarantee that we will perceive it.* We first must look at an object, of course, before we can see it, but we may not be able to see even what we *do* look at: Certain "organizational" requirements must be

[1] This does not imply that the physical world is more or less "real" than the perceived world, inasmuch as the term "reality" has no specific scientific meaning; however, the physical world is consistent in ways that, as we shall see, the perceived world is not—and vice versa.

met. These are not easy to explain at this point, but we shall discuss them in Chapters 4 and 5. For now, though, we can illustrate this point. Look at Figure 2*A*. It contains a picture of an old woman. The picture is not covered up in any way. Each part of that picture is just as exposed to your gaze as are those of the young woman (in fact, the same parts do double duty). Can you see it? Can you read the hieroglyphics in Figure 2*B*? If you turn to footnotes A. and B. on p. 7, you will then be able to observe these previously invisible objects. For advertising or courting purposes, it is desirable to be highly visible. For concealing oneself from unfriendly eyes, it is good to be invisible. Both man and nature have developed effective techniques for achieving these ends (Figure 2*C, D*).

A.

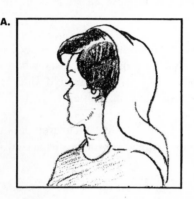

FIGURE 2. Objects may be physically present, yet they may not be observable. *(A.)* Can you see the old woman? (After Boring.) Every *part* is clearly visible. *(B.)* Can you read the symbols in the row? *(C.)* Artificial invisibility: man-made camouflage. *(D.)* Natural self-effacement: "protective coloration."

B.

C.

D.

In addition, two observers may respond very differently to the same event, even though it confronts their sense organs equally. Such differences may arise because the two observers have not had the same history of perceptual learning, a factor that is most clearly evident in reading and listening to speech, a topic we consider in Chapter 6B. Or such differences may arise because the two observers do not *pay attention* to the event in the same way, a vitally important factor discussed in Chapter 6B and C. For example, you can look at this page with no intention to read it at all; you can skim it, with the intention of extracting its meaning; or you can search for misspellings (there are two on this page). The same page of text results in different perceptions, depending on how you deploy your attention; we will see that we cannot really discuss perception at all without discusing as well the observer's attention and intention.

In short, the perceived world is not identical to the world we learn about through physical measures, and one of the primary tasks of the study of perception is to discover the relationship between these two worlds. This study cannot be a *purely* psychological discipline, because physics and mathematics are needed to determine what physical energies act upon our sense organs. On the other hand, no amount of study of the physical energies alone, nor of the physiological structure alone, well teach us anything about perception.

The study of perception is therefore *primarily* psychological. In fact, the problems of perception were once central to all other fields of study in psychology. Until the early part of this century, the main aim of psychology was to explain all of the possible thoughts or ideas we have by their origin in past and present sensory experience (see Chapter 4A). This goal has been pretty much abandoned, and perception has vacated the central position it once maintained. As a discipline in its own right, however, perception is still usually regarded as "basic," even though the attempt to rest all of psychology upon it is no longer seriously entertained.

B. *Outline of the Book*

We will discuss the topic of perception primarily as a set of scientific problems, problems that permit factual answers. This approach leaves out a great deal of what has been said on the subject. At the same time, we will try to consider research problems and findings in terms of relevance either to practical application, to the furtherance of coherent human knowledge, or both.

In Chapters 2 and 3 we shall survey the study of how we perceive very simple physical events such as a spot of light of a particular wavelength or a sound wave of a particular frequency. Many psychologists still view the results of such research as the basic groundwork on which our other perceptual knowledge must rest. Otherwise, this research is mainly of interest to sensory physiologists, to the medical profession, and to engineers who design signal lights, instrument panels, high-fidelity sound and video systems, set the limits for how much noise a landing aircraft can make at a given airport, and so on.

In Chapter 4, we shall consider attempts to use these findings to explain how we perceive the world, and the difficulties that confront these attempts. The major theoretical approach we start with is *classical structuralism,* an attempt to explain perception in terms of simply sensory experiences (based on the activities of identifiable sensory *receptors*) and the elaboration of these by more cognitive processes (based on the perceptual learning we undergo in interacting with the world of objects and people). This theory, although wrong in some basic respects, is important to us because it sets the problems that later approaches are attempts to solve, and because it provides the viewpoint from which most other disciplines regard perceptual psychology. In the last decade, moreover, certain central features of the classical approach have undergone a vigorous (if not always a self-conscious) revival.

In Chapter 5, we consider theories that attempt to deal more directly with more complex and more natural events, notably Gibson's attempt at a "direct" theory of perception and the Gestalt theory of organization and its descendants, in Chapter 5C. The objects and properties studied in Chapters 4 and 5 are still "physical"— sizes, distances, lightnesses—but here they pertain much more closely to the world of normal observation and are thus of more general interest, especially to artists and designers of visual aids.

Chapter 6 discusses nonpictorial communication (reading texts and listening to speech, Chapter 6B) and pictorial communication (still pictures and motion pictures, Chapter 6C) in the context of the problems of selective attention and sequential integration—that is, the problems of how we tune in on only certain features of the world and how we put our perceptions of the world together out of the fragmentary glimpses of it that we usually receive from eye movements or from movie "cutting." The theoretical approaches that dominate this chapter are those of *information processing* and what has been called *constructivism.* These approaches, not yet fully separated, have important points in common with the classical theory of Chapters 3 and 4. In addition, both are of considerable relevance to practical questions of some social importance (for example, how best to promote literacy among the culturally deprived, and how motion-picture cutting can best convey meaning and maintain interest).

Chapter 7 samples the field of social perception, an area still in its infancy. The objects studied here include people, their social relationships, and their personal qualities, all of which are of potential interest to social and clinical psychologists, advertisers, and theatrical directors. Although research in this area is still quite sparse, its promise is great.

Following this organization, which is roughly the chronological order in which investigation has proceeded, allows us to view experimental research within the context of its purposes, and the objects of perception become increasingly more natural and meaningful from one section to the next.

Because the different senses have not been equally explored, and because they are not equally important for the questions asked in each of our sections, we shall not treat each sensory system every time. Instead, we shall first survey the sense of sight and introduce the others only as problems necessitate. This source of distraction may be relieved somewhat by the fact that visual perception will predominate through most of the book, reflecting both the importance of visual perception to our knowledge of the world and the ease of presenting examples of visual phenomena on the printed page.

Wherever possible, I have presented miniature experiments to illustrate important phenomena and to circumvent more lengthy descriptions. You are urged to perform these experiments, and thus to transform an abstract discussion into concrete demonstration.

And wherever possible, I have tried to place more advanced or technical material in the figure captions and footnotes. *Sticking to the text, and only glancing at the figures as they are needed,* should provide a relatively simple presentation.

A. A slightly changed version of Figure 2A appears in Figure 51C-3. p. 99. Is the young woman easy to see in *that* version?

B. The word "concealed" in Figure 2B is *word.*

The Sensations and Their Measurement

HOW WE PERCEIVE VERY SIMPLE STIMULI

chapter two

A. The Separate Senses

We observe the world through our several senses, or *modalities of sensation.* Imagine that a songstress is performing: If you close your eyes, the song continues, but you can no longer tell whether the singer is blond or brunette. If the sight is more pleasing than the sound, you can reopen your eyes and plug your ears with your fingers. The world as we perceive it is in some sense composed of these separable *kinds* of experiences (e.g., sight and sound).

It is easy in most cases to separate the sensory channels of seeing and hearing. But some of the other senses are not so easy to separate. For example, taste and smell are closely intertwined (so that pinching your nostrils closed, or catching a cold, results in truly surprising losses in flavor). And the position senses, as we shall see, are almost inseparably involved in the process of seeing.

Here is a listing of the major senses. Those that will engage us in this book are marked with asterisks. Note that there are more than the traditional "five senses."

1. *The major distance senses:* Seeing* and hearing.*

2. *The skin senses:* Touch,* warmth, cold, pain, and the closely related chemical senses of taste and smell.

3. *The deep senses:* Position* and motion* of muscles and joints (kinesthesis), the senses of equilibration* (vestibular sense), and the senses of the internal organs.

For each sense, we have specialized sense organs that are most readily affected by one particular class of physical energy, or *stimulation.* Their *response* allows us to *detect* or *discriminate* the presence or absence of that physical energy.[1] Thus, although we can detect intense light—say, sunlight—with the skin of our shoulders (by its warmth, and by the subsequent blisters), the eye is immensely more sensitive to the presence or absence of photic energy, or light energy. Moreover, only the eye's response produces the experience of light or darkness.

THE PHYSICAL AND PHYSIOLOGICAL BASES
OF OUR SENSATIONS

Each modality of sensation normally results from a definite sequence of events (see Figure 3), starting, of course, with the physical object that we perceive.

Distal objects, proximal stimulation, and specific nerve energies. What matters to us in the world is objects and their properties, but our major sensory systems are *not* directly in contact with these objects at all. Therefore, psychologists call objects *distal stimuli* (the doorbell, *A,* in Figure 3), indicating that they only stimulate our nervous system indirectly, by the patterns of light energy, sound energy, and so on that they reflect or radiate. The patterns of energy that do reach and affect our sense organs are called the *proximal stimuli.* In Figure 3, these stimuli are light energy (1), pressure waves in the air ("sound waves," (2)), pressure on the finger tip (3). *We can only know about the distal, physical world—the world of space and objects and people and motion—through these proximal stimulus distributions acting on our sense organs.* If the stimulus (say, light energy) is prevented from acting on a sense organ (say, by closing one's eyes), no experience of light will be obtained. Con-

[1] As we shall see, each sensory system is designed to receive the *information* that is carried by a given kind of energy rather than to respond to the energy itself, but that distinction will not be clear until later on.

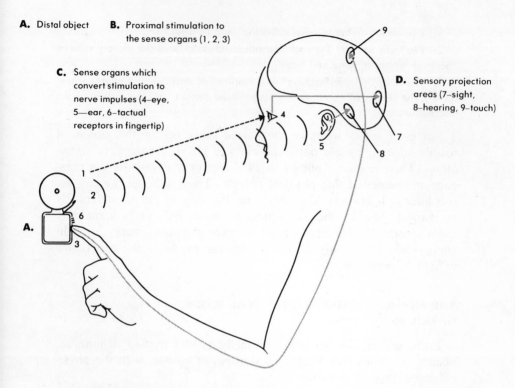

A. Distal object **B.** Proximal stimulation to the sense organs (1, 2, 3)

C. Sense organs which convert stimulation to nerve impulses (4–eye, 5—ear, 6–tactual receptors in fingertip)

D. Sensory projection areas (7–sight, 8–hearing, 9–touch)

FIGURE 3.   A brief outline of the sequence of physical events essential to perception.

versely, if the sense organ can be stimulated by some other means (say, by applying an electrical current to the eye), an experience of light will be obtained even though no light energy is present. *One stimulus can therefore act as a* surrogate, *or substitute, for another if both stimuli affect the sense organ in the same way.*

The classical explanation of the relationship between stimulation and experience is as follows: For each modality of experience, there exists a specialized class of *receptor neurons.* A receptor neuron is a nerve cell that responds most readily to a particular kind of physical energy. Thus, in Figure 3 there are receptors at the back of the eye (4) which respond to light energy, there are receptors in the ear (5) which respond to sound energy, and receptors in the skin (6) which respond to pressure. When a receptor is *stimulated,* it stimulates other nerve cells deeper in the nervous system, which in turn relay their activity to a special *projection area* in the brain (represented in Figure 3 by numbers 7, 8, and 9 for the modalities of sight, hearing, and touch, respectively) and from there to the surrounding regions called the *association areas.*

The response of a receptor neuron, incidentally, is often called its *specific nerve energy* because it was originally thought that each nerve acted differently from all others; now, however, we know that what is important to perception is *where* the impulse enters the cerebral cortex of the brain—that is, the receptor's projection area. If it were possible to hook up the receptor organs from your ear to the projection areas in the brain that are normally served by your eye, and vice versa, you would presumably hear light and see sound.

More modestly, if you press with your finger on your closed eyelid, you will see *pressure phosphenes* of faint purplish light, even though no light energy has entered your eye. What happens is that the finger's pressure stimulates the tissue of receptor neurons at the back of the eye (the *retina*), which normally respond to light energy; and their response to the pressure, when transmitted to the visual projection area in the brain, results in the sensation of light. (Meanwhile, in response to the same mechanical force, the nerves in the finger and in the eyelid, of course, convey sensations of touch.) Thus, if a proximal stimulus is lacking, we can stimulate the sensory nerves by other means, electrically or mechanically, for instance, or an experience of light can be produced, without any sensory basis, by direct stimulation of the appropriate sensory projection area in the cortex.

In short, we do not "see" objects directly. We see neither the retinal image nor the excitation in the optic nerve. At most, we might say that what we see is the final effect on the projection area of the cerebral cortex, and even that is debatable (for reasons that we shall discuss in Chapter 6C).

We can perceive only what affects our sensory systems. In this sense, the modalities of experience that we listed above comprise analytic units; that is, all experiences must be composed of these modalities *in various combinations,* and what doesn't affect one or more of these sensory systems will not be perceived.

The elementary physical variables and their sensory correlates. We can perceive an unlimited number of different things and occurrences. The first step in understanding how we do so is *analytic:* We must find some smaller number of perceptual elements or processes in terms of which we can explain the infinite variety of things we actually perceive. The separate sense modalities offer us, as we have seen, a rough set of analytic elements. All the physical world as we can perceive it is composed of what we can sense with those relatively few modalities (e.g., light, sound, pressure, etc.).

We can, of course, tell much more about the world than that it is light or dark, noisy or silent. With each sense organ, we can make many different observations; in fact, *within* each sense modality, there is an almost unlimited number of different physical things we may confront and perceive—for example, the number of different scenes that might confront the eye. Yet they can all be reduced to, or *reproduced by,* a much smaller number of *elementary physical variables.*

Thus, all the many millions of different things we see on a TV screen are reproduced by a relatively small number of spots of color at various points on the picture tube. Similarly, the entire range of things that we can hear—all of the speech and poetry and music and noises—can be reproduced by a loudspeaker that varies only in the intensity and rapidity (or frequency) with which it vibrates. And with sufficient care, and precautions (some of which we will discuss in Chapters 3 and 4), what we see on the screen and hear through the speaker can be made indistinguishable from the real events themselves.

This is one beginning: We can analyze the physical world into a relatively small number of physical variables with which, in various combinations, we can cause people to perceive anything at all. Having analyzed the world of stimulation into elementary physical variables, we must do the same for the experiences that they cause.

Within each separate sense modality, certain qualities seem to recur in various combinations in the objects we observe around us— qualities such as "blue," "red," "cold," "hard," "loud," "high-pitched," and so on. To discover that light energy is the physical stimulus for the experience of "light" versus "dark," for example, and that the eye is the visual sense organ, is relatively simple. To discover the physical stimuli and the anatomical equipment that are responsible for the different qualities that we can discern within each modality of sensation presents far more challenging and fundamental problems. What aspects of stimulation, and what sensory equipment, are responsible for seeing that the apple is green and not red? that the boy is nearer than the man? and that the boy is pleased whereas the man is worried?

Traditionally, two quite different sets of procedures were used to discover the lists of different sensory qualities (called *sensations*) that we can perceive, and to discover the differences in physical stimulation that are responsible for these differences in sensation. The general procedures are termed *sensory psychophysics* and *analytic introspection.* We shall examine each of these procedures in some detail, because the first one is still in use and a grasp of the second is essential for understanding most modern perceptual problems.

B. *Purposes and Principles of Sensory Psychophysics*

The most precise way of trying to catalog the "sensations" (that is, the different experiences that we can distinguish *within* each sensory modality), and of discovering their physical bases, is called sensory psychophysics. Although each sense organ can do much more than tell us merely whether or not physical stimulation is present (for example, whether it is light or dark), each still detects only a limited number of physical differences. Just as there are physical energies (like radio waves) that we cannot observe directly because we lack the sense organs that are sensitive to them, we cannot observe changes even in those energies for which we do have sense organs, if those changes are too small. One of the first tasks of sensory psychophysics is to discover what differences we can observe.

The smallest change in any physical stimulation that we can observe with our unaided senses is called the *difference threshold, discrimination threshold,* or *Difference Limen,* which is usually abbreviated *DL.* There are several uses for these measures, and a great many *psychophysical methods* have been designed to obtain them.

THE PSYCHOPHYSICAL METHODS
AND MEASURES

Classical psychophysics: Thresholds as measures of sensitivity. The psychophysical methods were originally designed to measure thresholds. The concept of thresholds is quite simple, and the psychophysical methods are equally simple—*in principle.* The most straightforward way to measure a difference threshold would be to start with two stimuli that are physically equal; then change one gradually over a number of trials until the two stimuli are barely different enough physically for that difference to be noticed—barely different enough for the two stimuli to appear unequal or different. The physical difference on the last trial might be taken as the DL, or difference threshold. If we start with no physical stimulus energy at all, and by small increases discover the smallest quantity that the observer can detect, that quantity (the difference from zero, so to speak) is called the *absolute threshold.*

For example, we might measure the DL for light with two incandescent lamps of the same wattage, both connected to dimmers. We would keep one lamp unchanged, calling it the *standard stimulus.* We would turn up the current in the other lamp, the *variable stimulus,* until its output of light energy just exceeded the difference threshold and it no longer looked identical to the standard but was instead just noticeably brighter.

This procedure is subject to one major complication, however. When an observer tries to decide which one of two almost identical objects is brighter (or larger, or heavier, or louder), his judgments fluctuate—now one looks brighter, now the other. The task is like straining to hear a very faint whispered signal in a hearing test: What at first seemed to be a very quiet room now seems to be filled with creaks and echoes, and even the rushing sound of the blood in your own ears makes it difficult to decide whether you actually heard the signal, or whether that last sound was simply a bit of the varying background noise.

For these reasons, "the" threshold is not a simple fixed value; instead, the threshold varies over a range of measures, in part because the motivation, attitudes, and expectations of the observer vary. Even if we change the stimulus abruptly from one level to another, the subject's judgments will not usually follow suit, nor will he always make the same response to the same stimulus. He might, for example, detect a small stimulus difference only infrequently—say, on only one trial in every ten (point *i* in Figure 4*A*)—and detect a larger difference more frequently—say, on nine trials in ten (point *iii*

(Text continues on page 16)

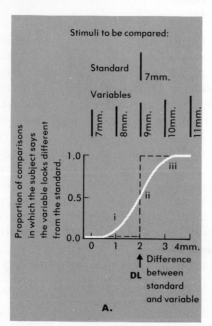

A.

FIGURE 4.

A. An imaginary experiment to measure sensitivity to differences in length. The standard stimulus is paired with each of the variable stimuli many times, and each time the subject must say whether they are different. The *difference threshold,* is usually taken to be that difference that can be detected 50 percent of the time. As the gray curve shows, the subject judged the 9-mm variable to be different from the standard (which was 7 mm.) on half of the trials on which the two were compared, so the DL is 9mm. − 7mm. =2mm. Because of variability in the sensory processes, the threshold is not abrupt (like the dotted line); instead, the subject sometimes notices differences that are smaller than 2 mm. (point *i*) and sometimes fails to notice larger differences (point *ii*).

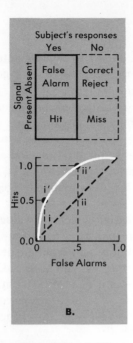

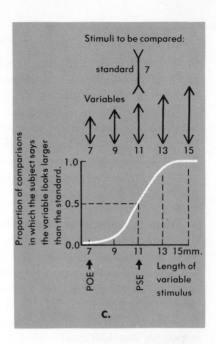

B. Signal detection theory. In the simplest psychophysical experiment, the subject can either say Yes (i.e., the two stimuli are different) or No; and the stimulus presentation can either include a *signal* (i.e. the two stimuli are in fact different by some amount) or not. When the subject cannot detect the signal at all and is only guessing, whether he says Yes more often than No depends only on his expectations about how frequently the signal will be presented and on how much he is motivated to avoid each kind of error. These factors affect his *criterion* of decision, but we can measure his sensitivity separately as follows: If the signal is present on only half the trials, and the subject is only guessing, it is obvious that each time he says Yes his answer is as likely to be a *false alarm* (i.e., the signal was not really present) as a *hit*. The measure d' is a function of the proportions of hits and of false alarms. Regardless of the proportion of trials on which the signal is present, this measure corrects for guessing in the sense that when the subject makes as many false alarms as hits, $d' = 0.0$. In the graph at *B*, when the proportion of false alarms and of hits are equal, the subject's judgments fall on the diagonal line, regardless of how often he says Yes: At point *i*, the proportion of trials on which he says Yes is 0.1, whether or not the signal is present; at point *ii*, it is 0.5. To the degree that the subject's sensitivity (d') is greater than 0. his responses fall above the diagonal. The white curve shows the ratio of hits to false alarms that would be obtained with a given d' and each possible criterion. Such a curve is known as an *ROC* (Receiver Operating Characteristic) function

C. How can we measure an illusion? The standard stimulus is paired with each of the variable stimuli, and the subject must decide in each case whether or not the variable is longer than the standard. The white curve shows that the subject judges the 11-mm. variable to be longer than the 7-mm., standard no more often (i.e., 0.50 times) than he judges it to be shorter. The *Point of Subjective Equality* (PSE), therefore, is 11 mm. The variable that is really equal to the standard is, of course, 7 mm., which is the *Point of Objective Equality* (POE). When perception is perfectly accurate, the PSE = POE. The *Constant Error* (CE) is the difference between PSE and POE; in this case, CE = $11 - 7 = 4$ mm., which shows the illusion to be CE/POE = 4/7 = 57 percent of the true length, in this example (it is usually closer to half that amount).

These kinds of measurement procedures have provided the quantitative basis for most of what we will discuss nonquantitatively in Chapters 2 through 5.

in Figure 4*A*)—so that the graph we obtain by accumulating and plotting his judgments (represented by the gray curve in Figure 4*A*) may not be at all abrupt.

Therefore, more complicated and sophisticated procedures are needed to help us decide somewhat arbitrarily on the value of each threshold. Traditionally, this *difference threshold* is taken to be the physical difference between the standard stimulus and the variable stimulus that will be detected 50 percent of the time—that is, the difference that is *just as likely as not* to be discriminated (point *ii* in Figure 4*A*).

These procedures provide a way to assign a definite value to the threshold, even though the subject's responses vary from trial to trial. But because the subject's expectations and cautiousness usually affect his willingness to decide that the two stimuli are different, more elaborate procedures and analyses are needed to control and assess these cognitive and motivational factors, and to separate them from his sensitivity. That is the task of signal detection procedures, which we consider next.

Signal detection methods Because the very nature of the threshold problem requires us to use experimental situations in which the observer cannot be sure whether or not he really detects the object for which he is searching, he might well mistake the background noise for the signal—an error called a *false alarm*—or he might make the opposite mistake and *miss* the signal. These fluctuations afflict all threshold decisions so that an observer's relative willingness to commit either false alarms or misses (his so-called *response bias*) will affect the size of the difference threshold. By introducing *catch trials* in which no stimulus (or no stimulus difference) is present, we can separately measure the subject's *sensitivity* (how small a difference influences his judgment) and his *criterion* (the point in the uncertain mixture of *signal* and *noise* at which he will decide that the stimulus is indeed present). If he is only guessing, he should make as many false alarms as hits (the diagonal line in Figure 4*B*). How much better he does than that indicates his sensitivity; these measurement methods are sketched in Figure 4*B*.

Position on the x-axis is a function of the subject's criterion: at *i* he is much more conservative than at *ii*. His criterion can be affected in many ways. In recent years, subjects' motivation and expectations have been deliberately manipulated in order to study the problem of how people make difficult decisions—a far cry from the original simple goals for which thresholds were measured. Thus, with rewards of 10 cents for each correct report of a signal, and 5 cents for each correct report of its absence, and a penalty of 5 cents for each error, the number of false alarms will rise, even though the stimulus is not changed in any way. On the other hand, we can keep constant both the stimulus and the system of rewards and punishments (called the *payoff function*) and merely change the proportion of catch trials. This will change the observer's expectations about how frequently he should be noticing a difference, and again his criterion—but not his sensitivity—will change. For a lucid introduction to this new approach to an old technique, see E. Galanter, 1962. For a more advanced discussion, see Engen, 1971, or Snodgrass, 1975.

Thresholds and their limitations. It should now be clear that "the threshold" is a mathematical abstraction, not a real dividing line. In fact, if we use a signal-detection measure (like d' in Figure 4*B*) of how sensitive a subject is to a particular stimulus variable, there is no point at which we can say *Here* is the threshold. This should be recalled when we find that subjects can be affected by words or pictures that are set "below threshold" and that this set of results has often been taken as demonstrating the participation of the unconscious mind in perceptual processes (see Chapter 7A). Properly interpreted, however, the results of these psychophysical experiments provide the foundations on which our study of perception must rest.

Thresholds have, of course, been used to discover what stimulus changes our senses can detect, and we will use that information shortly when we consider the sensory receptors of the eye and the ear. In addition, however, they have been used for another and quite different purpose, which we shall now consider briefly.

PSYCHOPHYSICAL LAWS AND SCALES

Suppose we have found that in order for an object to be noticeably heavier than one that weighs 100 g., it has to weigh at least 102 g.—that is, when the standard is 100 g., the difference threshold = 2 g. We might at first think from this that any two weights that differ by more than 2 grams will be noticeably different. This is not true, however, because the difference threshold increases as we increase the standard. Thus, for a standard of 150 g., the variable would have to weigh 153 g. to be just noticeably heavier, and for a standard of 250 g., the difference threshold = 5 g. As these difference threshold results suggest, although the difference threshold is not a constant, the *ratio,* difference threshold divided by the standard, *is* constant (over a moderate range of values of the standard). This law was discovered by E. H. Weber in 1830, and the Weber fraction, difference threshold/standard, or dI/I, is known to be constant in the middle ranges of stimulation for a wide variety of sensory attributes.

When, in this example, the variable of 102 g. appears to be noticeably different from the standard of 100 g., it seems different in a particular way: It is *heavier.* Similarly, a stimulus of 104 g. seems heavier than 102 g. As the weight of the object increases, the sensation of heaviness increases. So for the other senses, as photic energy increases, a light appears *brighter;* as sound-pressure waves carry more energy to the ear, a sound gets *louder.* The magnitude or quantity of a sensation seems to increase when the stimulus energy increases. How are the two kinds of increases related? Does doubling the weight in grams result in double the sensation of heaviness? In order to answer that question, we would need two scales. One scale would measure the number of grams of weight as physical units; the other would measure the amount of experienced heaviness as a *sensation.* But sensations are experiences, not things: How can we construct scales that measure sensations?

Gustav Theodor Fechner, a physicist and originator of most of the psychophysical methods, proposed in 1860 that *each just noticeable difference (or JND) measures an equal change in sensation.* An increase of, say, 10 JNDs therefore appears twice as large as an increase of 5 JNDs. The difference threshold is a measure of how much a stimulus must be changed in order to be just noticeably different. Taking Weber's Law into account (by a mathematical transformation which need not concern us here),[2] this would imply

$$S = C \log M$$

where
$S =$ the magnitude of the sensation,
$M =$ the physical measure of the stimulus, and
$C =$ a constant for a particular sense modality, derived from the value of the Weber fraction.

This is Fechner's Law, that "sensation is proportional to the log of the stimulus measure." It is still accepted by some engineers and psychologists, although the results of a recent wide-ranging survey of various sensory qualities by S. S. Stevens and his colleagues, us-

[2] Briefly, by treating the Weber fraction, *dI/I,* as a derivative and integrating it. In fact, if you will continue the scale of weights that we started in the example above, you will find that it is a logarithmic scale: 100, 102, 104, 106.12, 108.2, 110.4, 112.6, 114.9, 117.2, 119.5, ...

ing a very different sort of psychophysical method called *magnitude estimation,* support a different law (1961). His observers are asked to estimate the apparent magnitudes of different stimuli *simply by assigning appropriate numbers to each stimulus.* The magnitude estimates that subjects make generally fit more closely to a power function—say, $S = M^c$—than to Fechner's logarithmic function. Mathematically, this is equivalent to saying that *equal ratios of stimulation produce equal ratios of sensation,* a fact we shall discuss in Chapter 5.

Just as the existence of a threshold has been challenged (p. 17), the meaning of scales derived in this fashion and the validity of the power law have been seriously questioned,[3] but the logarithmic function and the power function do not differ enough as far as the subject matter of this book is concerned to warrant further study here.

Regardless of these questions, the psychophysical methods and measures remain important to us for two reasons: The first is that the methods of sensory psychophysics have produced a great deal of reliable and precise information about our sensitivities to various kinds and degrees of physical stimulation. Second, the psychophysical methods also give us quantitative methods to answer very different kinds of questions than we have considered up to this point.

THE PERCEPTUAL USES OF THE
PSYCHOPHYSICAL METHODS

The psychophysical methods are not only measures of sensitivity. Suppose we want to know how large the illusion is in Figure 1. Figure 4*C* sketches a simple example of how we would use the classical procedure to measure the *Point of Subjective Equality,* which is the size of the variable stimulus that *appears* equal to the standard. In this case, the setting at which the two parts of the Müller-Lyer pattern look equal. By comparing the Point of Subjective Equality to the *Point of Objective Equality*—the setting at which the two parts of the pattern are physically, objectively equal—we can measure the magnitude of the illusion. (In this case, it is $(11.0 - 7.0)/7.0 = 57$

---

[3] Some psychologists believe that it is seriously misleading to talk of "scales of sensation" in this way, and that the only reliable observation that one can make in sensory psychophysics is whether one stimulus appears the same as, or different from, another (Warren & Warren, 1963). Attempts to demonstrate that the method is valid, by showing that it gives consistent results when magnitudes in one modality are expressed in terms of stimulus magnitudes in another modality (called *cross-modality matching*), have not, moreover, been conclusive (see Anderson, 1974).

percent.) We could change some feature of the stimulus pattern (say, the angle between the "fins" and the "shafts") and determine how that change affects the size of the illusion. In ways like this, we can use the psychophysical methods to study how various conditions and manipulations affect how objects are perceived. It is this use of these methods, more than anything else, that makes them of interest to us in this text.

In Chapter 3 we shall survey psychologists' efforts to use the psychophysical information about difference thresholds to analyze the perceived world of objects, and in Chapter 4 we shall examine the attempts to reassemble those piecemeal observations into the world we perceive, using the kind of measures we have just considered above. In both of these enterprises, much use had been made of another method, *analytic introspection,* to supplement the procedures of sensory psychophysics; this method has since been justifiably discredited but is very difficult to discard entirely.

C. Analytic Introspection

Outside of the psychophysical laboratory, of course, the world we face is rarely so simple as a single spot of light that is allowed to change in only one simple way. In order to observe the elementary sensations in more natural environments, early psychologists attempted to develop a special procedure called *analytic introspection.*

To get some idea of the sense in which this was thought to work, look at the cube in Figure 5: You normally see it as a light, evenly colored tridimensional object with perpendicular corners and parallel sides. With a slight effort, however, you can separate it into patches of different lightnesses, converging lines, and so on. This is a simple form of analytical introspection, in which you have attempted to disregard the familiar "meaning" of the pattern (i.e., that it is a cube) and consider it only in terms of its component patches of light and shade. The task of analysis is far more difficult when you are looking at a real object such as a box or a cabinet than it is with a picture. With a real object, you will probably need to look at the various parts through a tube or through a hole in a piece of cardboard if you wish to detect the actual changes in local color from one region to the next.

Psychologists who considered that careful analytic introspection would show us the elementary sensations out of which they believed all of our perceptions of objects and events are constructed were called *structuralists.* The central structuralist assumption was this:

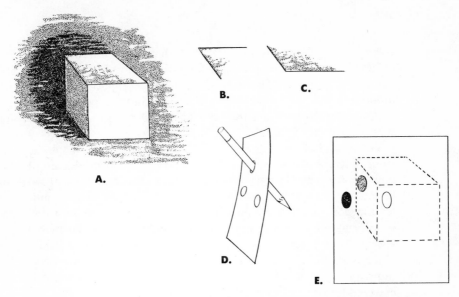

FIGURE 5. Applying analytic introspection to a simple object. To casual observation, the stimulus at *(A)* appears to be a light-colored cube; that is, it appears to have corners that are right angles, and a surface that is fairly uniformly light on all of its faces. As soon as the point is mentioned, however, you notice that *(A)* is nothing of the sort. With more careful dissection of the observation, you see that, as at *(B)* and *(C)*, the angles are very far from being 90°, and the local color grades from dark to light in a very marked manner. This is a particularly easy kind of analytic introspection to undertake since, after all, angle *(B)* really is an acute angle drawn on paper, and the gradation of ink from one point to the next is quite evident. If you punch three holes in a piece of paper with a pencil point, as shown in *(D)*, and place these holes on *(A)* so that different regions can be observed in relative isolation, as in *(E)*, you will have performed a primitive form of sensory psychophysics. It was once thought that, with suitable training, one could observe the same "pure sensations" both by means of sensory psychophysics and by analytic introspection. We now know that this is simply not true, as we shall see in Chapter 4. But the reasons why analytic introspection cannot do what it was intended to do are themselves important, and at least some of the assumptions that were made by the structuralist psychologists who had attempted this kind of analysis have been revived, in modified forms, in recent years.

that, with sufficiently painstaking analytic introspection, *the same "pure" sensations can be observed whenever the same stimulus energy falls on the same part of any sensory organ.* The appearances of the varied objects and events in the world that we can perceive were thought to be composed of just such elementary sensations in various combinations. In order to understand how we are able to perceive the world, therefore, we would have to understand first how we observe the elementary sensations.

This approach is really only the attempt to apply the law of specific nerve energies to our perceptions of things and happenings, as simply as it can be applied. As we noted before, stimulation of the ear (by pressure waves) results in the experience of hearing, and stimulation of the eye (by light energy) results in the experience of seeing. It is thus reasonable to say that our awareness of, say, a singer, consists of two separable experiences, sight and hearing. Similarly, it was hoped that the differences we experience *within each modality* — e.g., all of the different colors that we perceive when we look at a landscape — are the responses of different sensory receptors within each sense organ.

As we shall see, however, both the method of analytic introspection and the structuralist approach that motivated it must now be viewed with very serious reservations. But the search for the elementary sensations, and for the specific nerve energies and receptor mechanisms that presumably underlay them, yielded a great deal of information essential to any understanding of how we perceive.

Summary

The commonsense view of the perceptual process is that somehow the outside object gets inside, and then our minds can examine it. The analogy that the eye is just like a camera, and that our minds examine the upside-down images of the objects on our retinas, or on the sensory projection areas of the brain, is only slightly more sophisticated, and equally incorrect.

In fact, there is no duplicate of the object in the brain. Rather, there are characteristic neural processes set up in the nervous system, processes that are initiated by the physical energies that stimulate our sensory organs. Structuralist psychologists thought that for each detectable elementary physical event, a specialized receptor neuron responding to the event could be found, and that a corresponding elementary experience (or sensation) could be identified. Just as we can reduce all possible patterns of proximal stimulation to the various combinations of different elementary physical variables (e.g., all possible scenes can be reproduced by sets of colored dots on a TV screen), so they hoped to analyze our perceptions into combinations of elementary sensations corresponding to those elementary physical variables.

In order to identify the component sensations, procedures known as the *psychophysical methods* were devised to map out the repertory of different sensations that we can experience — i.e., to measure our sensory thresholds. By *analytic introspection,* it was hoped that the trained observer would be able to dissect his perceptions of the world into those same components.

Although we now know that this approach was seriously flawed, it cannot be forgotten. The theoretical consequences of this enterprise motivated the analysis of our sensory processes as physiological mechanisms, and affected the ways in which other disciplines approach the problem of how we know and interact with our physical and social environment.

The practical consequences provided information that made it possible to remedy sensory defects in a systematic fashion and also provided measures (chiefly, the psychophysical methods) of sensory sensitivity to those many industries that depend on them (audio hi-fi, colored textiles, video, etc.).

MORE ADVANCED READING

KLING, J. A., and RIGGS, L. A. (Eds.) *Woodworth and Schlosberg's Experimental Psychology.* New York: Holt, Rinehart and Winston, 1971. Chapters 2 and 3, by T. Engen: Psychophysics 1. Discrimination and detection (pp. 11–46), Psychophysics 2. Scaling methods (pp. 47–86).

SCHARF, B. (Ed.) *Experimental sensory psychology.* Glenview, Illinois: Scott, Foresman, 1975. Chapter 2, by J. G. Snodgrass: Psychophysics, pp. 17–67.

Human Sensory Capacities and Their Physiological Bases

THE PERCEPTION OF ELEMENTARY PHYSICAL EVENTS

chapter three

The perceptions of simple physical events are convenient to study because we can vary and measure the stimuli with ease and precision. In this chapter, we shall discuss the visual sensory system in some detail and the auditory system in much less detail; we shall deal with the other senses only as they happen to contribute to our discussion of the visual and auditory perception of the world of objects and events in space in Chapter 4.

A. The Visual Sense: Structure and Function

STRUCTURE

The visual system has several parts, of which the eye is only one. The structure of the eye is outlined in Figure 6. Within the eye, the light energy of the optic array is transformed into neural activity in the receptor neurons of the *retina*. The retinal system includes rods, cones, and connective cells. The *cones,* of which the *fovea* is composed exclusively, also occur in decreasing numbers in other zones of the retina. They are responsible for color vision and for seeing

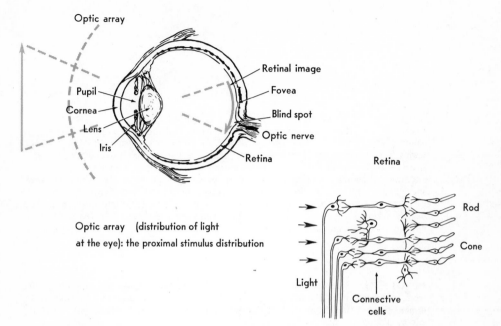

Optic array (distribution of light
at the eye): the proximal stimulus distribution

FIGURE 6. *The eye and its major parts (side view).* The lens, a transparent tissue, focuses light rays, which enter the cornea, to form an image on the retina. The iris is a diaphragm of pigmented tissue controlling the size of the pupil, thereby regulating the over-all amount of light reaching the retina and partially compensating for illumination changes. The retina is composed of a layer of receptor cells (rods and cones), which are neurons that are sensitive to light and to changes of light, and a layer of bipolar and gang-lion cells. These latter cells are not themselves sensitive to light but are stimulated by interconnected groups of receptor cells. The fovea is a small region, central in the retina, that is highly sensitive to detail and consists entirely of cones. The optic nerve is the bundle of nerve fibers from the retina of the eye to the projection area in the cortex (via a relay center called the thalamus); it leaves the eye at the blind spot, a small region which has no receptors sensitive to light.

small details. The *rods,* which are absent from the fovea, are "color blind" and are much more sensitive to low levels of light energy than the cones, so they are responsible for night vision. The *connective cells,* of which there are several kinds, collect the output of groups, or "fields," of receptors (rods or cones) and organize them in ways that we are only now discovering (Chapter 5B).

Aside from the eye, important related structures are as follows:

1. The *visual projection area* is the region in the brain which receives neural impulses that originate in the retina. This area is not simply a copy of the optic retina, however. The *nasal* (inner) halves of each retina send their impulses by one pathway, the *temporal* (outer) halves by another (Fig. 7 p. 28), and we still do not know precisely how the information from the two halves is put together again. We do know that in the cases of surgical operations

(Text continues on page 28)

FIGURE 10. The independence of wavelengths and the integration of hues. *A.* A beam of white-appearing light energy will spread out into a spectrum whose appearance varies from violet at the short-wavelength end to red at the long-wavelength end. *B.* If two narrow beams of light from this spectrum are recombined, they "mix" into a new hue; thus, a red-appearing beam and a green-appearing beam produce a yellow-appearing spot. The wavelengths of light energy themselves do not mix, however, since the combined beam can be redivided by passing it through a prism (C) into the two original beams, whereas a yellow-appearing beam taken from the spectrum at (B) would pass unchanged through a second prism.

FIGURE 11. The distinguishable sensations of color. Patches of color may differ from each other in brightness or lightness *(A)*, hue *(B)*, and saturation *(C)*, which is the dimension that runs from gray (or "colorless") to fully colored. About 350,000 JNDs can be distinguished.

FIGURE 12. The facts of trichromatic color mixture. Light taken from three different regions of the spectrum will, when mixed in the proper proportions, produce the hues of the entire spectrum, including white. At (A), they combine to form white. The graph at (B) shows the proportions of reddish-, greenish-, and bluish-appearing light energy needed to match the appearance of any point on the spectrum (the horizontal axis). Thus, to match 580 nanometers (yellow light), take about equal parts of 650 and 530 (reddish and greenish light, respectively). Note that you can't tell simply by looking at the curve in this diagram what perceived hue will be produced by each mixture (that is, 580 is yellow, not a reddish-green); rather, you have to look down at the labels on the horizontal axis to find out.

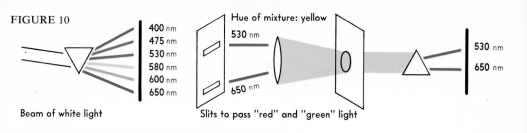

FIGURE 10

400 nm
475 nm
530 nm
580 nm
600 nm
650 nm

Beam of white light

Hue of mixture: yellow

530 nm

650 nm

Slits to pass "red" and "green" light

530 nm

650 nm

FIGURE 12

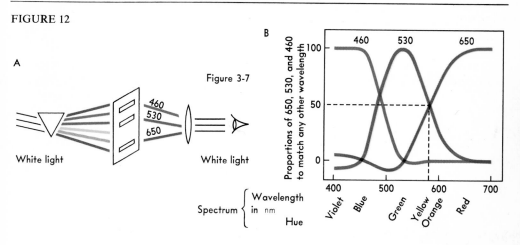

A

Figure 3-7

White light

460
530
650

White light

B

Proportions of 650, 530, and 460 to match any other wavelength

460   530   650

100

50

0

400   500   600   700

Spectrum { Wavelength in nm

Hue

Violet   Blue   Green   Yellow Orange   Red

FIGURE 11

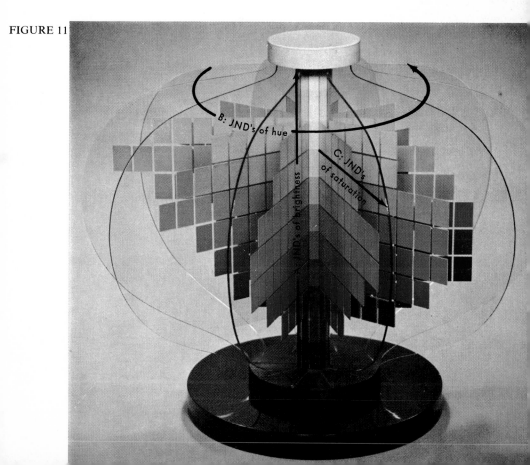

B: JND's of hue

C: JND's of saturation

JND's of brightness

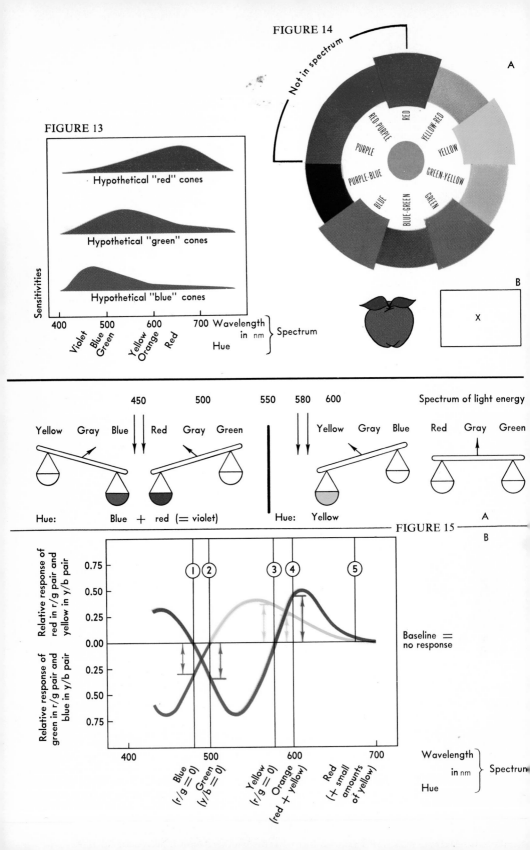

FIGURE 14

Not in spectrum

A

RED
RED-PURPLE
YELLOW-RED
PURPLE
YELLOW
PURPLE-BLUE
GREEN-YELLOW
BLUE
GREEN
BLUE-GREEN

B

X

FIGURE 13

Hypothetical "red" cones

Hypothetical "green" cones

Hypothetical "blue" cones

Sensitivities

400   500   600   700   Wavelength
                                in nm   } Spectrum

Violet Blue Green Yellow Orange Red

Hue

450   500   550 580   600   Spectrum of light energy

Yellow Gray Blue   Red Gray Green   Yellow Gray Blue   Red   Gray Green

Hue: Blue + red (= violet)   Hue: Yellow   A

FIGURE 15

B

Relative response of red in r/g pair and yellow in y/b pair

0.75

0.50

0.25

0.00

① ②   ③ ④   ⑤

Relative response of green in r/g pair and blue in y/b pair

0.25

0.50

0.75

Baseline =
no response

400   500   600   700   Wavelength
                                                  in nm   } Spectrum

Blue
(r/g = 0)   Green
(y/b = 0)   Yellow
(r/g = 0)   Orange
(red + yellow)   Red
(+ small
amounts
of yellow)

Hue

FIGURE 13. The Young-Helmholtz theory of color sensitivity. The simplest way in which to account for the color-mixture facts outlined in Figure 12 is to assume that there are three different kinds of receptors: cones maximally sensitive to 650 nanometers which when stimulated alone produce the sensation of red; cones maximally sensitive to 530 nanometers ("green"); and cones maximally sensitive to 460 nanometers ("blue"). In fact, these wavelengths do not really look like pure colors, appearing somewhat orange, green and reddish blue, respectively.

FIGURE 14. The color circle: complementaries, adaptation, and after-images. A. Without referring to wavelengths at all, we can summarize color phenomena as follows. There are four unique hues (red, yellow, green, and blue) that do not resemble one another; equal quantities of complementaries (hues that are on opposite sides of the circle) yield gray when they are mixed; unequal proportions of complementaries yield the color of the predominant component, but with a lower saturation. B. If you stare at any colored patch for some time — say, the apple in (B) — adaptation, or fatigue, will occur, and the color will become gradually less saturated (although that may not be readily discernable). Next, look at a white surface (as at X). An after-image of the first patch will be seen, but it will be of complementary color.

FIGURE 15. The opponent-colors theory (Hurvich and Jameson 1955, 1974). Assume that all hue sensations are produced by two pairs of receptors, one pair (r/g) producing either red or green sensation and a second pair (y/b) producing either yellow or blue. The two members in each pair are opponents: We cannot experience a yellowish-blue or a reddish-green. If both members of a single pair are equally stimulated, they cancel each other, leaving only gray; if one member is stimulated more than its opponent, its hue will be seen. Thus, the spectrum at 450 nm stimulates both pairs of receptors and looks reddish-blue (violet), while 580 nm stimulates only the y/b pair and looks yellow (A). All the hues that we can see are therefore either reddish-yellows, reddish-blues, greenish-yellows, or greenish-blues, and in order to predict exactly what hue will be seen with any given mixture of light, we must know the sensitivity of each receptor pair to the wavelengths of the spectrum.

How can the sensitivity curves of these receptor pairs be determined? The amount of the *blue response* at 450 nm is measured by adding just enough light that is pure yellow in appearance (about 580 nm) to cancel the blue. Similarly, the amount of *yellow response* at each wavelength in the yellowish regions of the spectrum is measured by adding just enough pure blue to cancel the yellow; pure red is used to measure the *green response* in the greenish regions of the spectrum, and pure green, to measure the *red response*.

The graph at B shows the amount of yellow or blue response and of red or green response that is produced at each wavelength, measured in this manner. Unlike the Young-Helmholtz sensitivity curves (in Figure 13), this graph tells us what hue will be seen at any given wavelength. Thus, at point (4), red plus yellow = yellowish-red (that is, orange); at point (1) (475 nm), r/g = 0, leaving *pure* blue; at (2) (500 nm), y/b = 0. leaving *pure* green; at (3) (580 nm), r/g =0 again, leaving *pure* yellow. Notice that yellow is present throughout the long wavelengths, (5). This is why a "red" of 650 and a "green" of 530 mix to give yellow: because light at 650 nm stimulates both red and yellow responses, light at 530 nm stimulates both green and yellow responses, and only the yellow remains after the red and green cancel each other (*not* because yellow is composed of red and green sensations, as the Young-Helmholtz theory asserts).

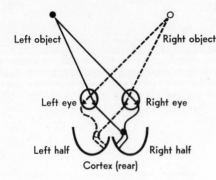

Left object

Right object

Left eye

Right eye

Left half

Right half

Cortex (rear)

FIGURE 7. *Optic pathways.* The outer *(temporal)* halves of each retina are connected to their corresponding (right or left) sides of the brain; the inner *(nasal)* halves, to opposite sides of the brain. Note that an object to the right of center affects the left side of the brain, and vice versa.

that cut the connections between the two halves of the brain, the subject behaves in some ways as though his skull contained two quite separate observers, each knowing the content of only the appropriate half of the total visual field. In such surgical split-brain cases, the separate accessibility of the two halves of the brain to visual stimulation makes it possible to study the differences in function that the two hemispheres seem to serve (Gazzaniga, 1970, has a review of this literature). Moreover, as we will see, the relay stations along the way and the cortex of the brain also contain special cells, each of which is stimulated by a relatively large pattern of neural elements in the retina. By the time all of these cross-connections and pattern-responding processes are taken into account, there can be little left of the "picture in the brain" that corresponds to the image in the eye.

2. From the *projection area,* neural activity spreads into the *visual association area,* the region of the brain adjacent to the projection area. It becomes very difficult to trace the effects of stimulation systematically much further into the nervous system.

3. The *oculomotor system* is a set of intricately coordinated muscles that move the eyes, permitting them to scan the optic array and to compensate for movements of the head and trunk.

We shall consider additional details of structure in the course of discussing how the visual system functions.

FUNCTION OF THE VISUAL SYSTEM:
THE "STATIONARY" EYE

Physical analysis of stimulation. The pattern of light that confronts the eye is called the *optic array* (*A* in Figure 8), as we noted above. The optic array (and the image on the retina) are found by drawing "rays" to the eye from each point in the object at which an observer is looking. At any such point the light energy may vary in the following ways that are known to affect the viewer's perceptions: in *intensity,* in *predominant wavelength,* and in the *purity* of the mixture of wavelengths.

1. *Intensity* is a function of the amount of physical energy present in the

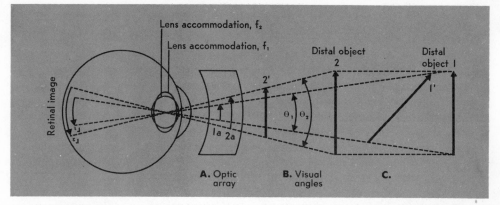

FIGURE 8. *The geometry of vision.* To discover what proximal pattern will be produced by any distal object, simple geometry will suffice. Objects (1) and (1′) subtend the same visual angle (θ), so they project the same optic array and the same retinal images (1a and r_1, respectively). Similarly, objects (2) and (2′) produce the same visual angle (θ_2), optic array (2a), and retinal image (r_2). However, to bring the retinal image into sharp focus, the curvature of the lens will have to be different for a near object (2′) than it is for a far one (2)—that is, the lens will have to change its *accommodation,* or focus, from f_1 to f_2.

light rays (as measured by the electricity generated in the photocell of a light meter at each wavelength, for example).

2. *Wavelength* is a measure of the distance between the crest of one wave and the crest of the next, when we consider the wavelike aspects of light rays, which, of course, are electromagnetic radiation. Electromagnetic waves range from 1/1,000,000,000 of a millionth of a meter to 100 million meters in length. Of this immense range, only the region between (roughly)

FIGURE 9. *The spectrum of electromagnetic radiation. A.* The total range of electromagnetic radiation. *B.* The visible spectrum of light energy (photic radiation).

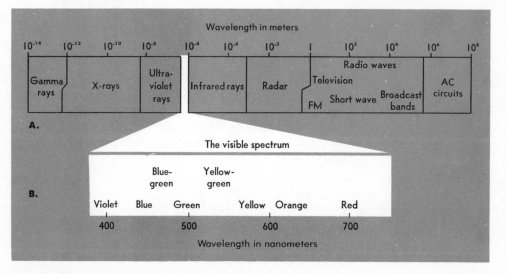

400 and 750nm. (or nanometers, which are 10^{-7} meters) is visible to the human eye (Figure 9B). If, as Isaac Newton showed in 1666, a beam of white-appearing light, such as sunlight, passes through a prism (Figure 10A [**Figures 10–12 face page 26**]), it will spread out into rays of different wavelength, and a band of different *hues* appears. This band is the *spectrum,* and light rays of any desired wavelength may be obtained from it by using a mask and a slit, as in Figure 10B. It is important to realize that light rays of different wavelengths can be mixed and separated indefinitely without affecting each other. When, as we shall see, "red light" and "green light" add together to form "yellow," *the yellow is in us, not in the light, which remains unchanged by the mixing* (Figure 10C).

3. *Purity* refers to the degree of predominance of one of the wavelengths into which the light ray can be separated by the prism. If all of the energy is concentrated at a single wavelength, the light is maximally pure.

What do we see when these physical stimulus attributes are varied?

The appearance of small patches of light: The sensations of color. As we vary a small patch of light energy, its appearance will normally change in the following simple manner:

1. *Intensity and brightness.* As physical intensity increases, the patch of light appears *lighter* or *brighter,* as indicated on the vertical axis (A in Figure 11).

2. *Wavelength and hue.* As the wavelength of the patch is varied, the *hue* of the patch changes from red, through orange, yellow, green, blue, and indigo to violet (B in Figure 11).

3. *Purity and saturation.* If a single wavelength of light is used, the hue appears strong and *saturated.* As other wavelengths are added, it will become diluted, grayer, and less saturated (C in Figure 11). Thus, a pure red is more saturated than a pink, even though the two may have the same hue and brightness, whereas a completely desaturated mixture in which all of the wavelengths are equally strong looks gray (or white, if it is intense, or black if it is very weak).

These correlations are by no means perfect.[1] The greatest lack of correspondence occurs between hue and wavelength. It is true that a single patch of light of a particular wavelength will, when viewed in isolation (that is, in black or gray surroundings), normally have one particular and predictable hue. However, the occurrence of that hue

---

[1] For a given wavelength, the hue and saturation change somewhat if the intensity is changed; and for a given intensity of light energy, *brightness will vary according to wavelength.* We call the effective intensity the *luminance.* Although these changes have been investigated in some detail, we can disregard them here. If we remember that our central purpose in this chapter is to discover the building blocks of the perceived world, a relatively simple story emerges.

is not limited to one particular wavelength: *Any hue in the spectrum can be produced either by a single wavelength or by a mixture of quite different wavelengths.*

The elements of color mixing: Facts and theories Let us consider Newton's prismatic experiment (Figure 10) and see why it was not simply an experiment in physics.

If we pass white light through a prism, it breaks up into all the colors of the spectrum, and if we recombine the entire spectrum, we again see white light. If, however, we repeat the experiment, selecting light from only three narrow bands of the spectrum — say, 650 (red), 530 (green), and 460 (blue) — we will also see white when we combine these tiny portions of the total spectrum. We have broken down the white light, kept only three colored portions of it, and recombined these to form white again (Figure 12*A*). And, as you might guess, if we can make white by mixing only three wavelengths, *we can match any hue in the spectrum by mixing those three wavelengths in varying proportions.* (In fact, we can make some colors that are not in the spectrum at all: The red in the spectrum always looks a little yellowish unless we add some blue; the color purple is completely missing from the spectrum.)

We can therefore describe the light of any hue in terms of the mixture of three standard wavelengths that will duplicate its appearance.[2] Many different mixtures of wavelengths can be used in this way to duplicate all of the hues. But because the three shown in Figure 12 appear to be relatively "pure" in appearance, it was believed for many years that they were the "primary colors." According to the *Young-Helmholtz theory* (which was proposed in 1845 by Thomas Young and developed in its widely accepted form by Hermann von Helmholtz 20 years later), there are three kinds of cones in the eye: Each kind of cone is maximally sensitive to one region of the spectrum (Figure 13) [**Figures 13–15 face page 27**] and each, when stimulated by light energy, would produce its specific sensation. The three colors were *red, green,* and *blue* (roughly speaking). All other hues were considered to be combinations of these. That is, although we can distinguish thousands of different JNDs of color, this immense catalog of observations may be accounted for by a much smaller number of elementary experiences.

This theory and its various modifications fit the facts of color-matching experiments well, and it was accepted as *the* explanation

[2] Because the three wavelengths' intensities can be expressed in a proportion that adds up to 1.0, specifying two of them will automatically determine the third as well, so that a standardized system can be set up using only two wavelengths. This is what is generally used in engineering applications.

of color vision for many years despite the fact that the colors produced by these wavelengths don't appear *really* pure (see Figure 15). There are several other difficulties; for example, we can observe spots of yellow which fall in regions of the retina where we cannot observe red and green; color-deficient observers may be "blind" to red and green, yet not to yellow. But the theory's greatest deficiency is that its explanations do not fit the perceived similarities and differences between colors: Violet does look like a reddish-blue, and aqua does look like a bluish-green, but yellow simply does not look like a greenish-red.

In fact, if all of the JNDs of hue are arranged so that each is next to those to which it appears most similar, we obtain the *color circle* shown in Figure 14. Notice that simply by arranging the colors in this way we learn some rules about how to combine them, and that these rules are *purely psychological facts*—that is, rules we can use to predict how colors will mix and combine without knowing anything at all about either physics or physiology.

The *opponent-process theory,* proposed in 1955 by psychologists L. Hurvich and D. Jameson (and based on an earlier theory [1872] of physiologist Ewald Hering) fits the apparent similarities and differences between hues very well. The opponent-process theory assumes that there are four basic hues (and their corresponding physiological processes), paired in two sets as diagrammed in Figure 15: a yellow-blue pair and a red-green pair. These two pairs, and a black-white pair, will account neatly for the facts of color mixture, for most color-vision defects, and for the appearances of "purity," "sim-

FIGURE 16. *A modern opponent-process model (Hurvich & Jameson, 1974).* To account for color vision three kinds of cones (alpha, beta, and gamma) are proposed, each responding most strongly to light of the wavelength indicated at *A*. These either stimulate (arrows) or inhibit (dotted lines) three kinds of central opponent pairs—cells that respond either "blue" or "yellow" (a b/y pair), "green" or "red" (a g/r pair), or "white" or "black" (a w/bk pair). This scheme is compatible both with the phenomena of color blindness and with current physiological knowledge. If you work it through, you will find that it also accounts for the facts in Figures 10, 12, 14, and 15.

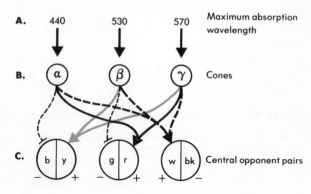

ilarity," and "dissimilarity" among the hues of the color circle (Figure 14).

There is some physiological evidence that retinal receptors exist that fit the Young-Helmholtz theory (although there is no evidence that they produce the independent sensations that theory requires); whereas more central mechanisms follow the opponent-process model. Photopigments found in the retina fit closely to the characteristics required of the three receptors in Figure 13 (Marks *et al.*, 1964) whereas cells are found in higher centers that increase their firing rate when a particular retinal region is stimulated by light energy of about 600 to 680 nm., and decrease their rate when the same region is stimulated by 540 nm. (DeValois & Jacobs, 1968)—which is just what we would expect from the red-green pair in Figure 15*B*. The diagram in Figure 16 is a plausible picture of how the system would work.

The elements of visual direction: acuity and local sign. So far, we have been considering single patches of light that differ only in their intensities and wavelengths. In addition, of course, such patches occur in different locations in the optic array; and if we could not distinguish one place from another, we could make little use of our eyes. We shall treat the problem in two parts: *acuity,* or the ability to detect a separation between two points, and *local sign,* or direction-sensitivity.

The importance, measures, and determinants of acuity. In order for us to perceive that one object, one facial expression, or one letter differs from another, there must be some specific difference in the way our receptors are being stimulated. We might conceivably have visual receptors that are sensitive to smiles versus frowns, *a*'s versus *b*'s, circles versus squares. This is both unlikely and uneconomical, however. Let us see what the most economical arrangement would be.

The simplest system that could respond differently to all of the shapes that we can see would be a mosaic of retinal receptors (as in Figure 17), each of which sends a single message to some separate place in the brain. How could such a system distinguish the letter *C* from an *O*, for example? By the fact that the gap in the *C* leaves one cell unstimulated. If the gap in the letter *C* were too small, we would see the *O* instead, as in *A*. Similarly, if the dots in *B* were too close together, we would see them as a single point. The ability to distinguish such fine separations is called *acuity,* and it has two general measures, one for diagnosis and one for research purposes.

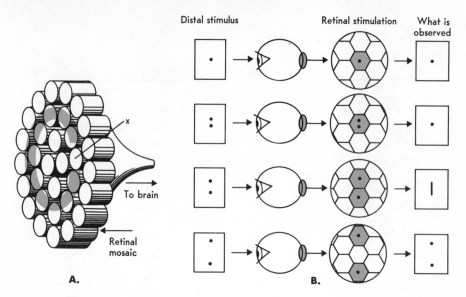

FIGURE 17. *The mosaic model of acuity.* A. Unless the gap in the letter C is large enough to leave one receptor, x, unstimulated, the C should be indistinguishable from an O. B. Similarly, only if an intervening receptor remains unstimulated, would we expect two points to be distinguishable from one (after Asher, 1961).

FIGURE 18. *Tests of visual acuity.* These are usually eye charts—for example, letters, as in the Snellen chart, or E's facing in different directions—in which a subject must see a gap between parts of the figure in order to respond correctly. (A.) Normal vision. (B.) Myopia: Near objects are focused readily; concave lenses needed for far objects. (C.) Hypermetropia: Far objects are focused readily; convex lenses needed for near objects (reading). (D.) Presbyopia: Loss of ability to focus near objects as age increases (see table). (E.) Frequency measures of acuity: At a distance of 2 feet from the eye, the grids at 1 are 30 lines per degree of visual angle, (see Figure 8 for an explanation of *visual angle*), those at 2 are 100 lines per degree at a distance of 5 feet. The number of pairs (or cycles) of light and dark bars per degree (they need not be sharp lines) may be considered the *spatial frequency*. When the grid's frequency is greater than the power of the subject's eye to resolve the individual lines, he cannot tell whether the grid is horizontally or vertically oriented.

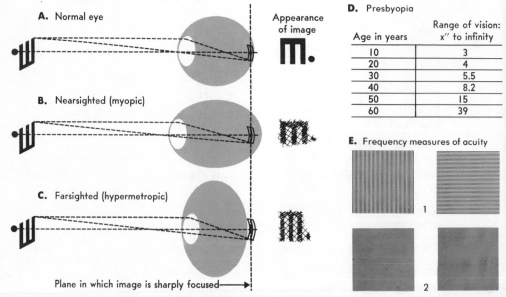

Diagnostic tests and measures. As was shown in Figure 8, the lens of the eye changes shape, or *accommodates,* in order to bring objects that are at different distances from the eye to the same focus on the retina. Many people (more than 25 percent of the population) are unable to focus equally well at all distances (see Figure 18). The resulting blur lowers the viewer's acuity. Because such defects can usually be corrected if we know the extent of the acuity loss, standardized acuity test charts have been devised. These are shortcut psychophysical procedures that measure difference thresholds of separation. Either the size of the gap which must be detected is varied from one line to the next on the testing chart, or the size of the retinal image is varied by having the viewer approach the chart until he can just make it out. By the first measure, if the average person can read the fourth line at 20 feet, and so can you, your acuity is a normal 20/20; by the second procedure, the number of feet from which you can read what the normal person can read at 20 feet is the measure of your acuity, and the higher the score, the greater your acuity. Because the various kinds of visual defects differ in the way in which distance affects vision, acuity tests should fit the tasks for which people are being selected.

Research measures: visual angle and grating acuity. For most scientific and technical purposes, the *visual angle subtended at the eye* is used to measure the size of a stimulus, because the retinal image's size remains constant for a given visual angle regardless of the object's distance (see Figure 8). Note that as the distance increases, it takes a larger object (or a larger separation between objects) to produce the same retinal image. In general, the normal observer can detect a separation between two points that subtends an angle of at least 1/60th of a degree (1 minute) at the eye. That visual angle is subtended by a separation of 0.005 inches at 1 1/2 feet (normal reading distance), of 0.05 inches at 15 feet, and of 0.5 inches at 150 feet. A smaller separation at each of these distances would be subthreshold.

One way to measure acuity is to use a ring with a gap in it—like a C—in varying orientations, as we did in Figure 17A. If the subject identifies the gap's orientation no better than we would expect him to by chance, then we know that we are below his acuity limit. Another similar measure uses a grid of lines, like those in Figure 18E. If the separation between the lines is too small, he cannot *resolve* the individual lines—that is, they all blur to a gray, instead of being clearly black and white lines—and he cannot tell which way the grid is oriented.

The grid has certain practical advantages in studying optical systems, such as cameras, microscopes, TV systems, and the human eye. One advantage is that it lets us describe that system in terms of how well it reproduces different *spatial frequencies.* "Spatial frequency" means the number of lines per degree of visual angle. The grids in Figures 17 *E1* and *2* are 30 cycles per degree and 100 cycles, respectively, when the former is viewed from about 2 feet and the latter from about 5 feet. The *modulation* between black and white stripes ("modulation" means the difference between the darkest and lightest regions) is not handled by the visual system at a frequency as high as 100 cycles, so you see only the average—a gray. The language of spatial frequencies is particularly suited to discussing video equipment, because it allows us to specify acuity in terms that can be directly applied to our equipment needs.

In addition to these practical advantages, we will see in Chapter 5B that there may be important theoretical reasons to think of the eye's functioning in these terms, as well.

The uses and applications of acuity measures.   One obvious use for acuity measures is to make sure that important details are large enough to be visible—that is, the gaps and serifs on the letters in a sign that is to be read at 150 feet should be *at least* one-half inch in size. Less obvious but at least equally important is the need to make dots and stripes *small enough so that they will blur* when we want them to. Let us see when we want this to happen.

In many applications, such as most methods of printing, television, and in much painting and drawing, shades of gray and mixtures of colors are obtained by using dots and stripes that are too small and close to be resolved (i.e., they are below acuity). All of the shades of gray and color that are printed in this book (for example, Figures 2C, D; 8; 11) are made of tiny dots. But in some figures, such as Figures 2A, and 5A, the dots or cross-hatching that are used to create the shading are clearly visible as black dots or lines.

This technique is also employed in paintings that are composed of numerous distinct patches of color, as in the work of such Impressionists as Monet and Seurat. Although individual patches are clearly visible, we can see shading, and the colors do mix. Why is that? Probably because the dots and patches are visible in the central region of the eye, but are more or less blurred in peripheral vision (see Figure 19). This fact is responsible for the peculiar vitality that such paintings have when viewed at the proper distance. Areas of color are seen now as dots, now as mixed color (see Jameson & Hurvich, 1975). Furthermore, there is a special "rightness" that the

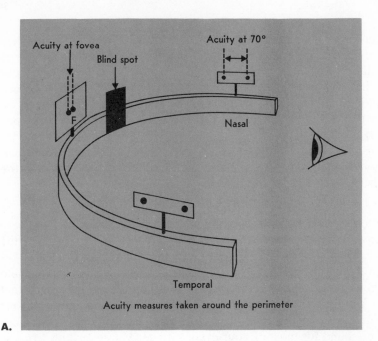

A.

FIGURE 19. *The surprising narrowness of the momentary gaze. A.* A perimetry experiment to measure acuity at various distances from the fovea. The observer is looking straight at the fixation point (F). Note that a wider separation is needed to distinguish the test dots at the sides. *B.* The percentages of acuity at different distances from the fovea.

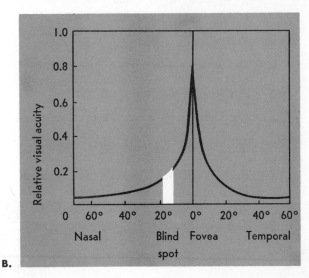

B.

eye discovers in them: When one looks away from a meaningless collection of dots and brings them from the fovea to peripheral vision, they turn out not to be meaningless at all, but to be just those dots that will snap into some clearly recognizable person or object. This kind of "discovery" is probably a major component of the esthetic response even though it can sometimes be achieved by such merely mechanical means.

This has raised an extremely important aspect of visual perception, namely the way in which acuity differs between the central and peripheral parts of the retina.

The distribution of acuity over the retina. Fine details can be detected only in the foveal region of the retina. Away from the central fovea, visual acuity deteriorates rapidly. By 5 degrees from the center, it has dropped 50 percent (Figure 19). The fovea itself is between 1 and 2 degrees. That is about 8 letters across, if you hold this book at a distance of 18 inches from your eye. This means that when you look at any larger scene or object, you see only that one tiny area as optimally clear during any one glance. You are therefore partially blind for most of your eye's surface. Moreover, the retina is *completely blind* where the optic nerve leaves the eye (see Figures 6 and 20). Why don't we normally notice the blind spot?

First, we are not aware of the blind spot because what we miss with the blind spot of one eye, the other eye usually picks up. Second, there is no empty or colorless spot in the world that we can observe, even with one eye alone: Things tend to "complete themselves" when interrupted by the blind spot (Figure 20), and a line that falls across that spot does not appear any shorter than when it falls elsewhere. Such filling-in processes are quite general in per-

FIGURE 20.   *The blind spot.* Close your left eye and fixate the X with your right eye. Adjust your distance from the page until the white disc at right disappears on the blind spot of your eye. See Figure 19 for further details. Is there an evident interruption of the checkerboard pattern when the white disc disappears?

ception (Figure 74*B*), but research into this quite fascinating phenomenon has so far been scant. The third and most important reason
that we do not see the blind spot is that it is far from the fovea; and
normally if we are interested in looking at something we look at it
with our sensitive foveas, much as you might cast about with a
flashlight in a dark room. *Normal vision is not stationary vision,* and
what we end up with after exploring the scene with our foveas is not
simply the sum of the details we have detected on each view. We return to this critically important topic in Chapters 5 and 6.

Local sign: Perceiving visual direction. It is not enough to be
able to detect that two patches are separated in space; we have to
perceive where they are *in relationship to each other* if our perceptual systems are to rebuild the perceived world out of these bits
and pieces into which we have been analyzing it.

Consider points *A, B,* and *C* below. Do we simply see that there
are three distinct points, or are *B* and *C* perceived as being situated
in different *directions?* A fourth point, *D,* is not merely one additional point: It is *in line with A* and *B,* and the four points taken together constitute a distinct spatial pattern—a *shape.* Each point thus
seems to carry some sensation of location, a *local sign,* in addition
to sensations of color (in this case, black).

C.

A   B   D

For a long time, it has been argued that no local signs—and no
shape perception—exist at birth, but that they are learned by making
eye movements. According to this theory, the brain registers the fact
that you must move your eye *down* from *C* to *A* if, when you are
looking at *C,* you wish to bring *A* to your fovea (i.e., to *fixate A*),
and then to the *right* in order to change fixation from *A* to *D.*
Whether local signs must be learned in this way is still an open
question to which we shall return later (Chapter 4B). However, we
do know that the actual performance of eye movements is certainly
not *necessary* for the perception of location and shape, because we
can discern shapes at exposures that are too short for any eye movements to be made (less than 0.2 seconds).[3]

---

[3] Although there were once powerful theoretical reasons for arguing that local signs
must be the result of learning via eye movements (see Chapter 4B), the main reason
today for keeping this possibility open is that there is evidence that a point's perceived location changes if the observer has been trained to perform different eye
movements in order to fixate that point (Festinger *et al.,* 1967).

Because only our foveas have good acuity, we must move our eyes about to see the world in any detail; as a moment's thought will tell you, such eye movements must change the location of any object's retinal image. Let us now discuss the effects of eye movements, and how they may be taken into account in perceiving an object's location.

THE MOVING EYE:
EYE MOVEMENTS AND REFLEXES

For a *stationary* eye and a *stationary* observer, the image of an object at any point in space is simply projected to some point on the retina and thence to the cortex (Figures 3 and 6). Given the position of the point in the retinal image, therefore, it is not difficult to understand how we manage to perceive the object's direction in space.

This stationary case is not at all the usual one, however. The viewer's body is in almost constant motion in the world, his head is in motion with respect to his trunk, and his eyes are in motion in his head. Moving observers need two kinds of eye movements to look at moving (or stationary) objects in a three-dimensional world:

Compensatory movements, smoothly and precisely executed, permit the eye to remain fixed on some point while the body moves. In addition, we have skilled *pursuit movements* that swing the eyes smoothly to keep them fixed on moving objects, and the adaptive mechanisms of *accommodation* and *convergence* that bring any object to which we are attending into clear focus and central location on the retina (Figure 21*B*).

In addition to these, *saccadic eye movements* bring the fovea from one point in the visual field to another, in rapid jumps that take only about 1/20 of a second to execute, but that take much longer—at least 1/5 of a second—to prepare for. That is, you can only make about four *saccades* (saccadic eye movements) per second. (If you consider the fact that you can only look at about four different places each second, and also recall the acuity distribution in Figure 19, you will begin to get some idea of how little you actually see clearly when you look at some large object or scene for a short time.)

Normal vision would be quite impossible without the cooperation of all of these muscular actions, and the viewer's perceptual system must in some fashion "make allowances" for the eye movements they produce before it can assign spatial meaning to any stimulation of the retina. In order to know where the distal object is in space, you have to know how your eye has moved. Only then can you in-

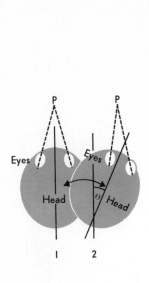

A. Compensatory movements **B.** Accommodation and convergence

FIGURE 21. *A. Compensatory movements, and B. accommodation and convergence.*
To experience this phenomenon yourself, fixate some point *P* that is straight ahead of
you. Keeping your gaze fixed on *P,* rotate your head from side to side. Do your eyes
seem to be moving? *A* shows the closely coordinated motions this task actually demands.
If you repeat this action, but nod your head vertically as you shake it from side to side
and also move your torso a little (in addition, the fixation point may be moving in space),
you will still be able to maintain fixation accurately and effortlessly – but we couldn't
begin to draw the kinds of complex compensatory movements needed to do this. As
a point to which we are attending approaches the eyes from far (F) to near (N), the shape
of the lens changes, or accommodates, from position 1 to position 3 to keep the focus
clearly on the retina (B2). Coordinated with this, the angle between the eyes changes, to
bring the point onto the fovea of each eye. This is the phenomenon of convergence.

terpret the image on your retina. Consider this example: Close one
eye and move your other eye from point *A* to point *B* below; the
page appears stationary. If, however, you produce approximately the
same change in your retinal image by first fixating point *B* and then
pressing at the side of the upper eyelid in order to move your eye-
ball back and forth, the page appears to move in space as the retinal
image moves across the eye. What is different in the way that retinal
image motion was obtained in the two situations?

          A.   B.

If we did not make some form of allowance for our eye movements, our perception of shapes would dissolve into kaleidoscopic

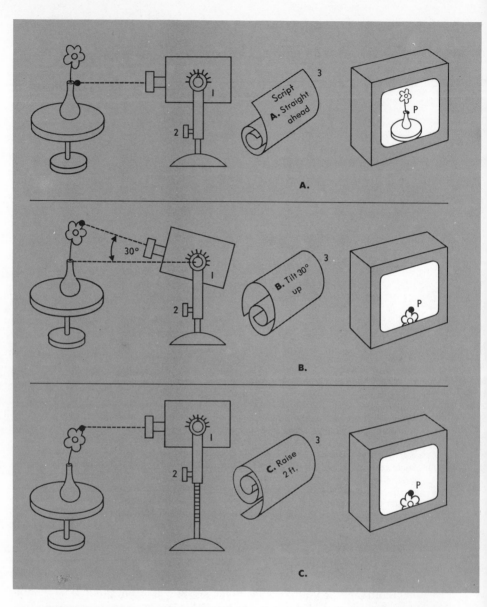

FIGURE 22. *The spatial meaning of a local sign depends on knowing the position of the eye itself.* The relationship between the movable eye and the fixed brain may be illustrated by the analogy of a fixed TV receiver on which is displayed the image picked up by a moving TV camera. The location of any point in space cannot be determined from the location of its image in the receiver alone, since the latter also depends on the position of the camera. We might know the position of the camera by receiving information about how it is tilted or raised (mechanisms 1, 2), as in (B) and (C). Analogously in the case of the eye, there might be sensations from kinesthetic receptors in the eye muscles that tell us which way the muscles are pulling the eye. We might also know about the camera's position from the script (3) that the camera is following. In the case of the eye, this would mean that the brain would have to keep track of the orders that are sent to the eye muscles. The relative contributions of these sources of information is still at issue, and we shall see in Chapter 5 that there are still other means by which the motion of the eye might be detected and "taken into account."

chaos, since the eye searches the world incessantly, bringing various points of interest into the clear spotlight of the fovea. The several ways in which we might get information about how our eye has moved are illustrated in Figure 22. Their relative importance is still under investigation, and we will consider some research to that point in Chapters 4 and 6.

This is a good place to stop and survey how much of the perceived world we can now explain, for we are now in possession of all the elements that would be needed to analyze our visual perceptions of things, people, and events, *if* the simplest structuralist assumptions were correct. Before we try to apply our visual analysis, however, we will take a very brief look at the other distance sense, audition, both to see whether we can find similar elementary units in that modality and because we will need to draw upon this information at various places later on in the book.

B. The Sense of Hearing

The sensory apparatus associated with the ear is not easy to visualize. In the simplified diagram of Figure 23*A*, we can identify the parts connected with hearing: *(1) The outer ear,* which brings the

FIGURE 23. *The ear in structure and function. A.* Pressure variations in the air (sound waves) are transmitted through the *outer ear* to the *ear drum,* which they set into motion. Those vibrations are transmitted by the small bones of the *middle ear* to the *oval window* of the *cochlea.* We examine the cochlea in more detail in *B.* The *auditory nerve* carries information from the cochlea to the auditory projection area in the brain (see Figure 3). (The semicircular *canals* are organs that sense changes in position; we discuss them on p. 65 in Chapter 4.)

B. Here the cochlea, greatly simplified, is drawn as though it were uncoiled and made partially transparent. The mechanical vibrations from the bones of the inner ear are transmitted through the oval window to the fluid that fills the inner ear and sets up ripples, or deformations, in the *basilar membrane* that runs the length of the cochlea. The basilar membrane carries the *organ of Corti,* which contains receptor neurons that are sensitive to any movement or strain in the basilar membrane. Sound waves of different frequency deform the basilar membrane most at different locations, as shown by the dotted arrows, and stimulate the auditory nerve in different characteristic patterns.

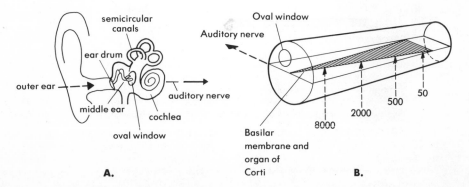

sound-pressure waves to the middle ear; *(2) The middle ear,* which transmits those waves to the inner ear; and *(3) The inner ear,* which contains a long ribbon of tissue, the *basilar membrane* (4) immersed in fluid. The basilar membrane (which is coiled into a spiral as shown in Figure 23*A*, but which we have "unrolled" in Figure 23*B*), supports the auditory receptors, which in turn transmit nerve impulses (through several relay stations) to the auditory projection area in the brain (see Fig. 3). The other structures in Figure 23*A* are the semicircular canals (7), which are involved in our sense of bodily position, and which we will consider in Chapter 4.

Sound waves entering the ear consist of pulses of different air pressures set up when the air is rapidly disturbed. The way pressure changes with time is shown for several kinds of sound waves in Figure 24. The simple *sine wave* that is produced by a tuning fork (or any other source of a perfectly pure musical note) can vary only in its *amplitude, frequency,* or *phase* (Figure 24A). When we vary the amplitude of the pressure differences in such a sound wave, we experience mainly a change in its *loudness;* when we vary its frequency (that is, how rapidly the pressure rises and falls), we experience mainly a change in its *pitch.*

By combining sine waves of different frequencies in varying mixtures and weights, more complex wave forms can be produced. That means that we can think of any one of the complex waves shown in Figure 24*B* as a collection of sine waves, and we can specify it in terms of its amplitude at each component frequency. In order to make graphs of nonrepeating sounds, like speech, we use *sound spectrographs* (like Figure 24*C,iii,* which as you see is composed of "slices," each one of which is like the graphs in Figure 24*C,ii*).

The mathematical technique by which we decompose a complex wave into a component set of sine waves is called *Fourier analysis.* In a proposal that is very similar to his theory of vision (Figure 13), Helmholtz suggested that the ear, in essence, performs a Fourier analysis of the sound waves that enter it. This is done when each different component frequency in the sound causes a particular place in the basilar membrane to vibrate (refer again to Figure 23*B*).[4] (This "place theory" of audition has been shown to be at least partially correct [von Békésy, 1947].)

The elementary physical variables would therefore be *frequency*

---

[4] It is easy to see how something like a Fourier analysis might underlie our perception of sounds. Less obviously, we will see that an extension of the frequency analysis to *visual* acuity, which we introduced on p. 33, permits a similar kind of analysis to be proposed as an explanation for shape perception. We will elaborate this further in Chapter 5B.

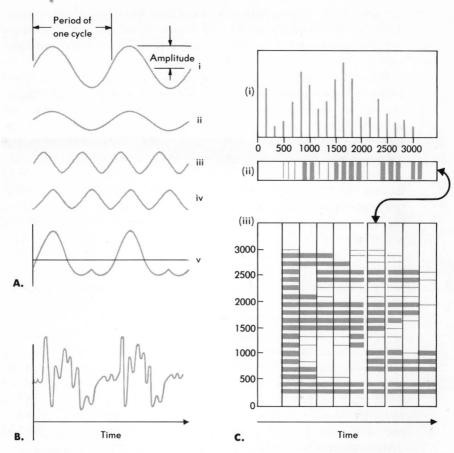

FIGURE 24. *Sound waves. A. Sine waves and their combinations.* The simplest auditory stimulus to describe is a train of condensations and rarefactions in the air that follows a sine wave *(i)*. Such sine waves can differ in their *amplitude,* in their *frequency* (how rapidly the cycle repeats) measured in *cycles per second* (1 cycle per second = 1 Hertz, or 1 Hz.), and in *phase* (how their cycles coincide). The waves at *i* and *ii* differ in amplitude; *ii* and *iii* differ in frequency; *iii* and *iv* differ in phase. At *v,* we have added together *i* and *iii,* point by point, and obtained a new wave. By a mathematical procedure known as Fourier analysis, we can reproduce any wave form as closely as we wish by adding together sine waves of the right frequencies and amplitudes.

B. A complex tone. A profile of the pressure waves produced by a musical instrument, it can be specified in terms of its fundamental frequency and a set of higher frequency components, or overtones.

C. Speech. A nonrepeating stimulus such as a speech sound can be described by mapping its energy at each frequency. This is done for a vowel at *i,* representing the amount of energy at each frequency by the height of the lines; the same vowel is mapped in *ii,* with the energy being indicated by the thickness of the line at each frequency. A sequence of sounds like a spoken word is represented by a *sound spectrograph (iii),* which is composed of momentary slices, each of which is like *ii.* The arrow shows where the vowel *(ii)* appears in the spectrograph.

and *amplitude.* The specific nerve energies would be given, respectively, by which receptors on the basilar membrane are stimulated and how much; and the corresponding sensations are *pitch* and *loudness.*

What about qualities of hearing besides pitch and loudness? For example, a note played on the clarinet and a note played on the piano may be identical in both pitch and loudness yet have characteristically different qualities, or *timbres,* by which we recognize them. Helmholtz showed that it was the particular pattern of higher frequencies, added to the basic pure tone, that determines timbre.

Although there are various complications that should be added to this simple picture, we appear to have a set of elementary units for the analysis of hearing just as we do for seeing, and we should be prepared to use them to explain our perceptions of objects in the real world.

C. The Distance Senses of Sight and Hearing: Summary and Preview

The objects and events of the world that we see affect our visual system only indirectly through the optic array, or pattern of proximal stimulation of light energy that reaches the eye. If we consider a small homogeneous patch of light energy at any point in the optic array, that patch can be completely specified in terms of its wavelength mixture, its intensity, and its position or direction in the array. (This *must* be possible in *every* case; we shall see later, however, that there may be much better ways in which to analyze and discuss the optic array.)

Corresponding to changes in these physical variables of predominant wavelength, wavelength mixture, and intensity, normally functioning human beings see such a homogeneous patch of light change its hue, its saturation, and its brightness.

Thus, for a small patch taken *from any scene at all,* we can predict the sensation it will produce (that is, its appearance in isolation) simply from those physical measures. The intensities of light energy at, say, 460, 530, and 650 nm. in wavelength, and the two spatial coordinates needed to locate the point in two dimensions—these five measures, taken together, will permit us to specify or duplicate the appearance of any point. In one sense, our analysis of the process of seeing is completed.

Using the physical properties of frequency and amplitude, and the corresponding sensations of pitch and loudness, we have done the same thing for hearing as well, although in a much less detailed way.

If we do stop here, however, almost all our normal observations of the world go unexplained. How does a near object differ from a far one? How does a smile differ from a frown? How do we perceive the infinite variety of nature and the subtleties of our civilized surroundings? In short, how can we assemble the world of perceived things and people from the observations of spots and patches, which is all we have studied up to this point?

The first solution (which we have called *structuralism,* and which we will consider again in the first part of the next chapter) was simply to add the sensations together — and, it must be admitted, for certain kinds of observations, this appears to work quite well. From this viewpoint, the perception of a near object might differ from that of a far one because we experience different sensations of muscular action when our eyes converge to fixate each of them (Figure 21*B*). A smile might differ from a frown in that the local signs of the individual sensations that "compose" the smile follow an upward curve, whereas those for a frown follow a downward curve, and we have learned to expect different interpersonal consequences for the two different aggregations of sensation.

In the next chapter, then, we shall attempt to put the pieces together. Instead of considering the perception of individual patches in a two-dimensional plane and the contributions of only one sensory system at a time, we shall apply what we have learned to the perception of solid objects in tridimensional space.

MORE ADVANCED READING

CORNSWEET, T. N. *Visual perception.* New York: Academic Press, 1970. Chapter 8: Color vision, pp. 155–267.

HURVICH, L. M., and JAMESON, D. *The perception of brightness and darkness.* Boston: Allyn and Bacon, 1966.

KLING, J. A., and RIGGS, L. A. (Eds.) *Woodworth and Schlosberg's Experimental Psychology.* New York: Holt, Rinehart and Winston, 1971. Chapter 5, by D. Kenshalo, The cutaneous senses, pp. 117–168; Chapter 6, by L. Bartoshuk, The chemical senses 1. Taste, pp. 169–191; Chapter 7, by M. Mozell, The chemical senses 2. Olfaction, pp. 193–222; Chapter 8, by W. Thurlow: Audition, 223–271; Chapter 9, by L. Riggs: Vision, pp. 273–314; Chapter 10, by R. Boynton: Color Vision, pp. 315–368; Chapter 11, by M. Alpern: Effector mechanisms in vision, pp. 369–394.

SCHIFFMAN, H. *Sensation and perception.* New York: Wiley, 1976. Chapter 4: The auditory system, pp. 32–57; Chapter 5; Complex auditory phenomena 1. Psychoacoustics, pp. 58–71.

Perceiving Objects as Structures of Sensations

chapter four

In some situations the findings of sensory psychophysics may be applied directly. How much photic energy is needed in order to see a lighthouse beacon from ten miles away on a dark night? How high in frequency must a hi-fi set go in order to reproduce every note that we can hear?

These are very simple stimulus situations, however, and most objects are vastly more complicated. How can we study those more complicated situations? The structuralist assumption was, as we have seen, that the sensations produced by individual physical stimuli remain unchanged even when those simple stimuli are combined into more complex scenes, and that they can then be studied by the careful kind of observation called *analytic introspection* (Chapter 2C).

A. The Classical Conception of the Perceived World

In some cases, analytic introspection of the world around us does indeed seem to reveal the component sensations—if we dissect our observations carefully enough (see Figure 25). This should not be easy

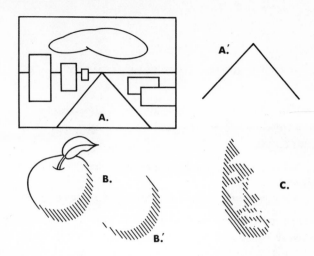

FIGURE 25. The world of "raw experience." The landscape scene at (A) can, with careful analysis, be seen to consist only of two-dimensional arrangements of lines: For example, the "road" is really only two lines which form the angle (A'). What are the "raw experiences" produced by (B) and (C)? See Figure 5 for another example. Now, look up from the page and, with one eye closed and your head stationary, inspect the room in front of you. With some effort, you will be able to see the room as a flat, disjointed arrangement of light, shade, and colors. To the extent that you are successful, you will have succeeded in taking the first step in the procedures of analytical introspection. This analytical procedure can be applied to your other senses as well. Consider a completely familiar word — say, "mother." It carries a host of meanings, memories, attitudes, and feelings. Now, repeat it aloud several times, while trying to listen to the sounds alone. With some effort and repetition, you may be able to hear those sounds without meaning — as though they were in some unknown language.

to do, however, because all of our previous perceptual efforts have been directed toward the perception of objects and events, and not toward discerning our sensations as such. Observers, it was thought, had to be trained to separate their "raw sensations" from their knowledge and from their memories about what the stimulus object is really like.

A limitation of this method is that it excludes most observers. We cannot study the insane, those too young to cooperate, or animals. Would this limit psychology too drastically? Not according to structuralist assumptions. Since the sensations of all men would be the same (and dependent on their specific nerve energies, Figure 3), the complete cataloging and study of the sensations would, when finished, be just as applicable to the very young children to whom we may wish to apply this knowledge as to the learned scientist who had undertaken the observations. After all, scientific observation usually requires long preparation, apparatus, and training, and the structuralists felt that there is no reason to expect the study of perception to be an exception.

The justification of this method depends, of course, upon the success with which one can in this way really uncover true elements, which presumably are the same for all men; otherwise the method is pointless.

PERCEPTIONS: SENSATIONS PLUS MEMORY
IMAGES

In line with what we have just said, the structuralists thought that the world of perception could be analyzed into two general classes of elements:

1. *Sensations,* which we observe when each individual receptor is stimulated; and

2. *Memory images,* which are the recollections of previous sensations.

Sensations were discussed in Chapter 3. As for memory images, they were presumed to be dimmer than, but otherwise similar to, the sensations whose "traces," or aftereffects, they are (Figure 26). Such images do not require sensory stimulation to be experienced. How do they occur without sensory stimulation? There is a very old theory about this: *If two sensations occur together a number of times, and if one sensation (or memory image) should occur alone, then the memory image of the other sensation will also be experienced.* (Do not confuse the *retinal image,* which is the pattern of light energy on the retina, with the *memory image,* whose existence is considerably more difficult to establish.) Thus, if the sight of a hammer's impact and the sound of a loud noise have occurred together frequently, the sight of the hammer alone will presumably cause the "bang" to be imagined (i.e., heard very faintly). There is no direct evidence to support this age-old theory, but variations of it continue to appear, and the versions offered by Helmholtz and by Hebb will be important to us throughout this book.

With these two classes of components—sensations and memory

FIGURE 26. Mistaking "images" for "sensations." Images and sensations were thought to differ from each other in degree, not in kind. If you were instructed to imagine an apple being displayed on a screen, and a real but very dim picture were actually projected on that screen, as in (A), you would probably not detect the picture as being real. Instead, even though (A) would be visible as a picture to any bystander, you would mistake it for an imagined apple (B) (Perky, 1910; Segal and Fusella, 1970).

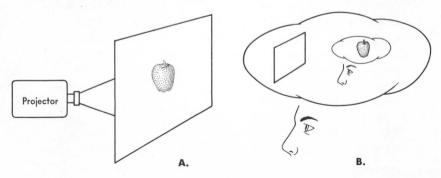

images—we should be able to account for all the things and happenings we can perceive, if we know the rules by which the components combine.

HOW DO SENSATIONS AND IMAGES COMBINE?

Most simply, sensations might just add together. The experience of a group of simple stimuli might simply consist of the *sum* of all the sensations that would have occurred if each stimulus had been presented separately, plus the memory images that have been associated with them. We shall call this the *addition hypothesis*. We will use it first to analyze the perception of visual space, which is a topic of particular importance. Let us see why it is.

THE SPECIAL IMPORTANCE OF SPACE

By the structuralist assumptions, all that we *see* consists of JNDs of light and shade, of points or patches of color. *We have no receptors for "motion," "approach," "causation"; we have no receptors for "anger," "cuteness," "sexual attractiveness."* How then can we perceive these qualities and events?

All possible events take place in space and time, and any object can be analyzed into a set of points in space. Once we have explained how we perceive each point in space, have we not explained the perception of all things we can observe? And isn't the perception of an object's movement explained if we understand how we see the object at different points in space at each moment in time, and put the whole sequence of images together in our memory?

The primary problem, then, was simply this: To discover how our visual sensations combine with the images acquired in our past experiences, in order to construct our current perceptions of space and spatial position.

B. The Perception of Two-Dimensional Shapes and Solid Objects at a Distance

The study of space perception had two early sources—although other reasons to be interested in it have arisen since then—(1) the practical, technical problems of pictorial depth representation—i.e., how to convey spatial distance where there really isn't any; and (2) philosophical questions about how (or whether) human beings can know the physical world.

The first task is epitomized by Leonardo da Vinci's penetrating analysis, in the sixteenth century, of spatial representation. The second task is represented by Bishop Berkeley's *New Theory of Vision,* written in the eighteenth century, which elaborated a detailed and tremendously influential psychological theory—in the course of attempting to prove a philosophical and theological point. Both of these sources have left their marks on present problems and prejudices in the study of perception.

THE PORTRAYAL OF DEPTH AND DISTANCE: THE DEPTH CUES

A *depth cue* (or clue) is *a pattern of proximal stimulation that contains information about the spatial locations of distal objects.* The monocular (or pictorial) depth cues convey information about space by the use of one eye alone; the binocular cues depend on the use of two eyes. The major traditional pictorial cues are interposition, linear perspective, size perspective, familiar size, and shadow distribution (see the descriptions in Figure 27). What makes them important to psychologists?

Pictures as surrogates for other distal objects. First let us see why the depth cues are important to artists. When an artist wants to draw a recognizable scene—say, a landscape—his intention is roughly as follows (although he does not phrase it this way): To create a stimulus object to which people will respond in much the same way as they would have responded to the countryside itself. That is, he intends to produce a *surrogate* of the countryside. He obviously cannot do this in its entirety. He must *abstract* only those aspects of the scene that are needed to obtain the desired effect yet which can be produced by pigment spread out on a flat surface of canvas or paper. One way to do this is to prepare a surface that reflects to the observer's eye the same proximal stimulus pattern as does the real physical scene. Figure 27 demonstrates the preparation of such a surrogate. The picture at *B* produces an optic array that is identical in many respects with the optic array produced by the scene at *A*.

Of course, there are ways in which artwork cannot match the optic array produced by a real scene. For example, if the spectator is free to use both eyes (see Figure 29), or to move his head (see Figure 59), he can usually see that he is only viewing a flat pigmented surface. But if he keeps his head motionless at the correct position

(Text continues on page 54)

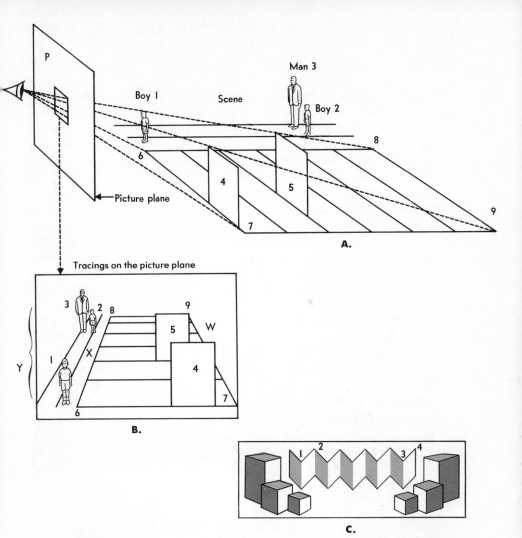

FIGURE 27. The monocular depth cues as prescriptions for painters. A. Side view of scene. The means of portraying tridimensional space on flat canvas were discovered by tracing the view on a "picture plane" of glass (P) held between the eye and the scene. Examining the tracings on the picture plane shows the cues that should be employed by the painter; some of these are listed below and are displayed at (B). B. Front view of scene. C. A demonstration of the cue of illumination (see explanation below).

List of monocular depth cues: (W) *Interposition.* Notice that rectangle 4 interrupts the outline of 5; this is a strong and effective depth cue, but it only indicates which of the objects is in front, not how much distance there is between them. (X) *Linear and size perspective.* Although lines 7–9, 6–8 are parallel on the ground, their tracings converge in the picture plane; similarly, 6–8–9–7 is a trapezoid on the picture plane, though it depicts a rectangle on the ground. This cue is called *linear perspective.* Following the same geometry, the same-sized boy (1, 2) and the same-sized rectangles (4, 5) produce smaller tracings when they are at greater distances: this is called *size perspective,* or the cue of *relative size.* Both of these sets of cues are effective. (Y) *Familiar size.* We know that the man (3) must be physically taller than the boy (1) yet they produce images of the same size in the tracing on the picture plane (1 and 3 in B); therefore, knowing their true sizes, we might deduce on the basis of their sizes in the tracing that the man is more distant than the boy. This is often a weak or ineffective cue (see Figure 56, pp. 118–120). (C) *Illumination direction.* Cover the right half of the picture in (C): which corner looks nearer, 1 or 2? Now cover the left half: which looks nearer, 3 or 4? Uncover both halves. What was responsible for the differences between 1 and 2, 3 and 4?

and closes one eye, then the optic arrays of picture and scene will be very similar, and he will perceive a convincingly three-dimensional scene even though what he is looking at is only a flat surface. To get an idea of how important it is to remove the cues that tell you that a picture is really flat, view with one eye any photograph of a scene through a small hole or tube that hides the picture's edges. It will then appear remarkably depthlike.

Like the artist's canvas, the retinas of our eyes are essentially flat. It seems reasonable now, as it did centuries ago, to believe that the monocular depth cues that cause us to perceive depth when we look at a picture also contribute to our perceptions of distance and solidity when we look at real objects in the real world. A number of these traditional cues are listed and explained in the caption for Figure 27. These depth cues are patterns that are likely to occur not only in the picture plane (Figure 27*B*) but also *in the proximal stimulation at the eye* when objects are scattered around in a three-dimensional landscape. It follows then that such indications of three-dimensional space are *necessarily* uncertain or ambiguous, for each cue by definition is a two-dimensional picture of some three-dimensional arrangement. Therefore, each cue must be ambiguous in the sense that the same proximal stimulation at the eye could be produced either by a two-dimensional pattern or by a three-dimensional arrangement of objects and surfaces. *Any theory that bases our perception of space on these depth cues must, therefore, consider space perception itself to be equally ambiguous.*

In fact, any given pattern in the optic array is much more ambiguous than that: The same proximal stimulus pattern can be produced at the eye by an *infinite* number of different three-dimensional arrangements. For example, all four quadrilaterals in Figure 28*A* stimulate exactly the same set of points on the retina of the eye. And the same reasoning applies to each individual point we consider in the retinal image. Although its local sign (see p. 39) will fix its apparent position in two dimensions, P', the very same point in the eye could be stimulated by an object at *any* distance from the eye: P_1, P_2, $P_3 \ldots P_n$.

This is a classical argument, much repeated ever since Berkeley offered it in the eighteenth century. As long as we consider our perceptions of objects to be composed of sensations, each of which corresponds to some *point* in the proximal stimulation, we must seek the explanation for visual space perception elsewhere than in the monocular visual stimulation.

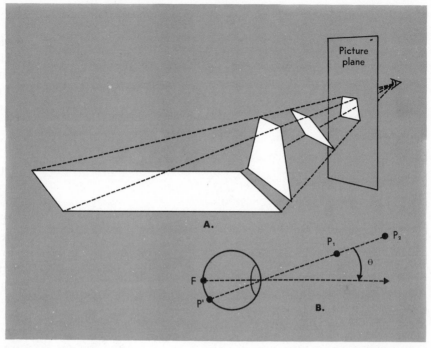

FIGURE 28. The ambiguity of a stationary monocular retinal image. *A*. Since the proximal stimulus pattern for the eye is two-dimensional, an infinite number of different tridimensional spatial arrangements will produce the same pattern at the eye. *B*. If we consider any single light-sensitive point on the retina (P'), it would respond in exactly the same way whether the distal stimulus is at distance P_1, P_2, etc.

INFORMATIVENESS AND LIMITATIONS OF
THE BINOCULAR VISUAL DEPTH CUES

Because the two eyes see the three-dimensional world from slightly different positions, the view each eye receives is somewhat different. Differences in these views provide two kinds of possible depth cues: double images and binocular disparity (Figure 29). Neither of these can be produced and used in pictures without special devices (or practice), and their absence contributes to the perceived flatness of ordinary pictures.

When the difference between the two views is large, double images are clearly visible, as in Figure 29*A*. When the difference or disparity between the two eyes' views is small, the double images can no longer be detected, but the disparity between them nevertheless comprises a sensitive and powerful depth cue. To explain bi-

(Text continues on page 57)

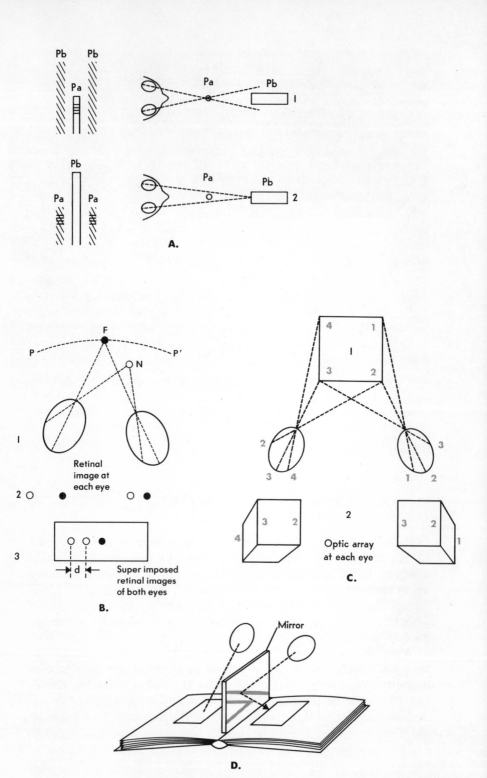

A.

Retinal
image at
each eye

Super imposed
retinal images
of both eyes

B.

Optic array
at each eye

C.

Mirror

D.

nocular disparity, we must first define corresponding (nondisparate) points: *Corresponding retinal points* are pairs of points, one on each retina, that would coincide if one retina could be slipped over the other. If a point in space projects its image to corresponding points on the retinas of the two eyes (like the black point, *F*, in Figure 29*B*), a single point of light will be observed. (As we shall see in Chapter 5, however, we can question whether such analyses in terms of points are the most appropriate for the perceptual process.) However, points that are farther or nearer than the distance for which the eyes are converged (like the white point, *N*, in Figure 29*B*) project their images to noncorresponding, or *disparate*, points. If the disparity is not too great (approximately 7 to 15 minutes of visual angle), it is still the case that only one point will be perceived — but the point will appear to be either nearer or farther than the plane *p–p'*, depending on the direction of the disparity (as explained in Figure 29*B*). This is often called binocular *fusion*, but the mechanism is not as well understood as that term might suggest. For a detailed yet clear discussion, see Kaufman (1974, pp. 263–361).

This disparity in itself can be a powerful depth cue. If we take

(*Text continues on page 59*)

FIGURE 29. *The binocular visual depth cues.*

A. Double images. Hold a pencil *(Pa)* vertically, about a foot straight ahead of you, lined up with some vertical edge on a more distant wall *(Pb)*. Fixate *Pa* (as at 1) and examine *Pb* carefully: It appears doubled, and you cannot tell, without closing one eye, which eye contributes each image. When you fixate *Pb*, double images of the pencil *(Pa)* appear. Notice from the diagrams that the disparity between the double images is opposite in direction between (1) and (2): it is "crossed" in (1) and "uncrossed" in (2).

B. Binocular disparity. Each eye receives a different view of any near three-dimensional arrangement. At (1) a schematic diagram illustrates the basis of the disparity; (2) shows what you would see with each eye separately. Note at (2) that the images of the black point *(F)* and the white one *(N)* are closer together in the right eye than in the left. If the viewer's eyes are *converged* (see Figure 21) on point *F*, all other points on the plane *p–p'* will produce retinal images at *corresponding points* in the two eyes, whereas objects that are nearer or farther than *p–p'* will fall on noncorresponding, or disparate, points, as at (3). As we saw in *(A)*, points nearer than *p–p'* produce crossed disparity, points further than *p–p'* produce uncrossed disparity. The direction and amount of the disparity, *d*, thus contains information about the points' relative distances, even though you are *not conscious of the disparity, nor of its direction.* (Remember that the retinal image is reversed within each eye, if you find the diagram at [2] confusing.)

C. Binocular difference as a depth cue was discovered in 1838 by Wheatstone, who also devised the first stereoscope, which is an apparatus for presenting the appropriate picture to each eye. At (1) we see a cube projecting different images to each eye (the front and rear corners have been numbered so that you can keep track of them). The pair of pictures at (2) is a *stereogram* of the cube, since if the left one is viewed by the left eye and the right one is viewed by the right eye, the respective eyes will receive the same patterns as they would receive from the cube itself (check the numbers on the corners).

D. A simplified stereoscope is shown that you can use with the stereograms in Figure 30. You can provide each eye with the appropriate picture by the following procedure: Place a small mirror on the gray center line. Adjust the mirror until the picture seen in the mirror appears to lie in the same plane as does the picture seen directly. Then fixate the picture in the mirror and wait for the stereo effect to develop. Proficiency will come quickly.

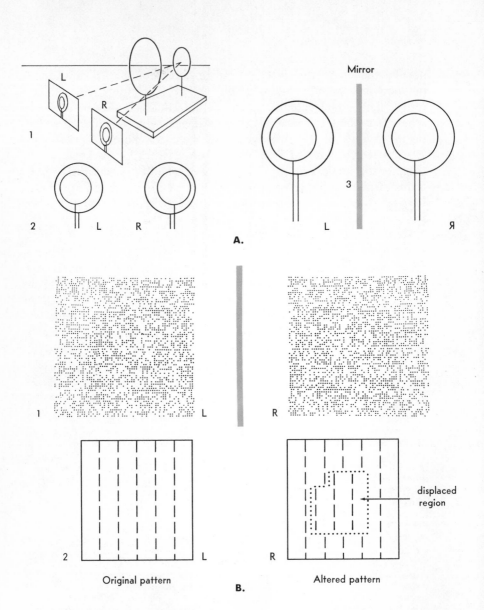

FIGURE 30. *Stereograms: Three dimensions from two views.* In *(A)* each eye receives a slightly different view of the two rings at (1). Although neither the left view *(L)* nor the right view *(R)*, as shown at (2), contains any depth cue to indicate which ring is nearer, if you present each view to the appropriate eye using the procedure shown in Figure 29D and the stereogram at (3) (in which the right view has been reversed because it will be viewed in the mirror), the correct three-dimensional spatial arrangement will appear after a moment's viewing.

The perception of a single three-dimensional scene is not simply a result of adding together the disparate views received by the two eyes. In *(B1)* no shape is recognizable in either view considered separately, nor can you detect any shape by looking for differences between the two views, but when the two patterns are viewed as a stereogram, a clearly visible object will appear, floating in space. Use the procedure of Figure 29D.

(Figure 30 continues)

two photographs of a scene, one from the position of each eye (that is, from about 65mm. apart), and then present each picture to its appropriate eye, a remarkably strong spatial effect will be obtained. Devices for viewing such disparate pictures are called *steroscopes*. A particularly simple procedure is illustrated in Figure 29*D* that will produce depth effects with the stereograms of Figure 30. (Not all viewers exhibit such stereoscopic vision, however, often because some imbalance between the two eyes results in some degree of suppression of the information from one of them.)

The cue of binocular disparity has been considered as an innate response to depth more frequently than any other. It is not too hard to imagine complex physiological connections that respond to the degree of disparity between two images produced by a point in space. Hering (1864) proposed a set of innate binocular distance signs, and recent electrophysiological recording has indentified cells in the brain that respond only to a given degree of disparity in binocular stimulation (Barlow *et al.,* 1967; Hubel & Wiesel, 1970). We

---

(Figure 30 continued)
Such stereograms, which provide a very important tool for probing the visual system (because they permit us to present shapes to the viewer's brain that are not present on either eye's retina), were originally devised and explored by Bela Julesz (1964, 1971). They are prepared by starting with two identical patterns of dots and then displacing an entire region (as shown at [*B*2]) in one of the patterns. Because the original pattern is random, the displacement of the region cannot be detected simply by looking at the altered pattern—it is still random. However, when the original is viewed by one eye and the altered pattern is viewed by the other, the displaced region then becomes visible, showing that the binocular visual system is directly sensitive to the *differences* in the stimulation at the two eyes. This sensitivity to binocular disparity is almost certainly innate.

You can make stereograms yourself that are much like the Julesz patterns by typing out arrays of letters or numbers that incorporate a disparity, and explore the machinery of binocular combination by formulating hypotheses and testing them (see Kaufman 1964a, b, and 1965; Kaufman and Pitblado, 1965). For example, what would you expect to see in the following stereogram? How could you increase the apparent distance that separates the *T*s and *H*s in depth?

OAUVTOMOHAOU   UOAXHMTWVUAO

OAUVTOMOHAOU   UOAXHMTWVUAO

OAUVTOMOHAOU   UOAXHMTWVUAO

Remember that one of the two views must be reversed, in order to use the mirror method of Figure 29*D*. We have done that here in the stereogram printed above, using letters that remain essentially unchanged by reversal. If you can master the trick of fusing stereograms without any apparatus (you have to relax your convergence, as though you were looking at something far away, even though you are accommodated for a near object), then you should not reverse one of the views when making a stereogram.

do not know whether such "disparity detectors" actually contribute to stereopsis, however.

We must keep in mind that all theories about binocular disparity are extremely speculative at present. And in any event, binocular disparity cannot be *the* basis of all space perception because one-eyed individuals may show good depth perception, even at very early ages (see p. 70n).

THE EMPIRICIST THEORY OF SPACE PERCEPTION

Having found that the monocular depth cues are inherently ambiguous, we must then ask how (and why) we see space as we do. For reasons that we need not review here, Helmholtz rejected binocular stereopsis as a possible innate basis for depth perception. Is there then some other sensory mechanism that we have missed, one which provides a specific nerve energy for depth and distance?

The earliest, easiest, and most persistent argument has been that there are no such mechanisms: that our list of elementary visual attributes is complete, and that our observations of "space" are not visual at all, but consist of the *kinesthetic* memory images (the memories of our movement and position sensations) that have become associated with the visual stimuli during our past experiences. This argument was formally proposed by Berkeley in 1709. As we will see, by adopting it, the structuralist explanation can get along with a remarkably economical set of analytic elements.

Berkeley's *New Theory of Vision*.   Whence do we get our ideas of space, size, solidity, and so on? Berkeley's hypothesis, now the traditional one, was that there could be only one such source—that is, *our memories of our past experiences with the world*—hence the name *empiricist* ("founded on experience"), which is frequently used for this theory.

Here is the heart of Berkeley's extremely influential argument in his own words:

> ... the judgment we make of the distance of an object ... is entirely the result of experience. ... a man born blind, being made to see, would at first have no idea of Distance by sight: the sun and stars, the remotest objects as well as the nearer, would all seem to be in his eye, or rather in his mind ... each ... as near to him as the perceptions of pain or pleasure, or the most inward passions of his soul. ... And I believe whoever will look narrowly into his own thoughts, and examine what he means by saying that he sees this or that thing at a distance, will agree with me, that what he sees only *suggests* to his un-

derstanding that, after having passed a certain distance, *to be measured by the motion of the body, which is perceivable by touch,* he shall come to perceive such and such tangible ideas [i.e., sensations of touch].

The nonvisual components of visual space. According to the empiricist hypothesis, then, an infant first learns the idea of distance through a combination of visual and kinesthetic experiences. The toy he wishes to grasp is, say, a full arm's reach away from him and subtends at that distance a visual angle of, say, 10° (Figure 31*A1*); by accident perhaps he extends his arm the full distance and grasps the toy to him. At another time, when the toy subtends a visual angle of, say, 30°, he may touch it while his arm is only half-extended (Figure 31*A2*). After many such experiences (according to

FIGURE 31. *The muscle-movement theory of visual space.* According to the empiricist theory, when the retinal image of some object brings to mind the memories of the grasping or walking motions that have been made in the past in order to reach that object *(A),* those memories *are* the idea of "distance" *(B).*

C. Normally, you do not perceive that your distance from some object or person has changed, but rather that one or both of you have changed location in space: your own movements must therefore be taken into account in the perception of space. Although the size of the retinal image has increased from 18° o 25° in both *(2)* and *(3),* at *(2)* the other person has changed his location, whereas at *(3)* the viewer has moved in space.

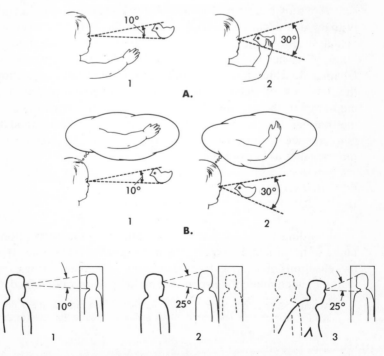

this theory) the child needs only to glance at the toy and recall the half-bent arm whenever the toy's image subtends 30°, or the fully extended arm whenever the image subtends 10° (Figure 31B). Thus he will acquire ideas of distance in space.

Moreover, reaching for, or walking toward an object are not the only kinesthetic memories that can contribute to our perception of the object's spatial location or depth. Our eyes also move in ways that might contribute; for example, in order to bring the image of any point at a moderate distance from the eye to sharp focus on the retina, the lens of the eye must be correctly *accommodated* (see Figure 21B). Similarly, the eyes must *converge* at some angle that is precisely related to the point's distance in order to bring the point's retinal image to the fovea of each eye. The kinesthetic sense of the degree of tension in the muscles responsible for these adjustments would thus provide an additional depth cue.

In fact, you can observe sensations resulting from these actions, with only a little effort. For instance, change your fixation rapidly from the horizon to the tip of your nose, and you will feel both sets of muscles in action. Moreover, the eye movement cues, as compared to the pictorial depth cues, would be relatively unambiguous. It is easy to imagine circumstances in which any of the pictorial depth cues would be wrong, but "fooling" accommodation or convergence requires special apparatus. For this reason, the nonvisual sensations of accommodation and convergence were thought to be primary depth cues in visual space perception.[1] Our experiences of visual space would then consist of three kinds of elements: (1) the "purely" visual sensations such as the color patches we discussed in Chapter 3, which are nonspatial; (2) the kinesthetic sensations from the muscles of accommodation and convergence; and (3) those memories of the previous kinesthetic sensations of reaching or walking that had become associated with the specific accommodation and convergence sensations, and with the visual depth cues, to lend *spatial* meaning to both of them.

COMBINING DIFFERENT SENSORY INPUTS
INTO A UNIFIED SPATIAL FRAMEWORK

According to the above explanation, then, the perception of distance is not a simple experience nor a purely visual one. It consists of sensations that arise from executing muscular actions (reaching, walking, accommodating, converging, and so on) combined with the

---

[1] Actually, despite this logic, it turns out that we do not use these distance cues much for near objects, and not at all for distances greater than two or three yards.

visual sensations that arise when the retina is stimulated in those contexts. This explanation therefore assumes that we possess sensory systems that keep us informed about those muscular actions with sufficient accuracy to account for our perceptions of space and distance.

So far we have taken into account only explanations of how we perceive the distance of some point from our eyes. But this is only a very small part of what we usually think of as space perception. Normally we don't see things as being at some distance and direction from *us*; instead we see things as being *at some place in space,* and we also perceive our bodies to be at some specific place within the same spatial framework. For example, if a person approaches you, he appears to get nearer, of course; if instead you walk (or lean) toward him, his perceived spatial location remains the same, while you perceive your own position to have changed (Figure 31C). The depth cues of accommodation, convergence, etc., may be identical in the two cases; what differs is that in the second case you supposedly "take into account" your own movements in space when using these depth cues.

An object's apparent spatial location does not, therefore, depend only on the depth cues that it provides the eye. It depends as well on how we perceive the positions of our eyes and of our bodies — on our *proprioceptions* (the perception of our bodily positions). And in order to be able to act effectively — to be able to place one foot in front of another, to stand upright, etc. — we must, of course, have sensory systems within our bodies that keep us informed about the spatial disposition of our limbs. We do have such proprioceptive apparatus: The sensory systems diagrammed in Figures 32 and 33, respectively, are normally capable of providing this sensory information, and we know that our perceptions of the main directions of space do draw on these systems.[2] Moreover, in addition to vision and kinesthesis, audition informs us about object's locations in space (Figure 34).

We have just described many very different kinds of sensory information, all of them referring to the *same space.* How do we combine all of these different kinds of sensory input into a single coherent perceptual experience?

The empiricist answer is that the physical world imposes its own consistency on our experience. Thus the degree of convergence of the eyes, their accommodation, their direction in the head, the size

[2] Howard (1973) provides a detailed and comprehensive outline of our position senses.

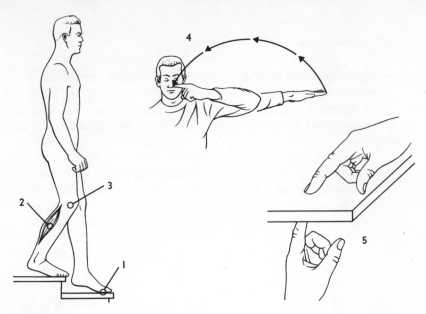

FIGURE 32. Locating the body in visual space: the kinesthetic and proprioceptive senses. Three types of receptors that are sensitive to pressure and strain are distributed as follows: over the body surfaces as the *tactile* sense organs of the skin (1); within the muscle bundles (2), to provide the *kinesthetic* system with information about the contractions of the muscles; and in the joints (3), to provide the *proprioceptive* information about the relative positions and displacements of the skeletal framework. Taken together with the senses of balance and acceleration (see Figure 33), they contribute to the body image, which refers to the spatial framework within which muscular behaviors are coordinated. Victims of diseases (such as locomotor ataxia) that have destroyed parts of the body image must guide each individual bodily movement visually, as in looking at each foot to see that it makes the proper movements for walking. To get an idea of the precision of the body image as a spatial framework, try the following tasks: (4) Close your eyes, stretch one arm to the side, at shoulder height, then bring the index finger of that arm in to touch the tip of your nose in one smooth motion. (5) Place the index finger of your left hand against the underside of a tabletop, out of sight, then place the index finger of your right hand on the topside of the table immediately over it. Now look under the table and see how close you came.

and direction of the retinal image, the size and direction of the arm movement that is needed in order to touch the object—these quantities are all determined by the geometry of physical space. Just because the physical world is consistent, the same patterns of stimulation of the visual receptors and of the kinesthetic receptors will occur together very frequently and so, consequently, will the corresponding visual, kinesthetic, and vestibular sensations (Figure 33A). Thus according to the empiricist theory, these very different sensations that are initially totally unrelated to each other will become associated because they occur together so frequently. Further, it hypothesizes that because each change in sensory input that results from a change in the viewer's bodily position is also fixed and consistent, *the viewer learns early in life that those changes are not due to the object's movement but rather to his own actions.*

(*Text continues on page 67*)

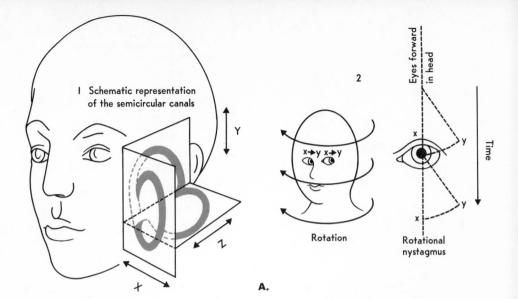

1 Schematic representation of the semicircular canals

2

Eyes forward in head

Time

Rotation

Rotational nystagmus

A.

FIGURE 33. Orientation and acceleration. *A.* The organs of equilibrium are located in the inner ear near the *cochlea,* which is the organ of hearing (see Figure 23). The semicircular canals (1) provide information to the nervous system each time a movement of the head along one or more of the three dimensions of space agitates the fluid in the appropriate canals. Other organs, called the vestibular sacs, respond with each tilt of the head against the downward pull of gravity. These organs are nicely suited to respond to changes in orientation or in velocity, and to provide the other sensory systems with the raw material needed to maintain a constant frame of reference with respect to the earth, even though the head on which those other organs are mounted is in continual movement. For example, if you whirl around like an ice skater or a ballet dancer, impulses from these organs set the eyes into an automatic compensatory reflex movement (called a *nystagmus*), which acts to help keep the retinal image still as long as possible during each glance at the world (2). If (x) is the straight-ahead direction in the head, the eye travels toward (y) against the motion of rotation, then rapidly snaps back in the direction of rotation and repeats the movement. Because of the nausea which attends any disturbance of these organs, and because of their importance in setting the spatial framework of perception, we could not be certain that normal perception would be possible in the absence of gravity ("free fall"). But recent prolonged orbital flights by U.S. and U.S.S.R. astronauts have shown that coordinated perception continues to be possible.

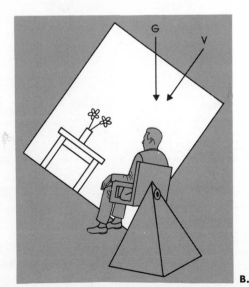

B. The fact is that our perceptions of the main direction of space do not depend completely on our organs of equilibrium and proprioception. Our visual environments usually contain obvious axes of vertical and horizontal orientation, such as walls, trees, and floors, and these provide a purely visual spatial coordinate system. The task of the observer in (B) is to adjust his chair until it is vertical, and his final setting is usually a compromise between the axis of gravity (G) and the main visual axis (V) (Witkin *et al.,* 1954).

Although there are great individual differences in the accuracy of performance on this task, the visual directions can readily be made to override the effects of gravitation (C). The "magic swing" occasionally found in amusement parks is a stationary suspended chair. The room (1) swings back and forth from (X) to (Y), around the ob-

B.

(Figure 33 continues)

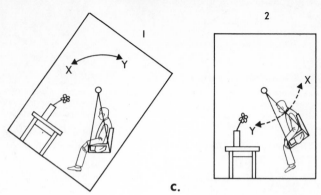

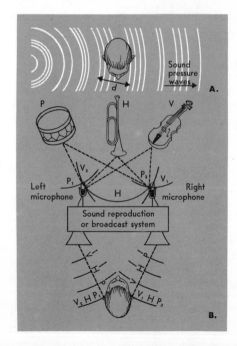

C.

(Figure 33 continued)

server. Such an enclosing visual framework exerts an extremely strong tendency to be seen at rest (see Figure 67), and, in consequence, the observer feels himself swinging to and fro, between (Y) and (X), as shown in (2)—to the extent that, if the room revolves completely, he will feel himself turning head over heels while the room appears to remain fixed and stationary (Wood, 1895). In the laboratory, if a rotating patterned cylinder surrounds a stationary viewer, he feels that he is rotating in the opposite direction (Brandt *et al.*, 1971); similarly, when viewing a patterned surface that rotates before him in the frontal plane, the upright viewer feels that he is tilting in the direction of rotation—just as though the direction of gravity had changed (Dichgans *et al.*, 1972; Held *et al.*, 1975). Peripheral vision is more important to this phenomenon than central vision, a fact that contributes to the greater effectiveness of wide screen motion pictures.

FIGURE 34. The auditory bases of space: stereophonic localization and other distance cues. Analogous to binocular disparity, the two ears receive pressure waves differently from different places in space. The pressure waves reach the nearer ear first, and this disparity, d (together with other binaural differences, such as the fact that a slightly lower intensity of stimulation reaches the farther ear because of a "sound shadow" cast by the head) permits the listener to localize the direction from which the sound is coming (Figure 34*A*).

Just as a stereoscope can present different pictures to each eye and thereby produce a three-dimensional effect, a stereophonic sound reproduction system can present appropriate binaural disparities and recreate many of the apparent spatial separations of the original recording session. The pressure waves of the violin in Figure 34*B* reach the right ear first, those of the drum reach the left ear first, and the horn reaches both ears together—as it should, since it is straight ahead during the recording session. This spatial separation permits a better appreciation of the contribution of each instrument than can usually be obtained in a monaural recording. The differences in arrival time are very slight—about 1/1,000 of a second. The time that it takes for the sounds of one's breathing and of one's footsteps to be reflected from the surfaces around one (about 1/1,000 of a second for each additional 6 inches of distance from the reflecting surface) provides the basis for what used to be called "facial vision" in blind subjects, enabling them to locate surfaces in space by ear. Some animals (especially the bat) depend almost entirely on this means of avoiding obstacles in space: Such creatures emit high-frequency sound waves and are guided by the time it takes the echoes to return.

The perception that some object is stationary at some place in space is, by this analysis, not at all a simple experience. It is a very complex mixture of visual sensations, tactual and kinesthetic sensations, and associations (or expectations) of what visual and tactual-kinesthetic sensations would result if the observer were to move his eyes or his body.

Because these structures of association are so well learned, the idea of an object's spatial location *seems* to be simple and immediate, which may make the above argument difficult to grasp. An early experiment reported by Helmholtz in 1866 will help to clarify the point, however.

By placing a prism in front of the eye, the direction of each point in the optic array is displaced, say, to the left. When the subject attempts to touch some object, therefore, it is not where it appears to be, and he reaches to the left of where it actually is (Figure 35*A*). His perceptions of visual direction and of tactual-kinesthetic direction are no longer in the same relationship. (Of course, the subject must *not* be able to see his hand while he is actually doing the reaching, else he will be able to guide his action by seeing where his hand is, relative to the object, at each moment.)

But after the subject practices at reaching for objects while wearing the prism, his errors decrease and finally disappear: The relationship between visual direction and tactual-kinesthetic direction has

FIGURE 35. *Prism adaptation. A.* How the subject tries to point at the target when first looking through the prism. *B.* How he points at the target after practice in guiding his hand while watching it through the prism. *C.* How he points at the target when the prism is removed. Note that his arm and hand are covered from view in all these tests. (This kind of experiment has been used as a tool to study perceptual learning, and we discuss it in that context on p. 98.)

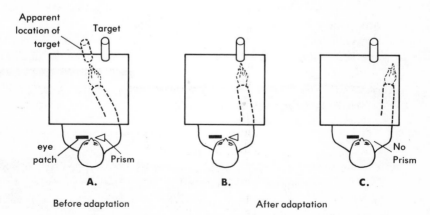

been relearned—*adaptation* has occurred (Figure 35*B*). In fact, when the prism is removed (Figure 35*C*), the subject now reaches too far to the *right* when he tries to touch the object.

These results show that a new relationship can be established between visual direction and reaching by exposing the observer to a new (but still consistent) physical arrangement. As we shall see later on (Figures 51, 52), similar adaptation effects have been demonstrated with a wide range of perceptual phenomena. Helmholtz thought that these findings proved the following: (1.) That the visual local sign of direction (the direction in space at which some point in the retinal image is perceived to lie) was changed in the course of wearing the prism; and (2.) that this change in visual perception occurred because the tactual-kinesthetic sensations that the subject experienced when he reached for and touched the objects while he looked at them through the prism, had provided him with a new structure of nonvisual associations which in turn gave a new spatial meaning to his visual sensations of direction. And, to Helmholtz's way of thinking, if visual space perception were not the result of learning in the first place (i.e., during the observer's childhood or infancy), it could not have been overcome and changed by conflicting tactual-kinesthetic experience in the adult observer.

Recent research has brought both these findings and the conclusions into question. The issue hinges particularly on whether it is vision or proprioception that has changed. Helmholtz concluded that vision had changed, because *intermanual transfer* occurred—i.e., the subject could point also correctly with his left hand after he had practiced with his right hand alone. This seemed to indicate that it was visual direction and not merely the felt position of his hand that had changed. Harris (1963) found adaptation to occur only with the practiced hand, however, implying that the felt position of that hand had changed rather than the visual sense of direction. Adaptation in both hands has also been obtained (Bossom & Held, 1957; see Harris, 1965), and changes in visual direction and in felt position have been found to develop at different rates in the course of the adaptation experiment (Hay & Pick, 1966). The fact remains that at least under some conditions it is proprioception rather than visual direction that changes, and this is enough to make Helmholtz's major conclusions unwarranted.

In any case, the experiment and its logic are good illustrations of the perceptual equipment that is needed for the traditional account of space perception. Our sensations of near/far, right/left, up/down are all compounded of nonspatial visual sensations to which are added the tactual-kinesthetic associations that the viewer has learned by his actions in the physical world.

This is the structuralist explanation of our perceptions of the spatial world, and it appeared to provide an elegant and unified foundation upon which to build an understanding of other more complex psychological processes.

Convincing though this argument has been for centuries, it faces some grave difficulties. Perhaps most striking is the fact that at least some creatures can make good spatial discriminations without ever having previously associated kinesthetic images to visual or auditory cues. An early case in point is Thorndike's classic experiment (1899) in which chicks were hatched and reared in darkness, and never had an opportunity to form visual-kinesthetic associations. When these chicks were placed on a test stand in an illuminated space, they were immediately able to use visual distance cues—i.e., the higher the stand, the longer they delayed in jumping (Figure 36*A*).

A.

B.

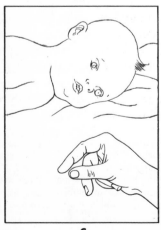

C.

FIGURE 36. *Space discriminations without prior visuomotor experience. A.* Thorndike's experiment with chicks. *B.* The visual cliff. *C.* Spatially coordinated behavior in the human infant. *D.* The kitten carousel.

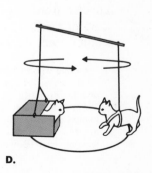

D.

Human infants, as well as a variety of animals, display the ability to use visual depth cues as soon as they are old enough to locomote. In the visual cliff experiment (Figure 36*B*) of Gibson and Walk (1960), infants placed on the center of a glass sheet, with patterned linoleum up against the glass on one side and a sheer drop-off on the other, avoid the cliff.[3]

In an ingenious experiment with an infant delivered without drugs (Wertheimer, 1961), it was found that the baby would consistently turn toward the source of a sound, only moments after birth. This seems to establish the existence of at least some minimum amount of spatially coordinated behavior at birth (Figure 36*C*).

However, such evidence should not lead us to conclude that visuomotor experience is not involved at all in the development of space perception: Kittens paired in a carousel (Figure 36*D*), with the passive partner being wheeled around in the light for one hour by the active one, were then returned to darkness for the remainder of the day. Both animals thus received the same amount of visual stimulation. The passive cats, however, showed marked inabilities on the visual cliff and in other visual tasks which require depth perception and visuomotor coordination. The active partners showed no such deficit (Held & Hein, 1963).

The facts represented by Figure 36*A-C* certainly cannot prove that *all* space perception is innate, but they do make Berkeley's logical argument that space perception *must* be learned (i.e., by the association of kinesthetic memories and visual sensations) quite unconvincing.

C. The Perception of the Qualities and Motions of Objects

So far, we have dealt mostly with points and places in space. Let us now try to assemble them into the objects of the world around us.

Imagine a flat mosaic, like a tile floor, built of sensitive elements. This is essentially the structuralist's model of the retina. The light reflected from an object produces an image on the retina, stimulating some of these sensitive receptor elements. The more intensely each is stimulated, the brighter the observed object should be, and its hue

[3] A child who had been essentially one-eyed from birth displayed the same choice on the visual cliff at age 18 months; this makes it clear that we cannot regard binocular disparity as being fundamental to space perception (Walk and Dodge, 1962). Subsequent research shows that *motion parallax*—a visual source of information about depth that we discuss on p. 126—plays an important part in performance on the visual cliff (Schiffman and Lore, 1975) and in infants' responses to objects in space (Bower, 1966).

and saturation should depend on how the different kinds of cones are stimulated by the mixture of wavelengths. With a larger object (at the same distance), a greater visual angle is subtended at the eye, a larger area of the retina will be stimulated, and the observed *size* should increase. We seem to have accounted for the perception of objects' perceived sizes and colors very quickly and directly. What about the perception of their *shapes* and *motions*?

Any shape that falls on the retina is, by this theory, simply a particular arrangement of points or patches. Some of these arrangements have occurred so frequently together that all the parts are associated with each other, and with the verbal names that we have given to them (such as "circle" or "face"). Until relatively recently, it was believed that our perceptions of shape are made possible only by the kinesthetic sensations caused by eye movements that are made as the fovea follows the outline of the shape. Despite a number of demonstrations that shapes can be recognized at exposures too short to permit eye movements to occur, this tenacious belief still reappears from time to time.

The perception of motion also seems easy to explain: When an object moves in space, the retinal image usually moves across a succession of neighboring receptors and will stimulate them one after the other. The successive sensations would naturally come to provide the components for our perceptions of motion (See Figure 48). Neither shape nor motion, then, seems to require the structuralist to seek any additional explanations beyond those already given for acuity and local sign (pp. 34–40). All the physical properties of the world of objects that we perceive are thus now accounted for—but with some surprising peculiarities:

If we introspect carefully, the visual sensations of every object's properties should appear to vary from one moment to the next in an astonishing manner. Size, shape, brightness—all change drastically in the optic array and in the retinal image, as both the observer and the objects that he looks at move about in the world (Figures 37, 38); our perceptions should, therefore, change accordingly.

Do we really perceive the world in this inconsistent fashion?

In fact, we see the physical attributes of objects both *more* correctly, and *less* correctly, than we should expect from what we know about sensory psychophysics. The basic structuralist attempt to observe the sensations that presumably compose our perceptions of objects and events has failed for every physical attribute of objects that has been studied! We can list these failures under three headings: the *perceptual constancies,* the *illusions,* and the facts of *organization.*

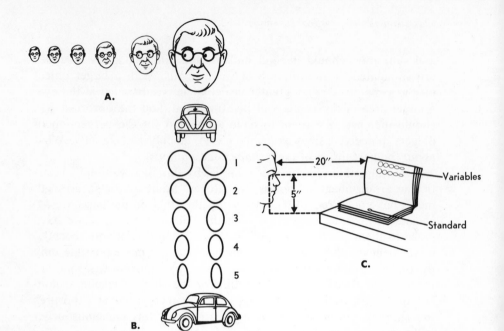

A.

B.

C.

FIGURE 37. Size constancy and shape constancy. *A*. The approximate change in size in the retinal image of a friend's face, as he approaches on the street. If you hold your thumb up at about eye level and move it to and fro, from close to your eye out to arm's length and back again, it will continue to appear roughly constant in size, that is, "thumb size"—unless you pay attention to the objects that it hides from view at different distances. At arm's length, the tip of your thumb can hide your friend's nose at 4 feet; it can hide his head at 20 feet; it can hide him completely at 150 feet. Does your friend appear to shrink to thumb-tip size when he is 150 feet away? Again, when your thumb approaches from arm's length to about three inches, the image of its tip in the optic array expands from being able to cover your friend's head, to hiding his entire body. Does your thumb appear to swell from head size to body size? *B*. Headlights of a passing automobile provide retinal images that vary from the perfect circle of a head-on view, through an ellipse of ever-narrowing proportions, to a sliver of light. Do you normally detect these changes in shape? *C*. Try the following experiment, however: Turn the book around so that you are facing it from the distances and at the orientation shown above, and then attempt to match the appearance of the *standard circle*, shown on the facing page, to the series of ellipses in (B). Which one of the ellipses matches the standard in retinal image? See the note on the bottom of page 75 for the answer.

THE PERCEPTUAL CONSTANCIES

The world we see is, by and large, a stable one. Only in unusual circumstances can we detect the tremendous changes of size that occur in proximal stimulation as we walk about, and the changes in the light reaching our eye from any object as the illumination falling on it changes. There is something that *does* in fact remain constant in the retinal image in each instance of the constancies; we shall consider this constant later (Chapter 5C).

Most generally, a friend does *not* appear to double in size with each few steps as he approaches; the headlights on a car do *not* seem to turn from circles through ellipses to lines as they pass us on the road (Figure 37); and a lump of coal does *not* change from one color to another when it moves from shade to sunlight. Object characteristics appear to remain approximately constant, even though the corresponding proximal stimulation changes. These general phenomena are variously called the *object constancies, phenomenal constancies,* or *perceptual constancies.*

It is tempting to explain the constancies as mechanisms by which the viewer "achieves" veridical, correct observations of the world because they are so necessary to his effective actions and survival. This is not really an explanation, however; it only recognizes that the constancies are useful, it does not explain how they come to be. Let us examine two important examples of the constancies and the structuralist attempt to explain these pervasive phenomena.

Lightness constancy and memory color. When light energy falls upon the surface of an object, some of that energy is reflected and some is absorbed (or transmitted, if the object is translucent or transparent). Under normal circumstances, if the object reflects most of the light energy that falls on it, it is usually perceived as light, or even white; an object that reflects little light appears dark, and one that reflects practically no light appears black. (It should be noted here that lightness and brightness are not identical. Lightness is the perceptual continuum running from white surface to black surface. Brightness is the apparent amount of light coming from the object. Thus, a piece of coal in the sunlight and a piece of coal in the shade will be of equal lightness [or darkness], if constancy is perfect, but the coal in the sunlight will appear brighter.)

The percentage of the light energy that a surface reflects is its *albedo,* or *reflectance.* This is usually constant—i.e., the object reflects the same percentage of weak light as of strong light. We perceive this reflectance with surprising accuracy, even though the amount of light actually reaching the eye from that object may vary widely (Figure 38).

The most obvious explanation that comes to mind is that we *know* the colors of coal and of paper, and that this knowledge (our *memory colors* of coal and paper) influences our judgments. This answer, though obvious, is wrong, inasmuch as lightness constancy is also attained with objects that are unfamiliar to the experimental subjects and whose reflectance is therefore unknown to them. How is this possible?

Consider an unfamiliar object that reflects a certain specific amount of light to your eye. In order to reflect that amount of light,

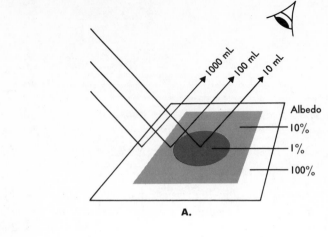

Albedo
- 10%
- 1%
- 100%

A.

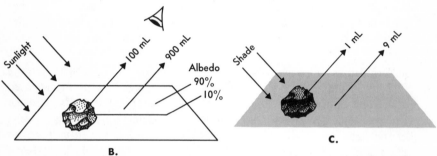

B.

C.

FIGURE 38. Lightness constancy. *A.* Even though the intensity of the light energy reaching the eye may change greatly from one moment to the next as the illumination on an object changes from direct sunlight to deep shadow, the apparent lightness of the object will remain relatively constant and unchanged. Light reflected or emitted by any surface is measured in units called millilamberts. *B.* In sunlight, coal may reflect 100 millilamberts (mL), and paper may reflect 900 mL. *C.* In the shade, the coal may reflect 1 mL, the paper, 9 mL. Does the paper look darker in the shade than the coal did in the sunlight? No: In normal situations, the coal looks black, and the paper looks white, in the shade as in the sunlight, regardless of the fact that much less light reaches the eye in the former case. (The paper does not look white in the diagram printed at *C,* of course; see Figure 54*A* to learn why.)

it must be more reflective if it is in low illumination than if it is in high illumination (Figure 38). Consequently, if the object appears to be in the shade, it will also appear to be lighter than if—without any change in the light reaching the eye—it appears to be strongly lit. Do you believe that you are making this kind of complicated calculation each time you observe the lightness of a surface? This same question arises in every one of the constancies.

Size constancy and familiar size. As the distance between an object and your eye changes, the object's retinal image undergoes tremendous changes in size, as we recall from our discussion of Figure 37. These changes are not usually perceived; instead, the object's size tends to be perceived as constant, a phenomenon we term *size constancy.* The term also includes the related tendency to see

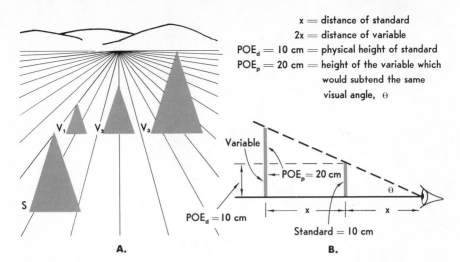

x = distance of standard
2x = distance of variable
POE_d = 10 cm = physical height of standard
POE_p = 20 cm = height of the variable which would subtend the same visual angle, θ

A.　　　　　　　　　　　　B.

FIGURE 39. *Constancy ratios. A.* Look at the scene through a tube of rolled-up paper or through a hole punched in a sheet of cardboard so that your field of view is restricted to the picture itself. The picture shows three triangles of varied size (V_1, V_2, V_3) in the middle distance and a standard triangle *(S)* nearer the viewer. Which of the variables (V_1, V_2, V_3) appears to be equal in size to the standard *(S)*? In the real scene that is represented by this picture, most observers would judge that V_2 is closest to being equal to *S*. At *(B.)* we discuss how to measure the degree of *size constancy* of such a judgment.

　　B. Note that in the scene that is represented at *A*, there are two different ways in which *V* can be equal to *S: (1.)* when the *distal objects* (the triangles themselves) are equal in height, as measured in inches or centimeters; *(2.)* when *S* and *V* subtend equal angles as measured in degrees, at the eye, and produce the same retinal images, or *proximal stimuli*. Recall from Figure 4 that the term POE means the *point of objective equality*, in which *S* and *V* are objectively equal, whereas PSE means the *point of subjective equality*, or the value of *V* at which the observer judges the standard and variable to be equal in length (using one of the *psychophysical methods*, Chapter 2B). As the diagram at *(B)* shows, there are two POEs in a situation like the one shown in *(A)*. One is the POE_p, which is the case in which *S* and *V* subtend equal visual angles at the eye, and the proximal stimuli are the same size. A second, the POE_d, is the case in which *S* and *V* are equal in size as distal objects.

　　One measure of perceptual constancy is the *constancy ratio*, $C = (PSE - POE_p/(POE_d - POE_p)$. In this measure, the PSE is the point of subjective equality. In the size constancy experiment represented at (B), if the subject were to judge a variable of V = 10 cm. to be equal to the standard, then PSE = 10, and $C = (10 - 20)/(10 - 20) = 1.0$, which would mean that the match is being made *solely* in terms of the distal sizes of *S* and *V:* size constancy would be perfect. If, however, the subject were to judge a variable of $V = 20$ cm. as being equal to *S*, then $C = (20 - 20)/(10 - 20) = 0.0$; this would mean that the match is being made in terms of the proximal stimuli, and that size constancy is completely missing. Most usually, some intermediate value between $C = 0.0$ and $C = 1.0$ is obtained.

large objects as large, and small objects as small, even when their proximal stimulus sizes are the same (Figure 39*A*).[4] Why do we see the man as being taller than the boy in Figure 40*B*?

[4] Figure 39*A* is a picture, which complicates the issue. In a picture (which is almost equivalent to the *proximal* stimulation that would be received from a real scene), $V_3=S$ *both* as a proximal *and* as a distal match, since *S* and *V* are really at the same distance from the eye. Constancy experiments can be performed with pictures by using the portrayed distance instead of the real distance when computing constancy ratios, with quite reliable results. If you look at the scene in Figure 39*A* through a tube of rolled-up paper for a few moments, you will most probably find that V_2 or V_1 seems much closer in size to *S* than does V_3. (See G. Sonoda, 1961; Yonas and Hagen, 1973.)

NOTE: The answer to the question in Figure 37: Ellipse 5 is closest in shape.

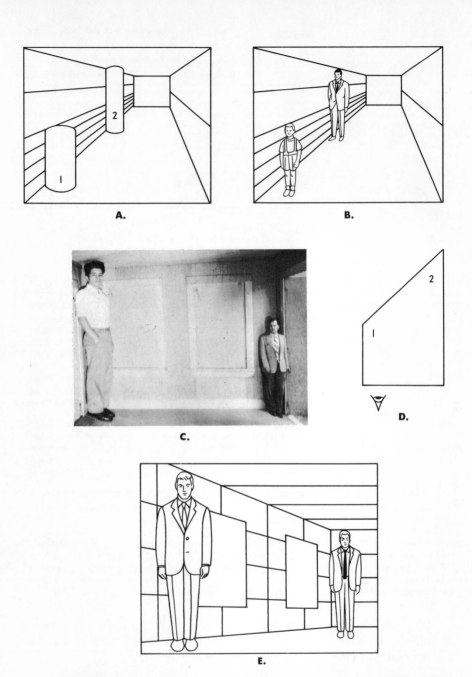

FIGURE 40. *The effect of context on apparent size. A.* Is the cylinder at *(1)* the same height as that at *(2)*? *B.* Are the boy and the man the same size? If you measure their heights with a ruler, you will find them to be the same in both cases. Now consider the two men in *(C)*. Both are of normal height, but one of them is considerably nearer. The room, of course, is quite distorted; looked at from above, it is shaped as shown in *(D)*. How is *(C)* related to *(A)* and *(B)*? (See Ittelson & Kilpatrick, 1952.) To monocular vision, the room appears to be rectangular, and our familiarity with the sizes of men is not sufficient to overcome this "assumption of rectangularity."

Analogous to the explanation offered for color constancy in terms of memory color, we might suppose that size constancy occurs because we *know* the true, physical sizes of men and boys. This is the traditional cue of *familiar size* (see p. 53). Yet size constancy is also obtained with completely unfamiliar objects. *By the use of false perspective, moreover, we can fool the eye into accepting two perfectly familiar, equal-sized objects as being at the same distances when they are really at different distances* (Figure 40C). The objects that would normally appear to be of equal size (and usually *are* of equal size) then appear greatly different, which is what one would expect from the distance framework in which they are set, *not* at all what one would expect from their familiar size.

Alternatively, size constancy might occur because the viewer somehow takes the object's distance into account in judging its size, just as we might try to explain lightness constancy as the result of taking illumination into account to judge reflectance. That is, perhaps the *size of an object is computed from the size of its retinal image and from its apparent distance,* just as an astronomer (to use Helmholtz's example) can compute the distances of the planets in space by using trigonometry. This is also an appealing possibility, as we shall see, which is still widely accepted in one form or another, but we must qualify it immediately: *The observer is not aware of making such computations, if in fact he does make them at all.* The implications of this fact must be considered because it really strikes at the heart of the structuralist program.

Unconscious conclusions from unnoticed sensations to explain perceptual achievement. This hypothesis of unconscious computation, or *unconscious inference,* implies that *sensations cannot in fact be observed,* but that instead they are hidden, or overlaid, by the unconsciously achieved conclusions. This explanation (which we get from Helmholtz) faces a number of difficulties, but it remains the most serious empiricist attempt to explain the fact that our perceptions are usually more like the distal objects of the real world than they are like the sensations we would expect from the proximal stimulation (and from the findings of sensory psychophysics). It can explain the constancies only if we abandon the belief that we can observe our individual sensations when they have been combined with others. Empiricism and structuralism, which supported each other so nicely in the first half of this chapter, appear to be in conflict here.

We shall see this same thing occur when we try to explain the other two kinds of discrepancies between proximal stimulation and appearance, namely the *illusions* and *figural organization.*

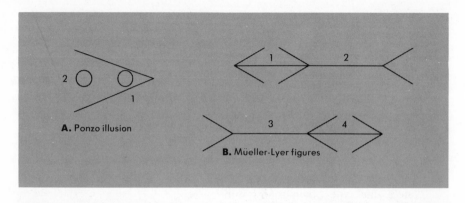

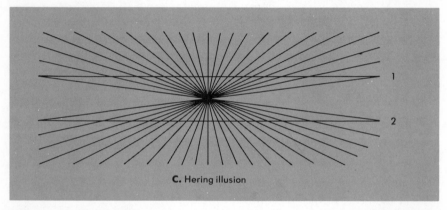

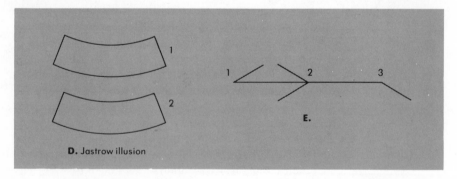

FIGURE 41. The geometrical illusions: erroneous perceptions of size and place. *A*. Circles *(1)* and *(2)* are really the same size. *B*. Segments *(1)*, *(2)*, *(3)*, and *(4)* are all the same size. *C*. The two horizontal lines are parallel, the distance between *(1)* and *(2)* being the same all the way across the figure. *D*. The two crescents *(1)* and *(2)* are the same size. *E*. This figure is explained in the text.

There are a great many different illusions of this general class, in which what you perceive corresponds neither to the proximal stimulus nor to the distal object. In general, they are even stronger than the constancies, to which at least some of them may be related. What is the common factor in Figures 41*A*, 40*E*, and 39*A* ?

ILLUSIONS

For every example of constancy and of perceptual achievement, we can find an illusion, or perceptual error. Whereas the constancies are examples of greater agreement between perception and the distal world than we would expect from the proximal stimulation, illusions show more discrepancy than we would expect: Figure 40*E* was an example of size constancy, yet Figure 41*A* is an illusion; Figure 38 is an example of lightness constancy, yet Figure 42 is an illusion.

Several illusions are illustrated in the Figure 41; others appear in later pages. These are not simple cases of "careless" observation that can be overcome by taking pains. The only way in which most illusions can be detected as such is by taking a ruler and measuring them. If no means of predicting their effects, or of anticipating their occurrence, can be found, the scientific study of perception will be impossible. Consequently, we cannot dismiss illusions as mere curiosities that demonstrate that "one can't trust one's senses."

At first glance, the pervasiveness and strength of the illusions appear to offer a particularly strong challenge to explanations based on perceptual learning from past experience: It is easy to believe that the constancies result from perceptual learning, because one would assume that our experiences with the world would teach us how to see it correctly. But it is not immediately evident why our experiences with the world would lead us to see it incorrectly, which is what an illusion amounts to.

Two famous illusions of size "inconstancy": The Müeller-Lyer illusion and the moon illusion. Many explanations have been offered to account for the illusions. One recurrent explanation is that they are due to the effects of eye movements. And in fact, eye movements directed toward the ends of the figures marked (*1*) and

FIGURE 42. Color contrast: erroneous perceptions of brightness and hue. In (*A*) the two halves of the gray ring are really identical, as we see when we view the ring without the split background in (*B*). Contrast will also induce illusory changes in hue: In (*A*) if (*1*) and (*2*) were red and green respectively, (*3*) and (*4*) would appear greenish and reddish, respectively. See also the "colored shadows" of Figure 53*A*. In general, color contrast results in induction of the complementary hue (the opposites on the color circle in Figure 14).

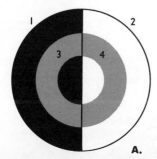
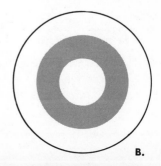

A.   B.

(2) in Figure 41B do initially undershoot the left-hand end of (1) and overshoot the right-hand end of (2) (Festinger *et al.*, 1968), and similar fixation errors occur when only a set of dots is used to replace the end points (Coren & Honig, 1972). Unfortunately for this explanation, even at tachistoscopic exposures that are too brief to permit eye movements, strong illusions are still obtained.

According to the *perspective theory* of the Mueller-Lyer illusion, for example, the "converging lines" at (1) and (2) in Figure 41E have been thought to "suggest" the depth cue of linear perspective. Therefore, it has been reasoned, segment 1–2 appears nearer than segment 2–3; because 1–2 appears near while subtending the same visual angle, it should appear *shorter* than 2–3. This would explain the illusion as being due to the *unconscious* use of a depth cue where there is, in fact, no real depth.

At first glance this doesn't make sense. Shouldn't an object appear to be larger if it appears to be nearer than it really is? Not according to the following reasoning, known in recent years as the *size-distance invariance hypothesis* (see Epstein, *et al.*, 1961).

Examine Figure 43B. In order to subtend a given visual angle θ (and, therefore, to produce a retinal image of a given size), as the object's distance increases, so must its physical size increase. In fact, where S = stimulus size, d = stimulus distance, and $k = \tan \theta$, $S = k \times d$, or $S/d = k$.

This is a simple physical invariance that is easily demonstrated by the procedure shown in Figure 43. If, as a result of learning (or by native endowment), our perceptions of the world agree with its physical characteristics, we should expect to find a *perceptual invariance*

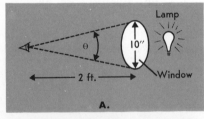

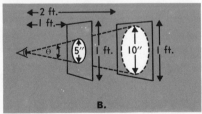

FIGURE 43. *Size-distance invariance hypothesis and Emmert's Law.* Prolonged staring at a light produces an afterimage (Figure 14). If an afterimage is obtained by gazing at the bright window in *(A)* from a distance of two feet, and then projected onto the one-foot-square paper in *(B)*, it will cover an area ten inches across at the same distance (two feet). If you now move the paper to a distance of one foot, how large does the afterimage appear to be? The apparent size of the projected afterimage is directly proportional to the distance from the eye to the surface upon which the afterimage is projected. This is known as Emmert's Law.

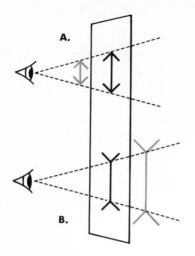

FIGURE 44. *The perspective theory of the illusions.* (A) and (B) are really at the same distance, of course, when they are printed on the page in Figure 41B. If, because of the perspective implied by the "fins," (A) appeared nearer to you (like the outside corner of a box), and (B) appeared further (like an inside corner), their sizes would be those of the gray figures. (See Figure 43.)

that reflects this physical invariance: *For a proximal stimulus which subtends a given angle (θ), as apparent distance increases, apparent size should increase and vice versa.* Such physical invariances hold for other physical properties such as reflectance/illumination, slant/shape—in short, for all of the attributes that display the constancies. This is a clue as to what remains constant in the constancies, and we shall return to some of these other invariances later on (Chapter 5C).

Now we can return to the "perspective explanation" of the Mueller-Lyer illusion. We have redrawn it in Figure 44 to illustrate this point: Because the retinal size of segments A and B are equal, but the apparent distance of A looks less than that of B, A looks shorter than B.

FIGURE 45. The "moon illusion." A. *The moon seems much larger when it is near the horizon (1) than when it is overhead. (2).* Although several factors such as the elevation of your gaze (see Holway & Boring, 1940) contribute to this illusion, recent research supports an ancient explanation: Distance cues in the terrain immediately adjacent to the horizon moon help cause the illusion making the moon look larger by making it look farther away (Kaufman & Rock, 1962). B. This illusion can easily be demonstrated in daylight. Obtain an after image by looking at a bright light, and then project it on the sky. Near the horizon (1), it appears larger than when it is projected overhead (2), even though the proximal stimulus (visual angle) remains constant (King & Gruber, 1962). Look back at Emmert's Law (Figure 43). What do these facts seem to imply about the distance of the sky at horizon and at zenith?

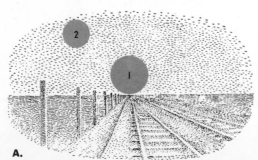

A.

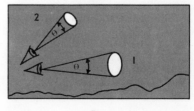

B.

This explanation can also be applied to many other size illusions. Consider the famous moon illusion shown in Figure 45. Note that this explanation is closely related to the unconscious inference explanation of the constancies. Let us consider that point.

Unconscious inferences and misapplied constancies. Helmholtz applied this explanation to the lightness-contrast illusion, arguing that it occurred because a bright surround leads us to assume that the illumination is higher, and therefore that the reflectance of the object is lower, than it really is. Helmholtz proposed this general explanation: the illusions result from the same judgmental processes that normally result in perceptual achievement—i.e., in the constancies. Usually, the observer perceives the object that would *most likely* produce the stimulus pattern he is receiving. Most often, when this happens, his perception is correct, and we then have an example of the constancies. But by the same token, he will sometimes be wrong, and we will then get "misapplied constancies" (Tausch, 1954)—the illusions.

The principle of unconscious inference (i.e., the observer unconsciously makes certain computations to arrive at the size or reflectance of an object) does seem to explain the illusions as well as the constancies—at least as a first approximation. If such inferences do explain these illusions, however, they are *not* calculations that the observer can report, nor do they depend on *knowledge* as that term is customarily used. Knowing that the Mueller-Lyer illusion lies on a flat surface does not dispel the illusion; knowing that the moon really remains the same size does not dispel the moon illusion. Moreover, the quantitative measurements of the illusions—the precise extent of the errors as measured in psychophysical experiments—do not agree exactly with what we would expect to find if this principle were correct.

For these reasons, unconscious inference and the "misapplied constancy" principle is really only an approximate rule of thumb. We shall consider alternate explanations later on. For now, let us note that for each of these illusions, we can find both proponents and opponents of a perspective explanation[4] so the issue is by no means as

[4] For example, for the Mueller-Lyer and related patterns, Gregory (1976) and Gillam (1971) support a perspective explanation, whereas Erlebacher and Sekuler (1969) and Hotopf (1966) support forms of a "confusion" theory (in which some feature associated with the different extensions of the auxiliary lines on the two sides affects the viewer's judgments of the lengths of the horizontal lines). For the moon illusion, Kaufman and Rock maintain the effects are due to size-distance invariance, whereas Restle (1970) sees the illusion as an effect of context (explained more fully in Figure 44, p. 81). Both factors may of course be at work, but Kaufman (1974) argues that the distance effect must be the major factor.

settled as some presentations would suggest. (And we will see in Chapter 5 that at least some of the constancies and illusions have more direct, and probably innate, bases.)

But even if the illusions were fully explained as special cases of the unconscious inference mechanisms that normally result in the perceptual constancies, they raise this uncomfortable feature: *They were explained after the fact,* not *predicted* by the theory. And with so many illusions around that we did not foresee, how many more are there that we don't know about? This difficulty will reappear in even greater force when we consider the principles of figural organization.

THE PERCEPTION OF SHAPE AND MOTION: A FIRST INTRODUCTION TO THE PRINCIPLES OF ORGANIZATION

As we have just seen, the illusions and the constancies reveal discrepancies between what we do in fact observe and what we should observe if our sensations were simply added together. When we turn to the perception of shape and motion, the sensations become completely unobservable. And what is worst of all for the empiricist position, what we do perceive does not seem to depend on what we are familiar with but rather on some new rules, or *principles of organization.*

Camouflage and puzzle pictures. In the structuralist scheme, a shape is simply the sum of the sensations of points of color and shade at a particular set of positions (see Figures 5 and 25). There are several familiar shapes in plain view in Figure 46A. Can you see

FIGURE 46. *Camouflage and puzzle pictures: invisibility through "organization."* *A.* Various numbers and letters are concealed in *(1)*, *(2)*, and *(3)* (after Kohler, 1929). Why are they invisible there yet obvious in *(1)*, *(2)*, and *(3)* in *(B)*?

(Figure 46 continues)

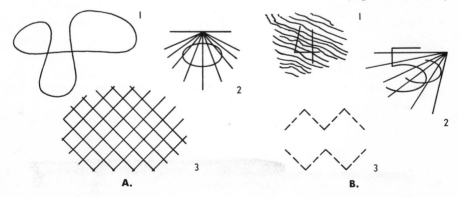

A.   B.

C. **D.**

Figure 46 *(continued)*
C. Two pencils: Which is easier to see, the one that is partly covered, or the one that is completely uncovered? *D*. Camouflage of an entire animal.

them? Is their invisibility due to the confusion caused by the added lines? No, this cannot be the answer, since in Figure 46*B* the same patterns are now embedded among even more lines (or suffer even more omissions) yet are clearly visible.

Is this somehow due to the artificiality of lines on paper or to human habits of looking at them? No, for we find the same principles of concealment used by animals to hide from other animals in the real world (Figure 46*D;* see also Figure 2*C*), and by pencils to hide from students (Figure 46*C*). What makes these shapes unobservable, even though their components are clearly above threshold?

We might try an explanation analogous to memory color (p. 73) and familiar size (p. 77): Is this simply a matter of seeing the shapes that we have learned to see? No, again. The demonstrations in Figures 46 and 47*A* show that what we might call familiar shape is no better a predictor of what we will see than were memory color and familiar size. As these demonstrations show, there seem to be "laws of organization" at work; and these—rather than our familiarity with the shapes with which they have been set in conflict in these demonstrations—seem to determine what we perceive.

These laws of organization form the heart of *Gestalt* theory, an alternative to structuralism that we shall examine in a more positive and detailed fashion in the next chapter. What makes them important to us here is this: Their demonstrations show quite dramatically that how we will perceive a whole object cannot be predicted simply

A.

B.

FIGURE 47. *Figure and ground, visibility and invisibility.* *A.* A set of Fiji island charms? A word is "concealed" here. In general, what is "figure" has a recognizable shape, while what is "ground" does not. *B.* You can either see as figure a black goblet on a white ground, or you can see two heads facing one another on a black ground. If you think that you see both, you are probably either alternating between the two or you see one region of the contour as part of a white profile and another region as part of a black vase.

by adding up our perceptions of the parts and that indeed the parts may become unobservable when combined with other parts.

The empiricist can offer a rebuttal: The Gestalt demonstrations may themselves merely reflect our experiences with objects. Although the shapes that we see in Figure 47*A* are less familiar than the shapes that we do *not* see there—i.e., the letters that have become formless and invisible—we may see the former because we have been provided with cues that they are the more likely to be objects. As with the constancies and the illusions, it is not through a particular memory (such as a memory color or a familiar size) that our experience with the world determines our perceptions, but by the unconscious inferences that we make as to what is most likely to confront us. *And the Gestalt demonstrations may work as they do because the features that they contain are* usually *good cues as to what is an object and what isn't.*

When we examine the Gestalt "laws of organization" in more detail, we shall see that the empiricist explanation is really a plausible one (Chapter 5D). But it is also clear now that it is an explanation that can only be offered after the fact: Neither introspection into what (and why) we see in Figures 46 and 47 nor our knowledge about what should be familiar to the viewer from his experience with the world, will predict these perceptual phenomena.

One last case, and we shall then have considered all of the physical variables of object perception.

Apparent motion. The simplest structuralist explanation of our observations of motion was that perceived motion is composed of the *sensations of successive positions* (that is, a sequence of local signs), accompanied by the memory images of having touched the same object at different spatial locations (Figure 48*A*). Are such sequential sensations necessary for the perception of motion? Not at all. We can observe perfectly convincing motion when no such successive stimulation occurs on the retina, as is shown in the phi phenomenon of Figure 48*B*. (Of course, there is really *no intervening path of stimulation in the retinal image* in such cases, a fact which has consequences that can be demonstrated by the appropriate experimental measures [see Kolers, 1963] so that we should not think that 48*A* and 48*B* are identical in all respects.) The general term for this kind of illusory motion is *stroboscopic motion,* because it is usually produced by a sequence of flashing lights. This apparent motion

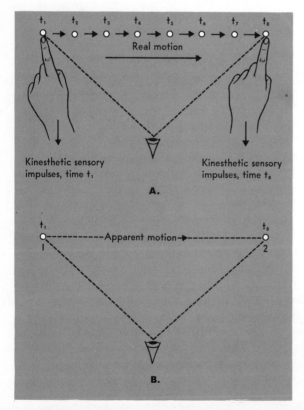

FIGURE 48. *A.* Sequential sensations: A schematic representation of the structuralist theory of the perception of motion. *B.* Lights turned on and off at *(1)* and *(2)* at suitable intervals are perceived as moving from *(1)* to *(2)*.

may actually be more convincing than "real" or continuous movement of the stimulus. The term *phi phenomenon,* strictly speaking, was used by Max Wertheimer (the founder of Gestalt theory) to describe the appearance of "pure motion," with no trace of any apparent object doing the moving, that occurs under the proper conditions. It was such apparent motion that led Wertheimer to decide that pure movement is just as direct an experience as any of the sensations for which we have sought specific nerve energies in Chapter 3, and led him to speculate about the nature of the organizational processes in the brain that might explain the phenomenon. The apparent movement of point *A* to point *B* was called *beta movement.*

Again, this phenomenon of apparent motion is not simply a laboratory curiosity that depends on careful conditions of presentation or attitude. All motion pictures, TV, and animated displays are examples of this principle. A series of still pictures is presented in brief, *stationary* exposures, or "frames," and the observation of motion is overwhelming. No one can see the individual frames in a movie regardless of how carefully he introspects.

D. What Can Be Saved of the Classical Theory?

THE DEMISE OF ANALYTIC INTROSPECTION

Analytic introspection clearly will not work as intended. This failure has enormous consequences—not only for the study of perception but for the entire complex scientific enterprise of understanding man's sensory system. In a nutshell, the whole interlocking structure of sensory physiology, sensory psychophysics, and analytic perception had its main assumptions pulled out from under it. We can no longer pursue old programs based upon these assumptions, and we have to understand the precise extent of the failures if we are to understand the prospects and limits of new programs in the study of perception. For new they must be, though they also must conserve what we have learned up to this point.

Where introspective structuralism failed. The structuralist procedure for studying perception was to discover the underlying fundamental sensations and their physiological bases (their "specific nerve energies"), and the laws by which these elements combine. With so many individual elements, the only way to keep the approach manageable was to assume that the elements combine by simple accretion, or addition: i.e., that our sensory experience is the sum of all of our sensations. All other perceptual qualities for which we find no receptors (such as distance, solidity, social attributes, facial expressions, and so forth) were taken to be simply sets of the fundamental sensations plus the images left by previous sensations, images that had become connected to those sets of sensations in accordance with the laws of association. This overall viewpoint gave a general purpose to the enterprise of sensory psychophysics and provided a unified picture of humans and of their perceptions of the world.

The basic failures lay in the addition hypothesis, in the technique of analytic introspection, or in both. We have examined all the building blocks (colors, position, distance, shape, size, movement) for visual perception, and in each case, we find that the data of sensory psychophysics do not predict the perceptions that result when those supposed building blocks are combined (Chapter 4C).

In many cases, we might explain the discrepancies as being due to unconscious inferences that we make, based on our past experiences. These explanations, whatever else they might do, cannot save analytic introspection, however, since with no amount of introspective effort can we overcome the effects of context and of past experiences to detect the "true" sensation (for example, that the lines are really equal in the Mueller-Lyer illusion).

However, if analytic introspection will not serve to dissect our perceptions of the world into the innate sensations, on the one hand, and memory images, on the other, how can we discover what is learned and what is innate? How can we investigate the empiricist assertion that the complex objects that we perceive are built up out of simpler sensations by some process of learning, and how can we tell what those simpler units are?

NONINTROSPECTIVE RESEARCH IN
PERCEPTUAL LEARNING

Ecological surveys. Some form of empiricism is still tenable. We may continue to suppose that there are simple sensory elements (like those studied in sensory psychophysics), which are combined by the effects of our past experiences into the complex things we see. However, since we must now recognize that we cannot use introspection to observe either these elements or their memory images (if such memory images are indeed the basis of perceptual learning, which is now very doubtful as we shall see), the only way that we can know what associations any observer has formed is to discover what he has been exposed to in the past. How can we do that?

One way we might attempt to do this would be to examine his normal environment, or ecology, in order to discover how often each visual depth cue is valid in that environment: For example, when converging lines appear in the visual field, what proportion of the time do they do so because they are parallel lines in depth that are providing the cue of *linear perspective* (as in Figures 27 and 40*B*, *E*), and how often do they converge because they are truly nonparallel (as in Figures 41*A* and *B*)—or fail to converge in the visual field as they should, for the same reason (as in Figure 40*C*)? By measuring the size of the illusions obtained with patterns like those of Figure 41, when the subjects were people who had grown up in a "carpentered world" having parallel lines and right angles (Europeans, Americans), on the one hand, or were people who live in round huts and restricted vistas (natives of primitive communities, forest dwellers), on the other hand, Segall, Campbell, and Herskovitz (1966) found that the former showed larger illusions than the latter—which is what one would expect if the explanation of the illusion given in Figure 44 is correct. This question is still at issue: subsequent cross-cultural research has sometimes corroborated these findings and sometimes given contrary results (Jahoda, 1966; Leibowitz & Pick, 1972). The fact that birds are subject to the same illusions, as Zanforlin (1967) pointed out, makes it hard to attribute the phenomenon entirely to one's culture. In any case, these studies illustrate how we can try to compile an inventory of what the world offers as raw material for the process of perceptual learning—in short, to perform what Brunswik (1956) called an *ecological survey*.

Such an approach follows in a straightforward way from Helmholtz's proposal that we perceive the most likely objects and events that would fit the sensory pattern that we are trying to interpret: After all, in order to apply that proposal, we have to know which objects are more likely than others.

An ecological survey is an immense undertaking, and few real surveys have been performed. There are several theoretical as well as practical problems that discourage such attempts. Perhaps the most critical problem is that of knowing *what* to measure in the environment. For example, we will see later on that the optic array contains much more direct and powerful sources of information about object properties, and about the viewer's own spatial location and movements, than any we have discussed so far, but that we must consider different aspects of the stimulus distribution if we are to find them (see pp. 123–131). In order to be useful, ecological surveys must be based on theories about what is important to measure, and for most purposes such an undertaking is premature because it is not yet clear what we should measure.

But even when we have such ecological inventories, we will not be able to use them directly, because we would need a very precise understanding of the processes of perceptual learning in order to use the results of the surveys. Consider Figure 40. In *B*, there is no conflict between the cue of linear perspective and the cue of familiar size (these cues were defined in Figure 27). If the two cues are set into conflict, however, as in Figure 40*C*, how can we tell which one will prevail? If we knew that the cue of linear perspective had been right 1,000 times and wrong 200 times in the life history of the viewer, and that the cue of familiar size had been right 900 times and wrong 50 times, could we then say which one would predominate?

Not unless we knew a great deal more about perceptual learning: We need exact and quantitative knowledge of the laws of perceptual learning before we can use the results of ecological surveys.

The search for the mechanisms of perceptual learning: Physiological models and electronic "perceiving machines." Where simple receptors could be found (or imagined) that might account for a particular simple perceptual experience (e.g., retinal cone = point of color), structuralists considered that experience to be an elementary sensation; otherwise, it was concluded to be a complex perception, assembled by the processes of perceptual learning somewhere in the inaccessible recesses of the central nervous system. In 1949, Donald O. Hebb offered a speculative but influential theory about such central processes that is outlined in Figures 49 and 50.

Hebb's proposal. In essence, this theory proposes that groupings of brain cells (called *cell-assemblies,* Figure 49) are formed as a result of perceptual learning. These groupings are tuned to respond to simple shapes (like an edge or an angle), to simple sounds (like familiar syllables) and so forth, in just as immediate a fashion as a single color receptor was thought to be sensitive to a particular wavelength. These would comprise a much more organized and plausible set of units than the independent sensations of Chapters 2 and 3.

These perceptual fragments, or learned elements, would still have to be assembled into the objects that we perceive, and into the speech or other familiar sounds that we hear. For this purpose, Hebb proposed sequential brain processes (the *phase sequence,* Figure 50): These are larger units in which the activity of one set of cell-assemblies makes it easier to activate a subsequent set after the first set of cell-assemblies has been started.

Hebb's general theory thus recognizes that there are different levels at which organization and perceptual learning *of different kinds and consequences* can occur; that elementary components of experience might themselves be the result of learning; and—most important—that the perceiver's *attention, set* or *expectations* must form an integral part of the perceptual process. This is the concept of the "phase sequence," in which the effect of a stimulus pattern depends on the processes set up by previous stimulus patterns.

Problems and consequences. Hebb's proposal is really much too complicated a picture of the nervous system to evaluate by any verbal discussion. Would such a nervous system *work?* Would it learn in the same way that humans really do? The attempt to answer this question has led to the construction of perceiving machines (or simulated nervous systems) which, by duplicating in electronic hardware or by a mathematical model some of the functions of particular hypothetical arrangements of neurons, seek to discover how such arrangements would work. These attempts must be *preceded,* however, by perceptual research with human beings: If we design a machine to duplicate what we consider to be a particular human performance, *and if we are wrong in our description of that performance,* our machine will be irrelevant to the human nervous system in both structure and function, no matter how well it does what it was designed to do.[5]

Hebb's proposal amounts to a general outline of a perceptual theory. It fails to provide for all of the structures (i.e., "perceptual fragments") that we now know are built into the nervous system and therefore need not be explained in terms of perceptual learning (Chapter 5B), and it really does not deal specifically with either the major problems of object perception that we have surveyed in this chapter, nor with those of attention and expectation that Hebb himself raised. But it is an outline that has continued to fit the findings (and the more detailed theories about various aspects of perception) that have emerged over the last twenty-five years, as we will note from time to time in the next two chapters.

(*Text continues on page 95*)

[5] Technical discussions of the mathematical models of "perceptrons" (machines that "learn" to respond differently to different shapes [Rosenblatt, 1958]), are found in Minsky and Pappert (1969). Examples of attempts to decide what machines would have to do to recognize objects roughly as we do (which is a different matter) are Guzman (1969) and Clowes (1969). See also Figure 73*B* in Chapter 6.

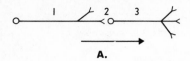

A.

FIGURE 49. **Units of brain action: cell-assemblies and receptive fields.** It was first thought that when any receptor neuron in a sense organ is stimulated, its activity is transmitted separately to the *sensory projection area* in the brain where it results in an elementary sensation. Elementary sensations were thought to combine into perceived objects as a result of neural processes in the *association areas* surrounding the projection areas. In this picture, the receptor processes were both the most important determinants of our perceptions, and the easiest to study. As we now know, however, individual receptor actions do not produce observable elements of experience that are simply shuffled into various combinations in the association areas. For this reason, recent years have seen a great increase in the study of (and speculation about) the brain processes that underlie sensation and perception.

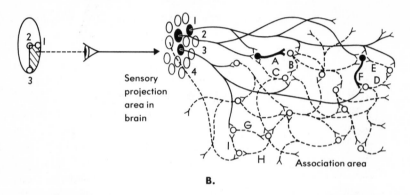

B.

Cell-assemblies. The neural circuitry in the cerebral cortex of the brain is immensely complex. Any attempt to explain perception in terms of cortical actions will have to use simplified analogies, or *models.* An influential example of such models is Hebb's *cell-assembly.*

Let us symbolize individual nerve fibers, or neurons, as at (1) and (3) in *(A).* When a neuron is firing, or *excited,* this excitation (which is bioelectrical in nature) is transmitted to another neuron in the direction shown by the arrow. In general, one excited neuron cannot by itself excite another, but if several firing neurons have a *synapse* with an inactive one (a synapse is the point of junction [2] between two neurons), they can make it fire. Thus, neurons 1 and 2, in *(B),* when acting together, might fire neurons A, F, etc., in the association area. In this way, the firing of particular neurons in the association cortex may depend on simultaneous stimulation by a whole *pattern* of sensory neurons.

Some of the neurons in the association areas are set into action by stimulation of the sense organs; on the other hand, the brain includes an immense number of "loop circuits" (such as A, B, C in [B], in which association fibers stimulate each other. These loops are the raw material from which cell-assemblies might be carved out, by the following process.

Assume that whenever two neurons fire together, some change occurs at the synapse so as to strengthen the ability of the first neuron to fire the second one. Further suppose that some frequently encountered pattern of stimulation on the retina causes neurons 1, 2, and 3 to fire in the sensory cortex, and these in turn fire fibers A, B, and C in the association cortex. Since A, B, and C fire together, the connections within this loop will eventually be so strengthened that stimulating one neuron sets off a *reverberating circuit* of excitation: A–B–C–A–B–C–A . . ., as shown in *(C).* If D, E, F is another loop which is also always fired at the same time by the same sensory event, the two loops will tend to coalesce into a single *cell-assembly,* and to fire as a unit. If either of two loops is also active by itself (without the other), however, they will remain separate

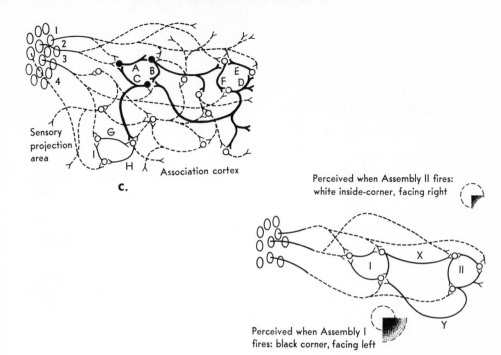

Sensory projection area

Association cortex

C.

Perceived when Assembly II fires: white inside-corner, facing right

Perceived when Assembly I fires: black corner, facing left

D.

assemblies that are "associated" in the sense that the firing of one loop (such as A, B, C) will increase the likelihood that the other loop (G, H, I) is fired when it is stimulated by still another source, like fiber 4, which would normally not be effective without such *facilitation* from A, B, C. Since some nerve fibers prevent others from firing, however, two cell-assemblies might *inhibit* rather than facilitate each other. Thus, if (X) and (Y) are inhibitory fibers in the arrangement at (D), either cell-assembly I or cell-assembly II would be fired by the sensory input, or they might alternate, but they could not both fire simultaneously.

(This "flip-flop" alternation between two mutually exclusive responses to one and the same sensory stimulus pattern characterizes the most important phenomenon in shape perception (the figure-ground phenomena discussed in Figure 47 and Chapter 5 C, D); without the ability to inhibit one of the two alternative shapes that are defined by the edge of each object, we should not be able to distinguish objects from the spaces between them.)

If this description of brain function is at all valid, these cell-assemblies, rather than the firing of specific receptor neurons would be the smallest units of perception. Each such cell-assembly would correspond to a simple common unit of sensory stimulation, such as a corner or a particular slope of a line in vision, a vowel sound in hearing, a pressure-pattern in touch. Whether or not such cell-assemblies do develop in the association areas, very similar units of complex neural action have been found in the sensory projection areas themselves.

Receptive fields. With very fine wires, called microelectrodes, the excitation of single neurons has been recorded from within the visual projection areas of various animals. Through this technique, neurons have been discovered that fire when some particular pattern (such as a line or an edge of a particular slope) stimulates an entire *field* of retinal receptors, and that do not fire when individual rods or cones are stimulated by points of light in the same retinal area (E) (Hubel & Wiesel, 1968). Unlike cell-assemblies, these line-sensitive and edge-sensitive cells are found in the sensory projection system. Like the cell-assemblies, they offer us a fresh approach to the study of sensory psychophysics, using much larger units of analysis (such as lines, corners, and edges of about ¼° by 4 to 8 degrees of visual angle in size) than those with which we first started—the specific nerve energies of punctiform receptor action. We discuss receptive fields further in pp. 107–110.

(Figure 49 continues)

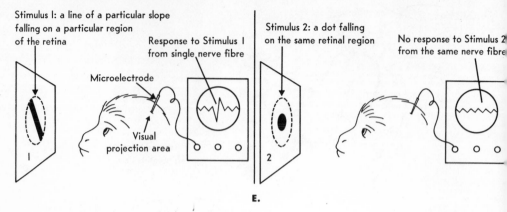

Stimulus I: a line of a particular slope falling on a particular region of the retina

Response to Stimulus I from single nerve fibre

Microelectrode

Visual projection area

Stimulus 2: a dot falling on the same retinal region

No response to Stimulus 2 from the same nerve fibre

E.

(Figure 49 continued)

Although these units of response are larger and more complex than those of traditional sensory psychophysics, they are still only fragments of the things we see. How might these cell-assemblies and receptive fields combine to form the objects and events of normal perception? Hebb's speculative sketch of this process is called the *phase sequence,* a version of which we shall consider briefly in Figure 50.

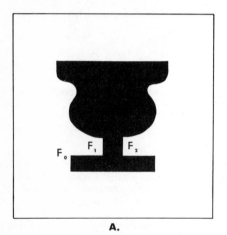

A.

FIGURE 50. The organization of cell-assemblies into phase sequences. When we look at an object, such as the silhouette of a vase in A., our gaze shifts from one *fixation* to another (say from F_0 to F_1 to F_2, etc.). Different sets of cell-assemblies will be stimulated when different patterns of stimulation— S_0, S_1, and S_2—fall on the fovea of the eye. Consider the first moment in time, T_0, with fixation F_0: the pattern of stimulation, S_0, facilitates the firing of cell-assemblies C_1 and Y_1 (to consider just two of many). If it were actually fired, C_1 might be experienced as "black-corner-pointing-left," while Y_1 might be "white-inside-corner-facing-right." (These two alternatives might well be mutually inhibitory, as shown

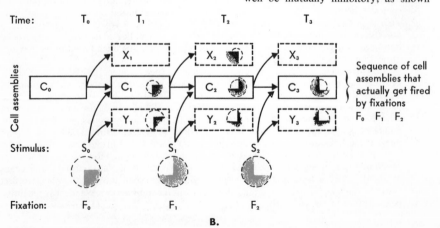

Time: T_0 T_1 T_2 T_3

Cell assemblies

Sequence of cell assemblies that actually get fired by fixations F_0 F_1 F_2

Stimulus: S_0 S_1 S_2

Fixation: F_0 F_1 F_2

B.

(Figure 50 continued)
in Figure 49E, in accordance with what we know about figure-ground perception (Figure 47).

Which cell-assembly, C_1 or Y_1 would fire? Which shape would be seen?

At moment T_0, the brain will not, of course, be idle: Reverberations will be continuing from the previous moment's visual (or nonvisual) sensory stimulation, and from whatever cell-assemblies had just been firing before S_0 fell on the eye. Let C_0 represent all the cell-assemblies that happen to be active at T_0. Their firing will facilitate the firing of other cell-assemblies, as we saw in Figure 49D. Suppose that C_1 and X_1 are the cell-assemblies that C_0 would facilitate. Of the three possible sets of outcomes (X_1, Y_1, and C_1), only C_1 would receive sufficient converging excitation to be fired and, in consequence, the observer would perceive a "black-corner-pointing-left."

Similarly, at the next fixation, F_1, the new pattern of stimulation falling on the fovea of the eye might facilitate two cell-assemblies (among others): C_2 ("black-inside-corner-facing-left") and Y_2 ("white-corner-pointing-right"). At this moment, T_1, C_1 will just have been fired by the events described above. If C_1 facilitates C_2 rather than Y_2—that is, if the observer "expects" C_2—the momentary pattern of stimulation (S_1) and the ongoing cortical processes (C_1) will both combine to produce the perception of "black-inside-corner-facing-left" at fixation F_1. As the observer continues to scan the object, the cortical processes set up by successive fixations will select the cell-assemblies to be seen at later fixations, and a smooth and consistent sequence of these elementary edges and corners will constitute the perception of the entire object—in this case, a black vase.

This description of a sequence of selection of alternative cell-assemblies (see Hebb 1949) is plausible in broad outline, but it is still to vague to make usable predictions about how objects will be perceived. Most particularly, it makes no provision for a very important principle that appears to govern this process of selection, the *Minimum Principle*, which we shall discuss in the next chapter.

Perceptual learning: Improvement and aftereffects. That there are effects of learning to perceive—especially for complex patterns of stimulation—appears certain. The change in appearance of a stranger's face after he becomes a familiar friend, our accommodation to the sounds of a foreign language (initially gibberish) as we are learning it, the difference between a text in a language that we can read and one that we can't, the tremendous difference between the appearance of a map or a circuit diagram before and after we have learned about such matters—all of these seem to guarantee that such effects exist (see Figure 51E).

There are many different kinds of perceptual change that can be demonstrated, and a number of these that have been the subject of particularly vigorous research are surveyed in Figure 51; some will be discussed further in Chapter 6. The fact is that few even approximate a simple process of association, and none of them yet offers the kind of knowledge about perceptual learning that would be needed to make the empiricist theory more than a loose hypothesis.

(Text continues on page 100)

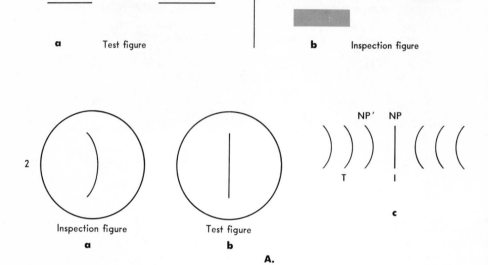

a   Test figure   **b**   Inspection figure

Inspection figure   Test figure
      a   **b**

A.

FIGURE 51. *Research in perceptual change.* Several varieties of perceptual change are currently receiving attention, partly because they seem to offer some hope of coming to grips with the fundamental problems of perceptual learning, and partly because they may help us discover sensory mechanisms (like the receptive fields we discussed in Figure 49) that respond directly to relatively complex patterns of stimulation.

A. Adaptation, aftereffects, and successive contrasts. As we have seen, the prolonged viewing of any color produces an afterimage of the opposite hue. Such effects are usually attributed to fatigue of the specific receptors that had been stimulated: the fatigued receptors fire at a lowered rate so that the remaining color receptors, being fresh and more active, contribute disproportionately to what we see. This seems like a simple and direct sensory explanation of a sensory process. But similar aftereffects of prolonged viewing can be demonstrated for such relatively complex properties as visual size, curvature, and motion (A, 1, 2, 3, respectively), and for location in haptic space (the space we know through our sense of exploratory touch). Do these facts imply that there are specific receptors responsible for such features of perception, in the same way that color receptors are responsible for the first stages of color perception?

We will return to the question of how such aftereffects can be used to identify sensory receptor mechanisms. Here, we consider the more general phenomena in which something like relearning, or recalibration, seems necessarily to be involved. We must note, however, that the question of whether a particular perceptual change is the result of learning or of the fatigue of a receptor mechanism, is usually very difficult to answer with real certainty.

First, to demonstrate some of the simple aftereffects:

1. Figural aftereffects. At (*a*) is a *test figure.* When you fixate point *X*, the sets of parallel lines on each side of the fixation point should appear to be equally separated. At (*b*) is an *inspection figure.* Fixate point *X* in the inspection figure for about a minute, and then return your gaze to the test figure. The separation should now appear to be greater between the right-hand set of parallel lines (Köhler & Wallach, 1944). This kind of phenomenon depends on keeping eye movements to a minimum and is quite local in effect.

2. Normalization. In Figure A2, if you run your eye up and down the curved inspection figure (*a*) and then fixate the test figure (*b*), the latter will appear to curve in the opposite direction. It is as though the straight line is a neutral point on a dimension that runs between curvature to the left and curvature to the right (*c*), and that by prolonged inspection of the test figure, the Neutral Point (NP) has been recalibrated

(Figure 51 continued)

in the direction of that curvature, and has moved to NP'. As a result of such normalization of the test pattern, then, the inspection pattern is no longer on the neutral point, but has shifted to the side opposite the test figure. Gibson argued in 1933 that this showed that curvature is just as direct a sensory response as color or temperature or any of the wide variety of sensory processes that show such adaptation. Similar changes will occur with a wide variety of perceptual features (Figure 52). These effects have recently received a great deal of attention because, by the logic of Figure *A2c* here, they seem to imply the existence of indentifiable mechanisms in the nervous system that respond directly to the perceptual feature in question, that can be fatigued only by that feature, and that therefore become amenable to study. We discuss some of these in the next chapter.

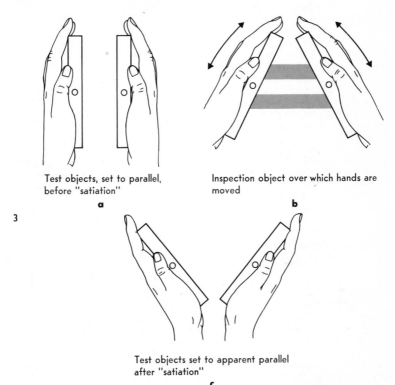

Test objects, set to parallel, before "satiation"

a

Inspection object over which hands are moved

b

3

Test objects set to apparent parallel after "satiation"

c

3. Kinesthetic and proprioceptive aftereffects. Even more dramatic aftereffects occur in the tactual-kinesthetic perception of shape and position. A blindfolded observer who rubs his hands back and forth across the inspection object obtains an astonishingly large aftereffect when he then adjusts two testboards between his hands so that they feel parallel. These aftereffects can certainly not be attributed merely to the fatigue of any conceivable set of sensory receptor neurons, since whole muscle systems are involved. Instead, the aftereffects occur in a space which transcends the individual tactual and kinesthetic receptors that are stimulated during the inspection period (Gibson & Backlund, 1963). This is called *haptic space,* the space we learn about by touch, kinesthetics, and proprioception (see Figure 32). More plausible than a change in peripheral tactual receptors is the possibility that the subject changes his expectations of how much pressure he will feel at different positions of his hands — that is, that a change in the correlation of touch and motion has been relearned, that the *sensorimotor correlation has been recalibrated.* A great deal of research has recently been done in this area, which we touch on next.

(Figure 51 continues)

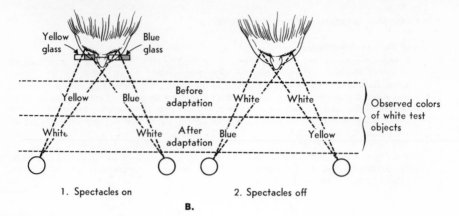

Yellow glass   Blue glass

Yellow   Blue   Before adaptation   White   White

White   White   After adaptation   Blue   Yellow

} Observed colors of white test objects

1. Spectacles on   2. Spectacles off

B.

(Figure 51 continued)

B. Changed relationships between the sensory modalities and sensorimotor recorrelations. The relationship between different modalities such as vision and kinesthesis readily changes with practice or adaptation. The relationship between visual up and down, and the meaning of these visual observations with respect to the body image (p. 64), can be at least partially upset and relearned—for example, by wearing inverting spectacles. When a subject first puts on inverting spectacles, he is virtually incapacitated. Within the course of a couple of weeks, however, he can even ride a bicycle. After removing the spectacles, the world now "looks upside down" (although it is not clear that this means what it at first appears to—see Harris, 1965), and the subject has trouble behaving appropriately in the normal world. There are many aftereffects of wearing distorting spectacles, especially prisms, that are purely visual, and these might contribute to the disruption of behavior that occurs when the spectacles are removed. For example, after adapting to spectacles with split-color lenses (B.1), when you remove the spectacles (B.2), the world looks yellow when you look to the left, and blue when you look to the right (I. Kohler, 1962). This effect has not turned out to be as robust as a similar phenomenon (which is harder to illustrate): Due to the way in which prisms bend light of different wavelengths (Figure 10), objects appear to be surrounded by a color fringe when the subject first puts on the glasses; after adaptation, the fringe of colors has disappeared or become more negligible, and when he removes the prisms, the fringes now reappear, but in the opposite direction (I. Kohler, 1962). We shall see that this may be a relatively peripheral, sensory phenomenon (Figure 52*D*). But there are changes in the relationship between vision and body image that require the subject to execute his own actions if adaptation is to occur, and these cannot be the direct or indirect results of purely sensory changes. An observer who is wearing distorting spectacles will undergo no adaptation while watching his hand move, in a situation similar to that in Figure 35, *if the experimenter moves his hand for him:* active, voluntary motion is needed for the adaptation and the aftereffects to occur (Held & Hein, 1958). An observer who is wheeled around in space while he is wearing distorting spectacles similarly shows no adaptation; but walking through the same environment, both displacement and curvature effects are obtained (Mikaelian & Held, 1964; Held & Rekosh, 1963). Precisely why voluntary movement is needed for adaptation to occur is not yet clearly established. Held proposed that these kinds of adaptation result because the subject learns a new correlation between the movements that he commands his muscles to make (the *efferent commands* he issues) and the visual changes that result from those actions, or *reafference*. This is essentially the third alternative represented in Figure 22. To what extent these aftereffects are changes within vision itself, within the body image alone (see Figure 31), or only in the correlation between the two, are questions that are not yet settled. But in any case, correlated eye movements and head movements are so intimately involved in the perception of visual space (see Figures 21, 22, and especially Figure 61c) that these distinctions are very hard to maintain on close analysis. In any case, this research is clearly dealing with something that we must call perceptual learning, and detailed quantitative knowledge of its course and conditions is being accumulated (Ebenholtz, 1966; Hay and Pick, 1966).

 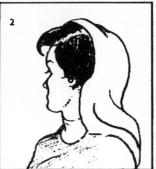 

C.

(Figure 51 continued)

C. Selective recognition of alternative organizations. Many situations are ambiguous in that we can perceive several quite different shapes or objects. Our previous experiences can influence which alternative we do perceive: At (*1*), we see a young lady in profile, at (*3*) an old woman. Subjects who had previously seen only (*1*) could at first see (*2*) only as a young lady; similarly, those who had first seen (*3*) could see (*2*) only as an old lady (Leeper, 1935). Similar effects have been found with reversible figures like those in Figures 62 and 63 (Rubin, 1921). The effects of prior experience with both alternatives is really very striking; it is as though the viewer needs some general schema or map into which to fit the details of any shape or object before he can perceive it, a point to which we will return in Chapter 6.

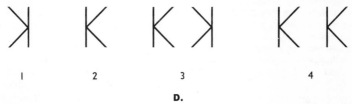

| 1 | 2 | 3 | 4 |

D.

D. Changes in recognition thresholds and reaction times. If we use light that is too weak, or exposure times that are too short, the viewer will be unable to discern the patterns or words that we show him. By gradually increasing the light or the duration, we reach a point at which the patterns can be recognized—that is, we will have a *recognition threshold* that can be measured by psychophysical methods (Chapter 2B). Practice, familiarity, and the viewer's expectation appear to affect these recognition thresholds. Thus, the mirror image of a letter (*1*) requires longer exposures in order to be correctly reported than does the shape in (*2*), which is a normally oriented letter (Henle, 1942). Does this mean that the shape in (*1*) is simply not seen at all at exposures that are sufficient to see that in (*2*)? No: Thresholds for judging whether two patterns are the "same" or "different," as in (*3*) and (*4*) are no higher for reversed or for rarely used letters than for normal and frequently used ones (Hayes, Robinson, and Brown, 1961). Moreover, subjects respond faster—that is, they display a faster *reaction time*—when they have to decide whether two letters are the same in shape (like *AA*) than when they have to decide whether they have the same name (like *Aa*) (Posner and Mitchell, 1967). Henle's results do not mean, therefore, that the letter's familiarity and name have supplied a shape to what otherwise would be a shapeless collection of points (see p. 85).

There is no doubt that past experience affects the recognition and report of the names and meanings of familiar letters, words, and shapes. If we wish to draw conclusions about the underlying processes of shape perception and about the ways in which the viewer decides on the names of the shapes that are presented to him, the question becomes a much trickier one. We will discuss the perception of words at

(Figure 51 continues)

(Figure 51 continued)
greater length in the section on *reading* (Chapter 6B). Words and letters seem at first to be ideal stimuli for studying perceptual learning because they present such a rich supply of alternative responses, but the ready availability of the spoken responses is itself a disadvantage.

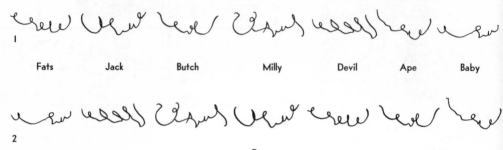

| Fats | Jack | Butch | Milly | Devil | Ape | Baby |

E.

E. Arabic scribbles and distinctive features. This is a demonstration of past experience which does not depend on reading skills, except in a trivial fashion. One effect of practice and experience is to increase our power of *differentiation* in what we perceive—that is, to enable us to see distinguishing characteristics and distinctive features by which we can respond differently to stimuli that previously looked all alike.

Indeed, the general trends that appear in the course of perceptual learning are *increasing differentiation, increasingly efficient direction of attention,* and *increasing economy of picking up information* (Gibson, 1969; Gibson & Levin, 1975). In the demonstration here (adapted from one described by E. J. Gibson, 1969), the row of curlicues running across the page at (*1*) has a row of names beneath it. Study the row carefully, trying to learn the name that goes with each scribble. The next row, (*2*) is a scrambled set of the same curlicues. Without looking at the first set, try to name the curlicues in the second set, and then check yourself. How many errors did you make? Finally, without going back to the first row, turn the book with the right-hand edge on the bottom, so that the set of curlicues runs vertically. Try again to name them. How many fewer errors did you make the second time? If you had fewer errors the second time, to what factors can you attribute the difference?

THE REMAINS OF THE NATURE-NURTURE DEBATE

What can we conclude about the empiricist theory of perception, once we have separated it from analytic introspection (and structuralism)?

Many of the issues raised by the structuralist enterprise remain active today. In most cases, their importance used to rest on a theorectical structure which, as we have seen, is now quite discredited. In consequence, though this is not always recognized, these questions are today quite different from their original formulations. The controversy about empiricism is a good example of this.

Do we see space (or shape, or direction) innately, or are such perceptual abilities learned, as the empiricist argument maintains? At first glance, one might think that the question would be simply settled. On the contrary, it entails extreme subtleties, and almost any sweeping statement made today about the relative contributions of nature and nurture is bound to be premature and irresponsible.

But this in itself tells us something about the problem. If the two alternatives offered clearly different predictions about perceptual abilities, or about the extent to which those abilities are educable or modifiable, they would be simple enough to separate and test. If, for example, an innate basis for space perception meant that perception would be fixed and unmodifiable, or if a learned basis for perception meant that it would be modifiable and educable (so that we could raise different people to perceive in different ways), then we would also, by the same token, have the basis for distinguishing between these two alternatives. Unfortunately, the issue is not so clear-cut.

It is perfectly possible that perceptual learning occurs in very early infancy, and resists further modification or relearning; at the other extreme, we might be born with a full set of perceptual abilities that are, although innate, subject to continual change and education.

With this in mind, the difficulty of deciding the nature-nurture issue becomes evident. But a further question then comes to the fore. If no such clear-cut alternatives attend either a nature or a nurture picture of perceptual development, under what conditions does this become an important issue?

Western tradition and common sense both incline toward an empiricist view. What conceivable innate mechanisms could explain space perception? Isn't it easier to imagine that this ability is learned? Not necessarily. Whatever the effects of learning may be, they must consist of changes in the nervous system, so that after the learning has occurred, the nervous system has a particular wiring, or set of interconnections. There is no reason why, as a result of millions of years of evolution, the individual cannot be born "prewired" — that is, born with whatever connections are necessary to perceive tridimensional space when presented with the appropriate stimulation. We discuss such possible mechanisms at several points (Chapter 5B, C).

The fact is that, at our present state of knowledge, one can find empiricist "explanations" of almost any perceptual phenomenon — even explanations of two mutually exclusive outcomes (see Figure 40C. If the same theory predicts that one object, *A*, will look nearer than another, *B*, and it also predicts the reverse, then such an explanation is rendered useless for predicting what we will perceive in any specific new situation, as well as being invulnerable to refutation. There has been a recent explosion of polemic about the heritability of cognitive capacities (that is, IQ) and the political consequences were such a theory proven true. One of the components of most intelligence tests is spatial visualization, which is usually tested with pictures much like those in Figure 72*A*. There are also repeated reports that African natives who are unaccustomed to pictures don't use perspective cues as well as Westerners (but see p. 136). But neither of the findings—even if we knew much more about their reliabilities and consequences than we do—really implies anything at all about nature versus nurture.

E. Alternatives to Structuralism

We have come to the end of any consistent attempt to build up the perceived world out of simple sensations that correspond to simple elementary physical variables. Next we will try "higher" units of analysis: *figures, edges, angles, and surfaces,* both stationary and in motion. Which of these are innately "prewired," and which result from perceptual learning, is still very much an open question.

Summary

In this chapter, we applied what we learned about the appearances of very simple stimuli to the perception of more normal and more complicated events.

Thus, in Chapter 3, we took the unit of visual response to be a sensation of a point of light whose apparent color and position depend on the stimulus, and on where the stimulus triggers some retinal receptor. Normally, of course, the scene that we face stimulates many millions of retinal receptors. Does what we see, then, consist only of the aggregate of the sensations produced by those receptors, varying in hue, saturation, and brightness from one part of a two-dimensional mosaic to another? Don't we also see shapes, distances, motions?

The traditional answer we have been exploring in this chapter is that in fact we don't *see* shapes, distances, or motion at all: that we *see* merely points of colored light in various arrangements, but that some of these arrangements have the memories of *nonvisual* sensations strongly associated with them. According to this theory, when we look at an object—say, an apple—what we actually see is only a red patch. If the apple is close to our eye, the red patch is large, and we remember that our hand need only stretch a small amount to touch it; if the apple is far, the patch is small, and we remember that our legs had to make some number of steps before our hand could touch it. The size of the red patch has thus become a visual "cue" that brings to mind those memories of reaching and walking that comprise the apparent depth or distance of the apple. Of course, there are many depth cues besides size (such as perspective, binocular disparity, and so on), and there are many other kinds of nonvisual memories that might be aroused by the visual sensations (the apple's tart taste, its smooth feel, and so on), but the basic theory (structuralism) has been illustrated. According to this theory, then, the multitude of different things and happenings we perceive are simply composed of the sensations, plus the memories of previous sensations.

If we could accept this structuralist theory wholeheartedly, the study of perception would rest directly on a set of fundamental elements—the sensations that are discovered by the procedures of sensory psychophysics. This in turn would give a clear purpose to studies of simple stimuli. Unfortunately, it is easy to show that complex stimuli are not perceived as we would be led to expect from the ways in which their parts are perceived. The same patch of light that is one color when viewed in isolation, looks very different when it is surrounded by light of another color. Similarly for shapes, sizes, motion: All of them usually appear quite different from what we should expect from this theory as soon as we depart from very simple situations. These differences may be classed under various headings, such as the perceptual constancies, the illusions, and the effects of organization. We have considered each of them in some detail, but they all add up to this: that what we have learned from sensory psychophysics will enable us to predict with assurance only how the very simplest stimuli are perceived.

We shall examine alternative approaches in the next two chapters.

MORE ADVANCED READING

FORGUS, R., and MELAMED, L. *Perception,* 2d ed. New York: McGraw Hill, 4: The auditory system, pp. 32–57; Chapter 5: Complex auditory phenomena 1. Psychoacoustics, pp. 58–71.

HABER, R. N., and HERSHENSON, M. *The psychology of visual perception.* New York: Holt, Rinehart and Winston, 1973. Chapter 15: The development of visual space perception, pp. 353–370.

KAUFMAN, L. *Sight and Mind.* New York: Oxford University Press, 1974. Chapter 7: The cues to depth, pp. 213–268; Chapter 8: Binocular stereopsis, pp. 270–321; Rearrangement of perceptual space, pp. 409–460.

KLING, J. A., and RIGGS, L. A. (Eds.) *Woodworth and Schlosberg's Experimental Psychology.* New York: Holt, Rinehart and Winston, 1971. Chapters 12 and 13, by J. Hochberg: Perception 1. Color and shape, pp. 395–474; Perception 2. Space and movement, pp. 475–550.

POSTMAN, L. (Ed.) *Psychology in the making.* New York: Knopf, 1962. Chapter 11, by J. Hochberg: Nativism and empiricism in perception. pp. 255–330.

SCHIFFMAN, H. *Sensation and perception.* New York: Wiley, 1976. Chapter 1976. Chapter 8: How size and shape constancy are mediated, pp. 146–169.

Higher-Order Units
in Perception

chapter five

In Chapter 3, we saw that the physical stimulation which reaches our sensory organs from the objects and events around us can be completely analyzed into a relatively small number of elementary physical variables, and that these local stimulus variables can be made to produce correspondingly elementary sensations (or simple perceptions). In Chapter 4, we saw that many discrepancies arise when we attempt to use the knowledge acquired in Chapter 3 to predict how entire objects (instead of elementary physical variables) are perceived. The classical remedy was to invoke our past experiences, in a particularly complex way (that is, by way of unconscious inferences) to explain these discrepancies. This complication is frequently unnecessary, as we shall see.

In this chapter, we return to most of the major questions of the last two chapters in approximately the same order in which we first discussed them. We will consider the nature of receptor units, color contrast and constancy, size and space, form and organization; but this time around we will study them in the context of perceptual theories that replace the classical explanations based on past experience and inferential processes with new explanations based on more organized direct responses to entire patterns of stimulation.

A. Sensory (Direct) vs. Cognitive Theories of Perception

HELMHOLTZ'S COGNITIVE EXPLANATIONS

Starting with what looked like the simplest set of sensory elements, Helmholtz had to explain *yellow* as an unconscious mixture of unnoticed red and green sensations, *lightness* as an unconscious judgment based on our unnoticed perceptions of the illumination, *size* as an unconscious judgment based on our perceptions of distance, and so on. For just about every quality of the objects that we perceive, our perceptions, according to this viewpoint, are based on calculations that are performed on other perceptions. We may call these *cognitive* explanations because they assume that our perceptions are based on (unconscious) mental processes similar to conscious reasoning.[1]

Such roundabout explanations are not inherently necessary, however. For the most part, they arise because of the particular set of sensory receptors that have been assumed as the unit of perceptual analysis. Let us consider other alternatives.

THE POSSIBLE SENSORY ALTERNATIVES

We have seen that there is probably a sensory mechanism that is directly responsible for the perception of *yellow* (p. 33), and that there may be neural structures that are directly responsive to the binocular indications of distance (p. 59). Is it possible to find sensory mechanisms that are also directly responsible for our perceptions of other object properties—for the *constancies, illusions,* and *organization?* These are all instances in which stimulus patches change their appearances when they are combined with other stimuli. If combining two stimuli changes the appearance of both, then there must be something about the combination itself which elicits that change.[2] That is, in addition to the local physical characteristics of each stim-

---

[1] You may detect a philosophical point here—that of one perceived event causing another—which alone has served to make many psychologists feel that this class of theory must be "mentalistic" and therefore unscientific. Inasmuch as it is perfectly possible to translate such "mentalism" into the language of computer programming, however, and computers are completely material devices, we can see that this misgiving, at least, is unwarranted.

[2] Whenever observers agree about what they see, the following must be true: No matter how complicated the stimulus is, and no matter how great the effects of past experiences (and of other unknown factors), *there must be some discoverable psychophysical relationship between the objects viewed and the perceptions that result.* If there were nothing in the stimulus pattern to govern their responses, there obviously could be no agreement (except by chance) among observers.

ulus, the *relationship between them* may be an important variable. A relationship between individual measures is what Gibson (1959) has called a higher-order variable. Let us see whether higher-order variables can be discovered that will account for the discrepancies of color, size, and form—the constancies and illusions and organizational phenomena that we encountered in Chapter 4.

This attempt has been pursued along *psychophysical* and *physiological* lines. The first consists of the search for aspects of sensory stimulation that correspond to what people in fact perceive: What information can we find in the proximal stimulus that accounts for the ways in which we actually perceive objects? The second is to try to find physiological mechanisms in the sensory system and in the brain that respond directly to such information.

In the following pages, we will see that a good start has been made at the first task—the task of finding stimulus bases to explain the phenomena of the constancies and illusions—and that there are enough indications that we have complex physiological response mechanisms available in the sensory nervous system to suggest that we can at least entertain notions of more direct or sensory explanations of those phenomena. We will see at the very end of this chapter, however, that such purely sensory explanations can only be a first step toward a complete understanding of perception, and that we have to draw upon cognitive explanations when we take into account how subjects respond to ambiguous stimuli, and how our perceptual systems must build up our perceptions out of successive sensory samples over time.

B. Higher-order Units in Sensory Physiology

The picture of the sensory nervous system that we outlined in Chapters 2 and 3 is, we now know, much too simple. Receptors do not function as independent points of sensory information, inasmuch as their outputs are in general collected by other cells that overlap many different receptors; and when one receptor is stimulated it generally *inhibits* the activity of its neighbors (Figure 52*A*). The results of such *lateral inhibition* are to accentuate differences in response to regions of different luminance (Figure 52*B*) and to produce *receptive fields* of various configuration and complexity (Figure 52*C*): At different stages in the visual system, categories of cells (like *2* in Figure 52*C*) have been found that do not respond when uniform light falls on the retina, but only respond when appropriate *patterns* stimulate the receptive fields on the retina to which they are connected.

(Text continues on page 110)

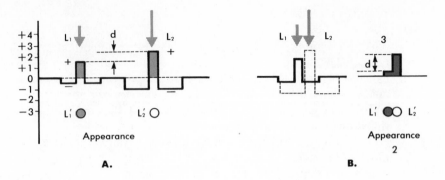

FIGURE 52. *Higher-order units of sensitivity.*

A. According to a very simple and elegant model of the effects of *lateral inhibition,* a spot of light increases the activity of the receptors that it stimulates, and it increases the activity of their surrounding neighbors (von Békésy, 1960): The retinal effects of two separate spots of light (L_1, L_2) are shown by the graph in *A*. Excitatory effects (+), shown above the base line (*0*), are flanked by inhibitory effects (−). The stronger light *(L_2)* produces more inhibition as well as more excitation. The spots' appearances are represented as L_1' and L_2'.

B. If the spots of light are adjacent instead of being separated, each spot's excitatory effect falls within the region of the other's inhibitory effects, as shown at B_1. Because the inhibition is greater around L_2 than that around L_1, the response to L_1 is diminished more than the response to L_2. This accentuates the difference (*d*) in responses to L_1 and L_2, as shown at B_2.

Even though lateral inhibition is only a slight departure from the independent mosaic model of Figure 17, we will see that it may be used to explain how the visual system is directly sensitive to quite complex patterns of stimulation (Figure 52C), and that it may also be used to explain most of the phenomena of color contrast and color constancy.

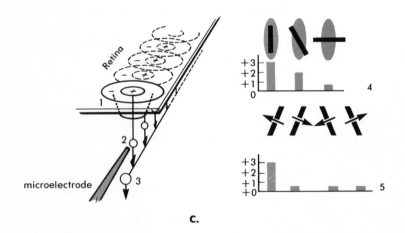

C.

C. By the use of microelectrodes to record the activity of cells in the visual system (see Figure 49), cells have been found which respond only when particular patterns of light stimulate particular regions of the retina. Thus, retinal ganglion cells (*2*) have been found which increase their firing rate when light stimulates the center of a field of receptors whose output they collect (*1*), and decrease their firing rate when the surrounding part of the receptor field is stimulated. These ganglion cells respond most strongly when their fields are stimulated by a central spot of light; other ganglion cells respond most strongly when a light ceases.

Collecting the output from a row of ganglion cells, a deeper cell (3) responds most strongly when a bar of light falls on a row of + centers. If the alignment of the bar with a row of centers decreases, so does the cell's response (4). At still deeper levels of the visual system, cells have been found (5) whose receptive fields respond to bars at a particular slant moving in one direction.

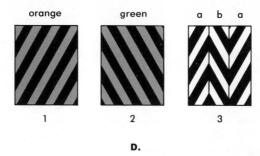

D.

D. Perceptual adaptation may provide a psychological tool with which to explore the psychological counterparts of consequences of the physiological phenomena described in Figure 52C. We noted in Figure 51B that one sees objects and contours to be surrounded by colored fringes after he removes prisms that have been worn for a while. McCullough (1965) found that if a subject looks alternately at the orange stripes at (*1*) and the green stripes at (*2*) for a few minutes, he finds that *a* and *b* appear greenish and pink, respectively, when he looks at the white stripes at *3*. According to the "fatigue" argument with which Gibson first used the normalization phenomenon as evidence that tilt and curvature were direct sensory properties (Figure 51A), these results may reveal the actions of cells that are sensitive to stripes of particular orientations and wavelengths. Similar aftereffects have been found that are specific to the stripes' colors and curvature (Riggs, 1973); and aftereffects of tilt and of movement (like those in Figure 51A and on p. 110) have been demonstrated to occur only when the inspection and test figures are of the same color (Held and Shattuck, 1971, and Favreau *et al.*, 1972 respectively). Note however that alternative explanations have been offered for some of these phenomena (Harris and Gibson, 1968; Murch and Hirsch, 1972), and that the meaning of these adaptation effects remains in question.

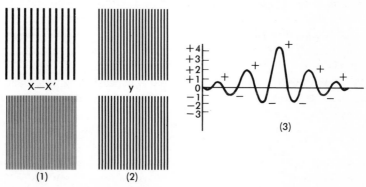

E.   *(Figure 52 continues)*

(Figure 52, continued)

E. If you keep your eye moving along the bar marked x–x' in (*1*) for a minute or so, and then fixate y in (*2*), the upper grating in (*2*) will probably appear more closely spaced than the lower one (Blakemore & Sutton, 1969). Such effects have been taken to show that the visual system responds directly to each of a number of different spatial frequencies (contours per degree of visual angle, see p. 36). This line of inquiry is still in its infancy. For a current and clear discussion, see Graham (1978), who also points out that by departing only slightly from the simplicity of the model of lateral inhibition in *C*, above — i.e., by adding auxiliary concentric bands of excitation and inhibition as at (*E, 3*) — we obtain a receptive field that would be tuned to a specific spatial frequency.

These cells in turn form the input to higher cells (Figure 52*C*,*3*), which are activated when their appropriate stimulus pattern falls anywhere within quite a wide region of the retina. To these, of course, we must add the receptive fields that we noted earlier in connection with stereopsis (p. 59).

These receptive fields have been discovered by microelectrode recording procedures (Figure 49), and we do not have any *direct* evidence of their function in perception. There is an additional large class of sensory analyzing mechanisms that were suggested by the phenomena of *perceptual adaptation and aftereffects*. As we noted in Chapter 3 (p. 27), after looking at one color, we get an aftereffect, or afterimage. This is due in part to the fact that the neural elements that have been stimulated become "fatigued": they respond progressively less to the stimulation while it is present, and contribute less to the balance of receptor activity when the stimulation ceases. Similar effects obtained with many other properties, such as shape, motion, etc., have been taken as evidence that those properties are also simple and direct sensory responses (Wohlgemuth, 1911; Gibson, 1933). This technique can be adopted as a general tool. For example, Sekuler and Ganz (1963) showed that after prolonged inspection of stripes moving in one direction, subjects needed more light to see stripes moving in that direction than in the opposite direction. Note that the effects were not due to any change in the subjects' eye movements (which would be the obvious explanation for the findings) because these experimenters used an image-stabilization technique similar in effect to the one described in Figure 53*C*.

Such procedures have suggested a wide variety of specialized sensory mechanisms, including ones that are sensitive to size (Pantle & Sekuler, 1968; Blakemore & Campbell, 1969); ones conjointly sensitive to color and orientation (McCollough, 1965), as shown in Figure 52*D*; and a series of experiments that seem to demonstrate that there are mechanisms in our visual systems that are directly sensitive to the spacing, or frequency, of repetitive patterns (Figure 52*E*).

We can now see why it is not totally implausible to think of the visual system, like the auditory system, as a device that analyzes the retinal image into a set of *spatial frequencies,* like the Fourier analysis described on p. 44. What we gain by such an analysis is another matter.

Some support for this proposal comes from adaptation experiments like that of Figure 52E, and some comes from the results of *masking experiments* like the following. When one pattern (like one of the grids in Figure 52E) is superimposed on another pattern, and the two patterns are presented either simultaneously, or separated by some short interval of time, the visibility of one or both is impaired. A similar phenomenon occurs in hearing: One sound will mask another if the masking sound contains a *critical band* of frequencies that bracket those of the masked sound; if the two sounds do not share the same component frequencies, then little masking will occur. In visual masking, the extent to which one pattern decreases the visibility of another one is also predictable from their shared spatial frequencies (Stromeyer & Julesz, 1972; Weisstein & Bisaha, 1972; Harmon & Julesz, 1973).

The existence of the sensory mechanisms we have outlined here is not yet well established. And in most cases, their function in normal perception remains to be demonstrated. It is clear, however, that the possibilities of direct sensory response to reasonably complex object-qualities are very real, and we will refer to such possibilities as we discuss the perception of various object-qualities in their turn.

C. Relationships as Stimuli

COLOR AND CONTOUR

Our sensory systems respond to change, not to stimulation as such. In Chapters 2 and 3, our simple assumption was that our receptors respond to the presence or absence of stimulation. That is not true. In fact, if a uniform color fills your field of view, termed a *Ganzfeld,* its color rapidly disappears (Hochberg, *et al.,* 1951; Cohen, 1958). You can demonstrate this for yourself readily if you follow the procedure in Figure 53B. Why doesn't vision always disappear as a matter of course then?

The reason lies in the very small, rapid movements the eye continually makes. When the field of view is *non*uniform, these small eye movements cause changes in retinal stimulation, as the boundaries between different parts of the retinal image move back and

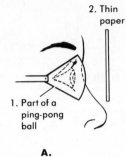

2. Thin paper

1. Part of a ping-pong ball

A.

FIGURE 53. *We cannot see with light alone—we need change, too.*

A. A simple means to obtain a homogeneous visual field (Ganzfeld). *1.* Half a ping pong ball, fitted over the eye. *2.* A diffusing screen. Because the light is uniform over the entire field of vision, it quickly fades to dark gray. When the eyes are closed and opened, the light returns briefly.

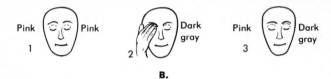

Pink 1 Pink   2 Dark gray   Pink 3 Dark gray

B.

B. A simpler demonstration. *1.* Close both eyes and look through your lids at a bright source; you will see a pink fog. Keep both eyes closed throughout this experiment. *2.* Cover your right eye with your hand. By this time, all the pink will have gone, even from your left eye. *3.* Remove your hand. Your right view will again be pink (briefly), in sharp contrast to your left view, which will be a dark gray.

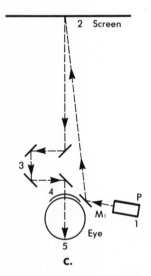

2 Screen

3

4

P

M_1

1

Eye

5

C.

C. Stabilized images. A projector (*P*) bounces its beam off a mirror, M_1, that is mounted on a contact lens (*4*) fitted snugly to the viewer's eye. The image reflects from the screen (*2*), and after a short path through some compensating mirrors at (*3*), enters the eye. If the eye moves to the right or to the left, the stimulus that is projected on the screen follows suit. Thus its image continues to end up at the same point on the retina. Because the picture projected to the eye produces the same image on the retina despite the eye's movements, it soon fades into invisibility. (Riggs, et al., 1953).

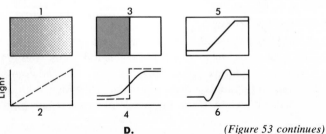

D.

(*Figure 53 continues*)

(Figure 53 continued)

D. What is a change? *1*. A gradual change from dark to light. *2*. In profile, a graph of the amount of light at each point in (*1*); the rate of change as indicated by the slope of the dotted line, is the *gradient* of light. *3*. An abrupt change on the printed page, between dark and light. *4*. The dotted line shows the stimulus change that confronts the eye; the solid line shows the image on the retina. Because of imperfect image-formation, even the most abrupt change in the stimulus is blurred and softened on the retina. *5*. A stimulus "ramp": the profile of a stimulus that is dark on the left and light on the right, like (*3*), but that has a steep gradient between the two. The retinal image is in any case just such a "ramp," no matter how abrupt the actual transition. *6*. The visual *response* to (*5*): The action of lateral inhibition between the units in Figure 52*B* accentuates the gradient in the retinal image, makes it sharp enough to form a contour, and makes the visual response more like the distal stimulus, which is a sharp and abrupt change, than it is like the blurred and gradually changing gradient in the retinal image—a primitive form of constancy. Less primitive consequences for the perception of object properties are discussed on p. 114. The "pips" on the response ramp in (*6*) are illusory stripes, called *Mach bands;* the fact and characteristics of their occurrence are nicely accounted for by von Bekésy's model (the units shown in Figure 52*A*), although that model does not account for the apparent brightness at some distance from the edge that separates the two regions (Hood and Whiteside, 1968).

forth on the retina. By using contact lenses that move with the eye, the retinal image can be made to move along with the eye (Figure 53*C*), achieving *image stabilization*. Because stabilized images do not change over time at each point on the retina, they fade from view, like the *Ganzfeld*.

The bases of contours and colors. So it appears that our eyes need differences in stimulation in order to see at all. What is more, the difference from one region to another cannot be gradual, or we will not see that the two regions are different: The effects of different *rates of change* (called *gradients*) from one region to the next, are shown schematically in Figure 53*D*. (We cannot actually demonstrate those gradients and their effects here on the printed page because the printing process is not sufficiently precise, so you will have to visualize them from the graphs which represent the gradient of brightness and the resulting apparent distribution of lightness in each case.)

When the difference in stimulation between two regions is sufficiently abrupt, they appear to be separated by a definite *contour*. Contours do more than form clearly perceptible boundaries between different areas: They also determine the colors of those areas. We can change the light in the middle of an area quite substantially, and as long as the gradient is too shallow to form a contour, the area will continue to appear homogeneous. In a remarkable demonstration to this point, Krauskopf (1963) presented an observer with a disc of one color that was surrounded by a ring of another color. Using image-stabilization apparatus (Figure 53*C*), the inner disc and its contour was stabilized in the retinal image; being stabilized, the whole inner disc faded from view. The outer ring was not stabilized, and when the inner disc vanished, the entire region homogeneously assumed the color of the outer ring! Thus the visual system apparently fills in colors between contours.

Only now are we ready to ask about the appearance of a patch of light: In order to have any appearance at all, it must be different from its surroundings, a point we would never have realized when we discussed the elements of analysis in Chapter 3. And this fact has considerable import for the phenomena of color constancy and color contrast.

Color constancy and color contrast. Vary the intensity of a patch of light, and its lightness changes. Keep its intensity constant, but vary that of a ring surrounding it, and its lightness again changes (Figure 42). Evidently the lightness of any region is not determined simply by *its* intensity; some relationship between the intensities of *two adjacent regions* must be considered. What is the simplest relationship between the intensities of two regions that might account for the apparent lightnesses of those regions? Let us try *ratios* of intensities (see Figure 54). If the apparent lightness of a region—say, the disc marked *?* in (*A*)—is proportional to the *ratio between its intensity and that of its surrounding region,* instead of simply being proportional to its intensity, the two inner discs should appear to be of equal lightness when *?* = 25 mL. In fact, that is what happens.

Both lightness constancy and the contrast phenomena discussed on pp. 73–79 seem simple to understand in these terms: Whether in sunlight or shade, the ratio between the light reflected from the lump of coal and its background (Figure 38), remains constant; this might therefore explain lightness constancy. Also the ratio of light reflected to the eye from regions *4* and *2* in Figure 42 is clearly smaller than the ratio obtaining between regions *3* and *1*, even though *3* and *4* are themselves equal; this might account for lightness contrast.

In general, simple *ratios* of stimulation will predict what we see far better, as a first approximation, than will measures of the individual patches, considered separately.

Even so, we cannot merely replace the simple addition hypothesis of Chapter 4A by an equally simple ratio hypothesis (Figure 54*A*); moreover, as the complexity of the stimulus pattern increases, the perceived lightness of any one region becomes more difficult to predict. There is also a hint of potential trouble to be found in the sketches in Figure 54*B*. We note there that the apparent lightness of an object may change even though the luminance distributions in the field of view remain substantially unchanged. You may observe

(*Text continues on page 116*)

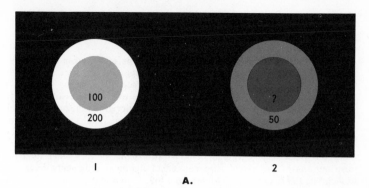

A.

FIGURE 54. Relative intensities and relative lightness.

A. On the left, disc (*1*) set at 100 mL.; on the right, disc (*2*), with variable luminance. Each disc is surrounded by a ring of light in an otherwise dark room, as shown. At what setting will disc (*2*) look exactly as light as disc (*1*)? Not at 100 mL., but at 25 mL.! The two discs are certainly not equal, then, in physical luminance; in what way are they equal? With a ring of 60 mL., disc (*2*) would have to be 30 mL. to match disc (*1*); with a ring of 100 mL., disc (*2*) would have to be 50 mL. The discs appear equally light, then, when the ratio of surround-luminance to disc-luminance is equal for each disc. Thus, if we increase the luminance of disc (*2*), but are careful to increase the luminance of the surround at the same rate so that the ratio of surround-luminance to disc-luminance is kept constant, the lightness of disc (*2*) also remains constant and equal to that of disc (*1*) (Wallach, 1948).

If the stimulus variable which determines perceived lightness is not the absolute amount of light energy, but is instead the *ratio* of light energies in adjacent regions, the phenomenon of lightness constancy (p. 73) becomes considerably easier to understand, since the ratio of intensities of light reaching the eye from each of several objects is in fact constant, regardless of changes in the illumination, as long as the reflectance of each object remains constant (see Figure 38).

In fact, this ratio hypothesis is too simple: at other levels of disc (*1*) and its surrounding ring, a constant ratio of surround-luminance to disc-luminance will not serve to keep disc (*2*) equal in apparent lightness to disc (*1*) (Hess and Pretori, 1894; Jameson and Hurvich, 1964). Jameson and Hurvich therefore propose a white/black opponent-process pair (see Figure 16, p. 32) such that the whiteness in any part of the visual field is the sum of the light energy falling on that part of the retina, plus an *induced effect* that is black if the surrounding regions are white and vice versa. Their theory provides a good quantitative fit to the data

(Figure 54 continues)

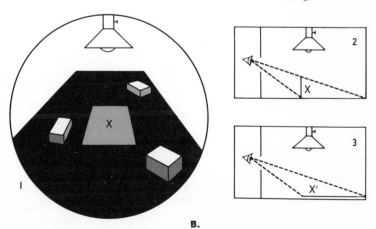

B.

(Figure 54 continued)

B. Can we really account for our perceptions of lightness completely in terms of relative luminances, as our discussion in *A* suggests? Perhaps not: If we change the amount of light that appears to fall on a surface, its apparent lightness may change also, even though the light energy entering the eye remains substantially unchanged! Object *X* in the view at (*1*) may look like an upright trapezoid in glancing illumination, which it really is (*2*), or it may look like a horizontal square receiving full illumination (*3*). When caused to change its apparent spatial orientation from (*3*) to (*2*) (for example, by waving a stick behind *X*), it may become darker in appearance (Hochberg and Beck, 1954). Similar demonstrations that factors other than the luminance distributions in the visual field can effect lightness judgments have been reported (Gilchrist, 1977; Gogel and Mershon, 1969; Coren and Komoda, 1973), but they are not always obtained (Flock, 1970; Epstein, 1961b) and, when they are, they may be due to differences in where the viewer has looked and what he is comparing the target to (Flock *et al.*, 1966). This issue remains undecided.

the same phenomenon by staring at an unevenly lit corner of the room that you are in and "forcing" it to appear flat—something you will be able to do with a little effort. When you succeed, the part that is in shadow will probably appear to become darker. This phenomenon (originally noted by Mach in 1886) seems very much like the result of some unconscious inference in which you calculate how light an object is by taking into account its apparent slant-toward-the-light and, hence, the illumination it appears to receive. As we noted in the figure, however, these effects are not always obtained; furthermore, they are not quantitatively what we would expect them to be in terms of Helmholtz's explanation (Beck, 1965).[3]

Regardless of such complications, however, the appearance of a region's lightness does appear to be determined mainly by its relationship to its surroundings, not by its own light energy. Similarly, the hue of any region also turns out to depend on the wavelength of its surroundings as well as upon its own wavelength (Figure 55). Thus, the stimulus basis for hue, like that of lightness, depends on the relationship between regions rather than on the stimulation within any single region.

ABSOLUTE, RELATIVE, AND FAMILIAR SIZE

With only one patch of stimulation on the retina of the eye, only one basis for a size response exists: the size of the retinal image (or visual angle subtended at the eye, Figure 39). This is called the *absolute size* of the stimulus. With more stimuli, a higher-order variable appears—the ratio of the size of one image on the retina rela-

---

[3] The apparent lightness does not vary predictably with the actual slant, as it should if unconscious inference were the basis of the phenomenon. The viewer may be answering a different question, when he is asked about uneven surfaces in uneven illuminations, than he does in the more classical experimental arrangements (Beck, 1972).

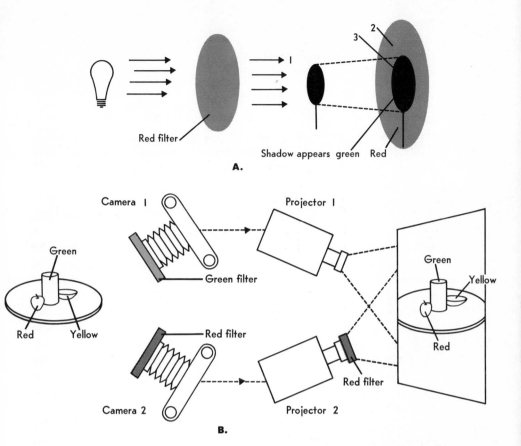

FIGURE 55. Colored shadows and "full-color" pictures from "one color." *A.* Light of 650 nm wavelength appears red; light of 530 nm appears green. A shadow *(3)* cast by such red-hued light of 650 nm *(1)* looks green, even though no light of 530 nm is present. The apparent hue of the shadow region *(3)* is determined by its relationship to the surrounding "red" region *(2)*, not to the absolute wavelength of the light coming from the shadow itself, as simultaneous color contrast, or induction, occurs (see p. 79). *B.* If a slide of colored objects, photographed through a red filter, is projected on a screen in red-hued light (650 nm), and another slide, photographed through a green filter, is projected in precise superposition in white (unfiltered) light, greens, blues, and yellows appear on the screen, as well as reds (Land, 1959). Can you explain why the green appears? How about yellow?

tive to the sizes of the other images. This is called the *relative size* of the stimulus. The structuralist approach assumed that our nervous system is responsive solely to the absolute sizes of the retinal images, and that any departure from this simple relationship is to be explained either by our knowledge about the real size, gained through our familiarity with the object, or by our calculations which take the object's distance into account.

As we saw in Figure 43 and on p. 80, there is a simple trigonometric relationship between size and distance. For a given size of visual angle, if the absolute size of the image is measured by angle θ, then

$$\tan \theta = S/D,$$

where S is the physical size of the object itself and D its distance. If we know the visual angle, or absolute size, and we know the distance of the object, we might calculate its physical distal size. Conversely, if we know the visual angle, or absolute size, and are familiar with the object's physical size, we might calculate its distance.

This introduces still another term: *familiar size.* In terms of Berkeley's original assumption, every familiar object is considered to have some *assumed,* or familiar, distal size that we have learned by our previous experience with the object. Does this familiar size tell us both the size of the object the next time we see it *and,* taken in conjunction with the absolute retinal size, allow us to calculate its distance unconsciously?

A classic experiment which is frequently quoted in support of familiar size is shown in Figure 56. Do the results of this experiment

FIGURE 56. *Familiar size.* A. Only Y is a normal playing card; X is twice normal size; Z is half normal size. All are at the same distance from the observer, but the base is hidden by the screen. Viewing all the cards at once monocularly, viewers judge X to be nearest and Z farthest, with Y appearing halfway between the two (Ittelson & Kilpatrick, 1952). Viewed one at a time, the cards yield no consistent differences as to the distances at which they are judged to be (Gogel, Hartman, & Harker, 1957; Epstein *et al.,* 1961). What other distance cues might have been working in (*A*) that are not present in (*B*)?

Although the efficacy of familiar size is still in question (Oyama, 1974; Mershon and Gogel, 1975), recent research has in general found it to work increasingly well when the targets whose distance the subjects are to judge are made more realistic (Epstein, 1965; Dinnerstein, 1967; Ono, 1969; Eriksson and Zetterberg, 1975).

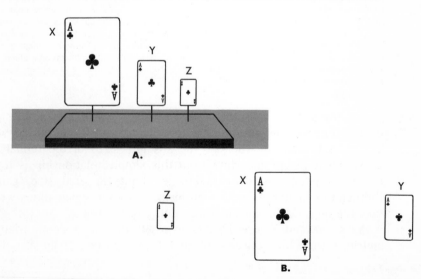

clearly demonstrate the operation of the familiar size cues? Not at all.

In this experiment, there are *two* possible depth cues at work, familiar size and *relative size* (the ratio of the images' sizes), and only the former, by its very definition, demands specific past experience (Hochberg & Hochberg, 1953). This will be an important theoretical point to us, and the distinction should be made clear.

Returning for a moment to Figure 27*B,* we see the two boys drawn in different sizes, which produces a cue of relative size as to their different distances, and you would not have to know either the absolute or the objective size of either of them in order to use that cue. The man (*3*) and the boy (*1*) are drawn the same size. In order for this to be a depth cue, therefore, you must know that the man is really larger (and hence further) than the boy — that is, you must know the *familiar size* of each. Most of the experiments that have attempted to demonstrate the latter actually employed relative size as well, and because the two cues have different properties — and very different theoretical implications — they must be separately studied.

Now if we repeat the experiment in Figure 56, but with only one card present at a time, relative size can no longer be used as a distance cue, and we can see whether familiar size alone can produce differences in apparent distance. There has been some question about that, but recent research has shown that subjects can indeed use an object's familiar size to judge its distance, with no other cue present. In general, such experiments use different-sized pictures or models of familiar objects and, the more realistic the model, the better familiar size works as a depth cue (Epstein, 1961; Dinnerstein, 1967; Ono, 1969). In fact, in a recent experiment in which subjects were shown real objects at various distances in the real world, but without any depth cues (the subjects were enclosed in a booth with a small aperture and shutter, all of which was mounted in an automobile), their immediate distance estimates were remakably good and stable (Eriksson & Zetterberg, 1975).

The Ittleson and Kilpatrick conclusions seem to be valid, and this implies that, at some level, the subjects must indeed make use of the absolute size of the retinal image and of some version of the size/distance relationship. This is a strong point for the empiricist position, and we will return to it later.

A decade ago, in the first edition of this book, the effectiveness of *familiar size* was very much in doubt. Figure 40*C* clearly demonstrates that this cue has strong limitations, and it is important to learn what these are. But the fact remains that familiar size does determine the perception of distance in the absence of other depth cues, and this implies that we have stored an "idea" of distance corresponding to the absolute size of each familiar object, just as Berkeley and Helmholtz argued (cf. Ittleson, 1951a). Regardless of how practically important or unimportant familiar size is as a depth cue, therefore, it is clearly *theoretically important* in the understanding of perceptual learning.

RATIOS AS STIMULI FOR APPARENT SIZE AND APPARENT VELOCITY

Even if we assume that we perceive the sizes of familiar objects because of our past experiences with them, we still must explain how we perceive the sizes of objects that do not have definite familiar sizes (such as an unfamiliar machine, a boulder, etc.), and how we learn the familiar sizes of objects that we have not actually touched. (Surely, we have not actually touched everything whose size we know; nor does the efficacy of familiar size prove that perceived distance and size are based on memories of reaching and touching.)

Do we take our perceptions of distance into account in arriving at our perceptions of size, by the kind of Helmholtzian unconscious inference process that we examined in Figure 44?

We saw in Figure 54 that if our perceptions of lightness are determined directly by the ratios of adjacent luminances, both lightness constancy and contrast are explained with no need to take illumination into account. The same is true of size and motion. Consider the size of the central *o*'s in the right-hand and left-hand groups:

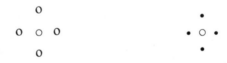

The two are actually the same size, of course, but the right-hand one comprises a larger proportion of its surroundings. If an object's apparent size is determined by its relative size—by the proportion of its surroundings that it occupies—then in most cases its apparent size will remain constant, regardless of the observer's distance from it. That is, the proportion of its surroundings that the object occupies will remain constant, even though the absolute size of each may change in the retinal image. So size constancy would be explained as a direct response to stimulation, without any need to take distance into account. And similarly, many of the illusions of size (such as Figures 40, 41) would be explained as the direct response to size proportions.

In fact, when observers are asked to match the lengths of two lines which are presented to them in apertures of different sizes in an otherwise dark room, their match is close to the ratio of each line to its aperture (Rock & Ebenholtz, 1959). Earlier evidence to the same point comes from research on perceived velocity, which is, of course, closely related to perceived size or extent.

If spots move across each window in Figure 43B at a rate of five inches per second, in one second the near one will cross its window, but the far one will only get half way. The two spots will not have moved the same retinal distance in both cases. The retinal image motion is not sufficient, therefore, to tell us how fast the spot is really moving. Do we take the apparent distance into account when we perceive the two as moving at the same speed? J. F. Brown proposed the transposition principle in 1931: that apparent speed remains constant if physical speed and the dimensions of the object and its surround remain in the same ratio; and Wallach pointed out (1939, 1959) that this would account directly for speed constancy, with no need to take distance into account.

As in the case of color perception, the possibility that we are responding directly to ratios of stimulation, whether by perceptual learning or by innate prewiring, may render the Helmholtzian cognitive explanation unnecessary. But it is very difficult in fact to test whether perceived size or perceived speed depends on perceived distance, because we have to remove all possible direct bases for the judgment of size and distance—we have to remove all possible *non*-cognitive bases. This would mean removing the context in which the object is presented. If an object is presented with no context to provide depth cues, how then can we change its apparent distance? The following experiments attempted to do just that by varying the binocular cues to distance.

As long as the viewer can use both eyes, he has binocular cues to distance (i.e., convergence, Figure 21, and disparity, Figure 29). In fact, both apparent size and apparent speed have been found to change as convergence changes (Heinemann *et al.,* 1959; Rock *et al.,* 1968; Gogel & Teitz, 1974; Hay & Sawyer, 1969).

A recent study makes a very strong case for the effect of *apparent* distance on apparent speed: When a subject is surrounded by a cylinder of moving vertical stripes, he feels himself to be rotating in the

opposite direction (the phenomenon is close to the one illustrated in
Figure 33*B* and *C*). Wist and his colleagues (1975) varied the apparent distance of the cylinder by placing a neutral filter (like one lens
of a pair of sunglasses) in front of one of the subject's eyes. Such a
filter produces the *Pulfrich phenomenon* (Lit, 1949), in which a moving object appears to be nearer or farther than it is, depending on its
direction of motion. (This presumably occurs because the filter lowers the intensity of the retinal stimulation in that eye, which in turn
lowers the speed with which the information from that eye enters
the central nervous system. Because *the object is moving over the
retina,* this lag in information transmission changes the degree of effective binocular disparity. This, in turn, changes the object's apparent distance [see Figure 29.]). Subjects' judgments both of their own
speed of rotation and of the stripes' distance increased as the experimenters increased the magnitude of the Pulfrich effect.

In all of these examples, it remains possible *in principle* to argue
that the subject is responding directly to some combination of stimuli, perhaps something like a ratio of retinal size to the amount of binocular disparity, although that seems farfetched when applied to the
last example. But try the following demonstration: Look at the left-
most box in Figure 66*C*. If you perceive the box with *its* left face
nearest to you, its left and right sides probably look reasonably
equal in size; if you "force" the box to reverse its orientation so that
its right side looks nearer to you (it will take some time and effort to
view the box as if from below), the right face will probably then look
much smaller. There are numerous cases like this, in which apparent
size or movement of precisely the same stimulus changes, depending
on how you perceive it (Sanford, 1897; Mefferd & Wieland, 1968;
Gregory, 1970): For example, if two fields of dots are moving equally
fast but in different directions, observers see two moving surfaces,
and the one that looks further seems to move more *slowly* (Farber
& McConkie, 1977). These are not merely curiosities: they show that
perceived distance can affect perceived extent, even when there is
no direct basis for that in stimulation.

This does not mean that we always go through this intervening
procedure of taking distance into account. Neither "size perception"
nor "motion perception" is a single experience, dependent on a
single underlying mechanism. (We know that movement thresholds,
shape constancy, and brightness constancy results are affected by
the time that the subject has in which to view the stimuli [Leibowitz,
1956; Leibowitz & Bourne, 1956; Leibowitz & Chinetti, 1957]; similar research, directed to the question of whether we normally take
distance into account in our perceptions of size and speed, might

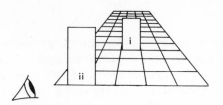

FIGURE 57. What is constant in size constancy? If the stimulus variable upon which we base our judgments about the size of an object were the number of texture elements it covers, where it touches the ground, we would have at least one explanation for the phenomenon of size constancy, since this variable will remain constant for a given distal object size, regardless of the distance from which the object is viewed (Gibson 1950, 1959).

show that the cases in which we take distance into account are slower—i.e., they take longer to reach a perceptual conclusion—than those in which apparent size and apparent velocity are direct responses to higher-order variables of stimulation.)

We should note that there are very different ways in which we may perceive an object's size, ways that do not depend on our taking its distance into account to infer its size, or vice versa. In a normal environment, our size judgments are made about *objects on a surface,* not about points in empty space. The surface on which the objects stand is likely to be covered with a reasonably uniform pattern or *texture* (see Figure 57). If we take the number of elements of texture that are obscured by the object *i,* where it touches the ground to be T_i, and the number of elements obscured by object *ii* to be T_{ii}, then the ratio of these two numbers, T_i/T_{ii}, provides us with a higher-order variable of stimulation that should under normal circumstances be in perfect correspondence with the actual physical sizes of the objects. That is, *it is possible to find variables of stimulation that automatically take distance into account, if we accept the possibility that ratios are stimuli to which the nervous system can respond.*

GRADIENTS AS POTENTIAL STIMULI:
TOWARD A PSYCHOPHYSICS OF SURFACES

A stimulus ratio measures how some variable differs in two regions of the optic array. It is appropriate to *pairs* of stimuli. The physical world, however, is not really characterized by pairs of regions (which is what we have been talking about so far in this section) any more than by individual points (which is what we had discussed in Chapters 2 and 3). We are usually confronted by continuous surfaces, by extended objects, by prolonged motions. The rate at which some measured property changes over a continuous, extended stimulus is called a *gradient.*

From Berkeley on, most philosophers, physiologists, and psychologists had started with the assumption that we cannot account for our perceptions of space in terms of information in visual stimulation, and had gone on from there to try to discover how we made up for this inadequacy. The first real challenge to this tradition came from James J. Gibson, who started with the inescapable fact that people *can* perceive space by means of vision alone, and concluded, therefore, that some kind of information must be present in visual stimulation. The *gradient of texture-density* is a particularly promising higher-order variable for this purpose. If you look straight ahead at a homogeneously textured surface, the density of the texture does not change from one part of the optic array to the next, so that the gradient of texture-density is zero; as the slant increases, the density of texture changes from the near edge to the far edge, and the gradient, or rate of change, increases. Figure 58 shows several ways in which the gradient of texture-density could provide the observer with precise and relatively unambiguous information about the distances, sizes, and slants of the surfaces and objects in the world.

The examples of Figure 58 provide an impressive analytical vocabulary. By assembling the proper texture-density gradients, we can produce almost any collection of objects and surfaces. If we take texture gradients as the physical stimulus variables, and perceived surface slant as the corresponding psychological unit, we *may* have *a new set of elements with which to analyze our perceptions of the physical world.*   *(Text continues on page 126)*

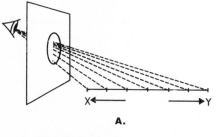

A.

FIGURE 58. Texture-density gradients as informative variables of stimulation. In *(A)* we see why a uniform texture on the ground produces a texture-density gradient at the eye, and, although the texture may vary *(B)*, the gradient itself remains the same for a given degree of slant. These gradients of texture-density carry information about the sizes of objects (familiar or otherwise) standing on the surface *(C)*, and, in addition, they carry information about the arrangement of surfaces with respect to each other.

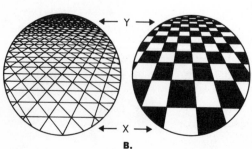

B.

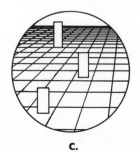

C.

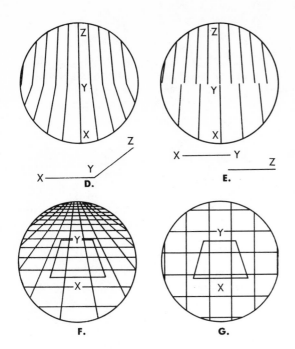

In (D) we see how an abrupt change in gradient results in an apparent dihedral angle (that is, an angle between surfaces); in (E), an edge or drop between parallel surfaces is indicated by a change in density and a constant gradient. Even shape constancy (see Figure 37B) might be accounted for in these terms:

In (F) the rear edge (Y) of the geometrical figure is the same number of texture-units wide as is the front edge (X), so that the figure can serve as a stimulus for "square-at-a-slant"; in (G), on the other hand, (Y) is a smaller number of texture-units wide than is (X), and the texture gradient itself is zero (signifying "no slant"), so that the figure is the stimulus for "trapezoid-in-frontal-parallel."

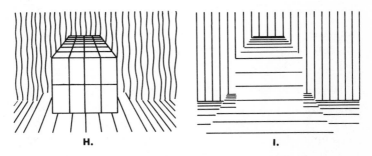

In all these illustrations (after Gibson, 1950), the gradient is the unit of analysis, not the points of light and dark of which any particular example is composed; thus, we could replace any or all of the surfaces in (H) by a quite different pattern (as in I), yet leave both the gradients and the apparent spatial arrangements of the scene unchanged. In (J), these sources of information about space are not used as fully as they might be. If they were, we would perceive the world of distal stimuli veridically (that

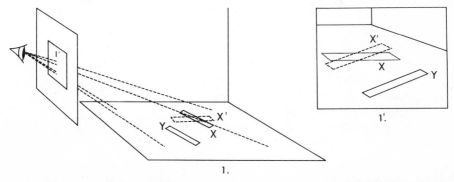

(Figure 58 continues)

(Figure 58 continued)
is, our perceptions of angles, sizes, distances, and so forth, would all be perfect). This
is simply not always true: Observers who are asked to set (X) so that it is parallel to
(Y) in (*I*), choose a setting approximately at (X'), which is more in accordance with
what is present in the optic array at (*I'*) than it is with the true distal arrangement at
(*I*) (O. W. and P. C. Smith, 1962).

With this method of analysis, there is no need to talk of unconscious inferences that take distance into account in order to arrive at
a perception of size, nor of taking slant into account in order to perceive shape: As Figures 57 and 58 show, the optic array usually
contains direct stimulus information about objects' sizes and slants
(i.e., their relationship to the texture-density gradient), so that size
and shape constancy might simply be *direct* responses to that information. Thus, a viewer might correctly perceive an object's size yet
not respond correctly to information about its distance (i.e., the
point at which the object intersects the ground plane). And, in fact,
there is often a poor correlation between how well size and distance
are judged (Gruber, 1954; Epstein & Landauer, 1969; Smith &
Smith, 1966; Oyama, 1974).

MOTION PERSPECTIVE AND SPACE PERCEPTION:
DETERMINING THE PERCEPTION OF THE REAL WORLD
FOR A MOVING OBSERVER

When the study of perception started with pure sensations and attempted to build up from these to an understanding of our perceptions of the physical world, there seemed to be no way to gain
unambiguous information about the world of objects, space, and motion by means of our eyes alone. We shall now see that, if we consider the higher-order variables which result from the observer's
own motions, the stimulation at the eye is almost completely unambiguous—at least in principle.

Berkeley "refuted." A single view of a scene may be ambiguous,
but successive glances rapidly reduce the ambiguity: Imagine a row
of fenceposts viewed from one end as in Figure 59*A*. As you walk
past it to the right, you will get successive views *5* through *1;* as you
walk past it to the left, you will get successive views *1* through *5*.
A succession of such views could give you visual information about
where you are looking from, within the scene, and how you are moving
around in it—as long as you assume that the objects are rigidly
fixed to the ground plane.

Now add to this the fact that *you can change your view at your*

(Text continues on page 129)

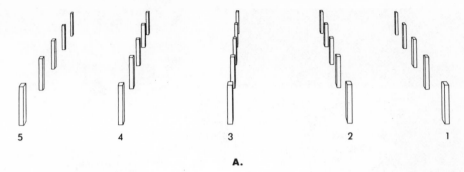

| 5 | 4 | 3 | 2 | 1 |

A.

FIGURE 59. *The visual information available to an active observer. A. Motion parallax.* The succession of views you receive as you walk past a row of posts, from left to right. To help visualize this, follow the instructions in Figure 66D, looking at marginal figures (*V*).

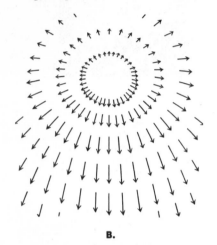

B.

B. The optical expansion pattern received by a moving observer. The pattern with which the distances between points expand in the optic array, and the rate at which the expansions occur, offer information to the observer about how fast he is approaching or receding from a surface, at what angle he is traveling with respect to it, and where he will collide with the surface if he continues to approach it. The "flow pattern" here derives from a 45° path of approach; the directions and lengths of arrows point the direction and rate of expansion, respectively, of each point in the optic array (after Gibson *et al.*, 1955).

C. Flow patterns for different elementary movements of the observer. At (*1*), the optical expansion pattern your eye receives when walking, driving, or flying toward the horizon (straight ahead); at (*2*), what confronts a pilot who is heading for a touchdown at the point; at (*3*), the view you receive as you look, at right angles to your

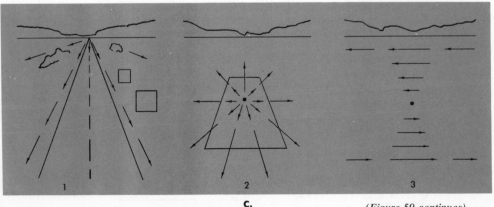

C.

(*Figure 59 continues*)

D.

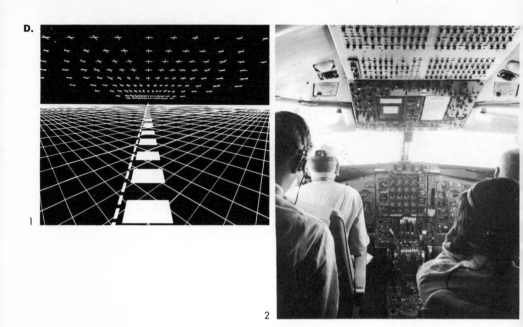

1

2

(Figure 59 continued)
movement, at the point shown (out of the side windows of a car, for example.(*1, 2, 3* after Gibson, 1950). At (*D*), we see the "contact analog" (*1*) developed by General Electric, to present to the operators of high-speed vehicles readily grasped information about the vehicles' movements, by means of such flow patterns and texture-density gradients. The contact analog is a computer-operated television-type tube which presents to the pilot a pictorial display that is visually analogous to contact flight. The visual

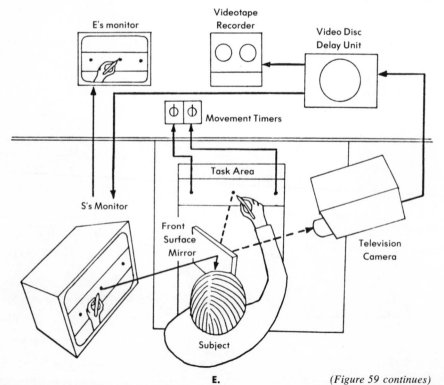

E.

(Figure 59 continues)

(Figure 59 continued)
cues displayed on the vertical screen form a three-dimensional background and a rib-
bonlike pathway along which the airplane is flown. Deviations from the intended
course or altitude cause the airplane to appear displaced from the pathway accordingly. Contrast this single display with the confusing aggregate of instruments a pilot
now must use (2).

E. The use to which we can actually put our visual feedback has been subjected to
experimental test only in recent years, as by using a TV camera to view the distal
scene while the subject sees the results of his actions in the TV monitor (at left). This
arrangement permits the experimenter to interfere with the feedback by inverting, re-
versing, displacing, or even delaying the picture presented on the monitor (K. U.
Smith & W. Smith, 1962: Bowen & Smith, 1977, reproduced from the latter by
permission). As the figure points out by its subject matter, this research ties together
the inquiry on space and distance, which we have been following on these past few
pages, with the questions of sensorimotor correlation and prism adaptation that we
discussed in Figures 35 and 51; a delay of as little as 0.3 seconds between the hand
movement and the visual feedback from it prevents adaptation from occurring (Held
et al., 1966).

own volition. As long as you were forced to sit passively, there is no
way, in principle, that you could distinguish between the succession
of scenes shown in Figure 59*A*, which might merely be the successive frames of a motion-picture film, and the change in viewpoint,
called *motion parallax,* which would result from real motion in a real
three-dimensional world. If, on the other hand, you are free to walk
left and right or to move your head about, there will be changes in
the optic array that are precisely tied to your voluntary movements—in the case of a real fence in real space—but which would
not occur in the case of the motion picture. When you are free to
initiate this *visual feedback* (the change in the optic array that results from motions made by the observer himself), then it becomes
difficult or impossible to fool you about the world. You should remember that the eye movements that you must make in order to
keep looking at an object while you move your head, must take that
object's distance into account (Figure 21); therefore, even the small
amount of motion parallax involved in the linkage between head
movement and eye movement makes the act of turning to look from
one point to another what Gibson (1966) calls a *perceptual system*
that is informative about space and distance.

Every time an observer moves toward any rigid surface, the elements in his visual field undergo a process of expansion; and this
gradient of expansion forms a pattern that will be different for each
orientation of surface, for each direction and speed of the observer's
motion, and for each distance of the observer from that surface in
terms of when he would hit it (see Figure 59*B*).

We do not, of course, thereby preclude *all* possibility of fooling
the viewer. We only make it more difficult to do without special apparatus, and therefore make it more implausible that the viewer will
see the world in some other (incorrect) fashion. This means that we

really do not address the original philosophical problem with which Berkeley started (which was: How can we be *certain* of what we know), and it means that we are talking about the *relative* ambiguity of different perceptual situations—a point that will concern us again (Chapter 5D).

We will return to this point in the next chapter when we discuss the construction and perception of motion pictures. For now, let us note how, by taking such *expansion gradients* as the starting point of the perceptual process—the sensory information that the viewer may (by nature or nurture) be able to detect and use directly—we transform our picture of psychological process in general and of perception in particular. The viewer need not calculate from cues: He need only learn *which variables in stimulation are invariantly related to important characteristics (e.g., reflectance [Figure 54], time-to-collision [Figure 59B]) of the physical world.*

We cannot overestimate the importance of these variables if they do in fact account for the constancies and for space and motion perception. Compared to anything we have encountered until now, they offer a very different kind of analysis; they require a different picture of the physiological processes involved;[4] and they set a different group of tasks for the psychologist (Gibson, 1966). If an observer's ability to use these higher-order variables is the result of learning at all, it is quite a different kind of learning from having to form associations between individual visual point-sensations and memory images of kinesthesis and touch (Gibson & Gibson, 1955).

Some cautions and limitations. Despite its great promise, however, this approach remains in its infancy, and certain cautions are in order.

1. It is still largely programmatic; we don't know, for example, what surface angles will be perceived when specific gradients are combined; that is, both the analytic units and the laws of their combination need quantitative psychophysical study. More critically; we don't know any of the *thresholds:* Can we generally detect such gradients over a wide retinal expanse, or do we need the acuity of foveal vision (see Figure 19)? *If the latter is true, we will have to confront the problem of picking up the information over a period of time by successive eye movements,* which makes the directness of the process much less convincing.

---

[4] Although there is no thought-out connection between the two, several psychologists have noted that the kinds of *spatial-frequency mechanisms* that we have mentioned on pp. 36, 109, 111 could be the first stage in detecting gradients of texture and motion.

2. The explanation is *too* good, for it provides the observer with enough information for the constancies to be complete, and for our space perception to be perfect, and neither of these is true (see Figure 68). We have to know whether we actually *use* these potentially informative stimulus variables before we can consider them to be explanations of the perceptual constancies.

3. Surfaces have important qualities in addition to their slants, and these will require different kinds of analysis. For example, they may vary from *rough* to *smooth,* from *matte* to *glossy,* and the stimulus properties for those appearances — e.g., the placement of highlights or reflections (cf. Evans, 1951; Beck, 1972) — seem to be at least as easily thought of as being "cues" as being higher-order variables.

4. Whether or not we do make use of the potential information in these higher-order variables, there is evidence that we use Helmholtzian cues, as well: We have seen that objects' familiar sizes can determine their apparent distances, in the absence of other distance information (p. 119), and that must depend on something like associative learning. We have also seen that subjects do seem to do something like take distance into account in their perceptions of size and motion (p. 122), and that might be explained at least superficially by Helmholtz's unconscious inference. Explicit provision must be made for these phenomena, and we must have some criteria, too, that will tell us when they — and not a direct response to higher-order stimulus variables — are at work.

5. Finally, "shape" itself has been left out. Nothing in our description of a texture-density gradient or an optical expansion pattern allows us to distinguish a square from a circle, a smile from a frown. And without some basis for accounting for our perceptions of shape, the psychophysics of color and surface are neither very useful nor satisfactory.

THE SHAPE AND FORM OF OBJECTS AND MOTIONS

We have considered all the physical attributes of a perceived object but one — its shape or form — and this is the most important and challenging of all. What might the higher-order variables be that determine what form will be perceived? We will consider this question in three parts. (1) First, the modern attempts to undertake a "psychophysics of shapes"; (2) *Gestalt theory,* which historically was the successor to structuralism, and which was above all concerned with the problem of form perception; and (3) the attempts to relate Gestalt theory to a more modern formulation in terms of *information theory.*

Attempts at a psychophysics of shape. We can call any two-dimensional pattern a *shape;* the three-dimensional volume that it occupies, its *form.* What can we want to know about them? We might try to ask the same three general questions that we asked about color and sound in Chapter 3: (1) How may different shapes can we perceive? (2) How many dimensions of stimulation, and of experience, will account for the differences and similarities between forms? (For these first two tasks, the analogy in color vision would be given by the *color solid* in Figure 11.) (3) What theories can we formulate and test that will account for the findings of (1) and (2)?

Stated this way, it is clear that we face a different kind of problem in shape perception, and that the first two questions cannot really be asked in a general fashion, let alone answered: In one sense, each just noticeable change in a contour or in the position of a dot in a pattern of dots, produces a new shape. And how can we decide what dimensions are needed to account for all our experiences of shape unless we can study *all* of the shapes while reaching that decision?

We can't consider all possible shapes, of course; we have to use a sample. Then we face the question of how the findings we have obtained with that sample, whatever these may be, will apply to other shapes that we have not tested.

One solution is to devise some procedure of *generating* shapes and of studying a randomly selected sample of all the shapes produced. If the sample is indeed random, our findings will apply statistically to all other samples of shapes (the *population* of shapes) that were generated according to that procedure. Most research of this kind has used the procedures suggested by Attneave and Arnoult (1956) which produce shapes like (*A*), or patterns of dots, like (*B*), in Figure 60. But even if the results with such stimuli can be generalized to other members of their populations, we cannot escape the problem of how to generalize to *other* populations, especially since subjects appear to take into account the entire set of stimuli from which the sample is drawn (see Figure 60*B*).

The primary use of these shapes has been to test theories, major and minor, of how we perceive form. Their value for this purpose is that, since they are constructed according to some *arbitrary* procedure, we can be sure that we have not selected just those stimuli that will prove what we want to prove. Their disadvantage is that they are not necessarily suited to test a given theory. They do not, for example, seem particularly well suited to test Gestalt theory, which has until very recently offered the most systematic treatment of form perception and the most dramatic (and most practically important) demonstrations.

(Text continues on page 134)

FIGURE 60. *"Nonsense shapes" for form-perception research.*
A. Attneave-Arnoult shape, generated according to random decisions about where a corner will occur, etc. Such shapes are convenient to produce with known characteristics, and collections of them (and lists of stimulus and response properties) have been published by Vanderplas *et al., 1965;* Brown and Owen, 1967; Zusne, 1970.

A.

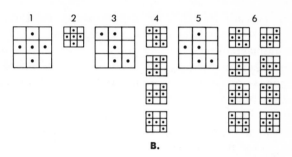

B.

B. Dot patterns are easy to generate according to the statistical properties desired, and have been widely used. The set here comes from research by Garner and his colleagues, designed to study the "goodness" of a stimulus pattern. Figure (*5*) is generated by a procedure that produces a large number of different shapes — that is, it is drawn from a large set (*6*); figure (*1*) comes from a much smaller set (*2*). The smaller the set size to which a stimulus belongs, the "better" subjects judge the shape to be, the better they remember it, and so on. This implies that subjects take into account shapes that they have never seen — that is, they take into account set *6* when judging stimulus *5,* set *4* when judging stimulus *3,* and so on. This ability to "infer" *abstract* properties about a set of things from individual members of the set is a theme to which we will return (Garner & Clement, 1963; Handel & Garner, 1965; Garner, 1970).

Another way of saying this is that the less likely it is that a particular arrangement could be chosen from a set of patterns to which it belongs, by chance alone, the "better" it appears to be. Although any *one* pattern in (*B*) is no less likely than any other pattern, it is more likely that one of the member of the set of patterns shown at (*6*) would occur than a member of the set of patterns in (*4*) or (*2*), simply because there are more of the former.

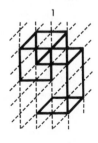

C.

C. Most of the traditional questions about form in perceptual research cannot even be asked with shapes like those in (*A*) and (*B*). The principle of generating stimulus shapes by an arbitrary procedure can, however, be applied to almost any kind of form. At (*1*), an arbitrarily generated reversible-perspective figure; at (*2*), one of the alternative ways in which it can be seen.

D.

D. One consequence of using nonsense shapes is that, of course, subjects cannot simply name the shape that they see, which is sometimes inconvenient. Arbitrariness and nameability can be usefully combined by embedding familiar shapes (lines, triangles, letters) in random and arbitrary arrays of dots, or of other features that degrade the shape in some way that can be statistically specified. The stimulus
(Figure 60 continues)

(*Figure 60 continued*)
here (a triangle embedded in random dots. or "noise") is like one of a series used by Uttal (1975) in testing a particular model of form perception that makes predictions about how detectable the shape will be. A very considerable virtue of this method is that it readily permits signal detection procedures (see p. 16) to be used with shapes by requiring the subject to judge whether any individual presentation is a shape plus noise, or noise alone.

The Gestaltists' laws of organization. Gestalt theory was the first serious attempt to deal with perception that did not start with an assemblage of independent point sensations. It initiated two intertwined programs for research. The first was to find natural units for the analysis of perception, units with which to replace the artificial sensations; this program is still in progress. The other was to explain these new units in terms of a totally revised picture of how the nervous system works. Although our understanding of the nervous system is indeed being thoroughly revised (see Figures 49, 52), the version that the Gestaltists proposed cannot be considered tenable today.

These programs were launched by Max Wertheimer in the 1920s; under the leadership of Wertheimer, Kurt Koffka, and Wolfgang Kohler, Gestalt theory dominated the study of perception during the next two decades and also provided most of the basis for the dialog between artists and psychologists (Arnheim, 1964, 1969).

Gestaltist aims, criticisms, and proposals. The Gestaltists' general aim was to reanalyze our perception of the world. *Gestalt* means "whole," "configuration," or "form," and the Gestalt position was itself something of a Gestalt, whose argument really makes sense only after you have gone all the way through it twice. The *Gestalt* criticisms of structuralism run as follows.

A percept is *not* composed of sensations. "Sensations" are artificial kinds of perception that appear only under the special conditions of the physiological and psychological laboratories. Sensations are *not* elementary experiences, and consequently all the speculations about independent receptors, and about individual specific nerve energies, are in error. For these reasons, the precise measurement techniques of sensory psychophysics are likely to be irrelevant until we first discover what it is we should measure, and those of analytic introspection are utterly invalid.

What then should we do instead?

If we take a new look at the world of perception, unbiased by any structuralist assumptions, what do we find as the most natural units of analysis? In the world of sight, not meaningless tiny patches of light and color, but whole shaped regions, set off or bounded by their contours, which appear the same whether they fall on one particular set of cells on the retina or on another: As you shift your gaze even slightly to one side of the number at the bottom of the page, a totally new set of cones is stimulated, yet the shape you see remains the same. In the world of hearing, not JNDs of pitch or loudness, but coherent sounds and melodies: Simply raising the key in which you play or whistle a melody alters every single note, yet the tune itself remains the same (and in fact the change of key may go unrecognized). *In both cases, the form we perceive remains constant, though the points of color or the musical notes may be completely changed.*

Before we undertake detailed psychophysical measurement, before we seek to understand the underlying physiological mechanisms, we must discover the rules that govern the appearance of shapes and forms.

Contours, shapes, and figures. Let us start with the fact that although any contour divides the stimulation at the eye into two regions (Figure 61*A*), the shape of both regions cannot usually be perceived simultaneously: Only one shape or the other will be seen at any one moment in time, although the two shapes may well alternate under prolonged viewing. (But having said this, we must qualify it immediately: As we shall see, the same continuous contour may make one area the figure at one point, and the other area the figure at another point [Figures 69*A*–*G*, *J*]). The side whose shape is visible is called the *figure;* it usually seems to be interposed between the observer and the *ground,* which seems to extend some indeterminate distance behind the figure. Looking at Figure 61*A;* either a vase or two faces are usually seen; when the pattern has the appearance of (*1*) in Figure 61*B*, then we say that the vase is "figure."

FIGURE 61. The one-sidedness of outline contours and of objects' edges. At (*A*), either a vase (B1) or two faces (B2) can be seen as figure. At (B), each alternative is illustrated in terms of the physical arrangement that would correspond to it. This one-sidedness of a contour—which delineates a shape to only one of the two areas it sepa-

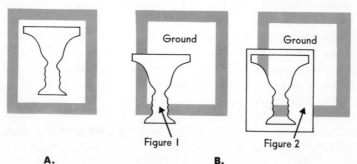

Figure 1

Figure 2

A.   B.

(*Figure 61 continues*)

(Figure 61 continued)
rates—is characteristic of real objects' edges as well. At (C), note that as your gaze crosses the edge of the nearer surface, there is an abrupt increase in distance to the next surface, which normally extends behind the nearer one, out of sight; note too that slight movements of the head, as from (2) to (1) will cause parts of the further surface to disappear from view as they are occluded by the nearer object, but that the visibility of the nearer surface, bounded by the edge, does not change with head movements (cf. Hochberg, 1962, 1972).

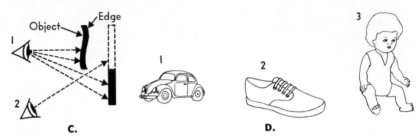

Do we recognize outline shapes because we have learned to associate line drawings with objects' edges much as we learn a foreign language at school? Are outlines drawn on paper merely learned symbols for the edges of things in the world? No. A child who had been raised without ever having had any opportunity to associate pictures with either objects or with object names (and who had seen very few pictures at all), still could correctly identify the pictured objects shown in (D) (Hochberg and Brooks, 1962).

As we saw in Chapter 4C, these phenomena at first appear to be difficult to explain in terms of a structuralist analysis into point sensations; the Gestaltists therefore offered them as evidence against structuralism. We should note, however, that the figure-ground phenomenon is not necessarily incompatible with Helmholtzian empiricism: The contour of a figure behaves in some ways like the edge of an object, which by its very nature has a shape on only one side: past that edge the object's surface ceases to exist (see Figure 61C). Is the fact that figural contours possess shape in only one direction the result of our past experiences with the edges of objects? We shall return to this possibility shortly.

We *do* know that the figure-ground phenomenon is not merely a matter of arbitrary artistic convention. The fact that we see objects where there are only contours or outlines on paper is not simply the result of our having learned to associate drawings with objects—that is, of having learned that outlines "stand for" objects' edges: A child does not have to learn specifically to see outline drawings by associating pictures with objects (Figure 61D)—as one might learn a foreign language. The perceptual properties that contours share with objects' edges are either innate or, if they are learned, they are learned from our experiences with objects in the world. The study of the figure-ground phenomena, and of how contours and outline pictures behave, should therefore be very useful to our understanding of how we perceive objects.

Ambiguous stimuli and the laws of organization. Inasmuch as a contour can produce a shape in either of two directions, it is ambiguous. How can we tell, in advance, which shape will be perceived?

Here is where the Gestalt psychologists made their chief contributions and provided visual artists with a set of tools with which to analyze and control the appearance of designs and pictures. Why are the soldier, the bird, the vase, and the letters and pencils difficult to see in Figures 2 and 46? Why doesn't Figure 63*B* appear as three-dimensional as does Figure 63*A*? (*Text continues on page 139*)

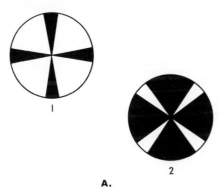

A.

FIGURE 62. Gestalt laws of organization. The patterns on this page are all ambiguous. That is, you can easily see more than one shape in each of them. By making some change in a pattern and observing how that change affects the relative ease of seeing each of the alternative shapes, Max Wertheimer, followed by other Gestalt psychologists (notably Koffka and W. Köhler), compiled a long list of factors that influence the perception of shape. Five of their most important "laws of organization" are illustrated here.

A. Area. The smaller a closed region, the more it tends to be seen as figure. Thus, as the area of the white cross decreases from 1 to 2, its tendency to be seen as figure increases.

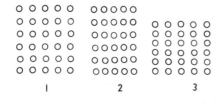

B.

B. Proximity. Dots or objects that are close together tend to be grouped together. In (1), you can see either horizontal rows or vertical columns with equal ease. As the dots get closer together horizontally, as in (2), horizontal rows emerge as figure; with increased vertical proximity (3), vertical columns appear. Examine the enlarged print of the eye at (4). How does this law contribute to TV or to photoreproductions?

C. Closedness. Areas with closed contours tend to be seen as figure more than do those with open contours. At (1), profiles of TV screens appear, at (2), profiles of apple cores, in accordance with this principle. These three laws are easy enough to measure and test; there are other laws however, of equal or greater importance, that can readily be demonstrated in an intuitive or common-sense manner, but which are extremely difficult to define in an objective, measurable fashion.

C.

(*Figure 62 continues*)

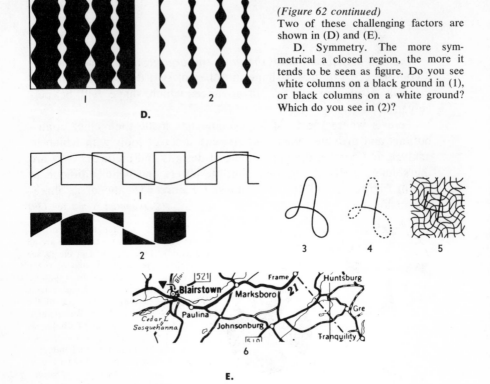

(Figure 62 continued)
Two of these challenging factors are shown in (D) and (E).

D. Symmetry. The more symmetrical a closed region, the more it tends to be seen as figure. Do you see white columns on a black ground in (1), or black columns on a white ground? Which do you see in (2)?

D.

E.

E. Good continuation. That arrangement of figure and ground tends to be seen which will make the fewest changes or interruptions in straight or smoothly curving lines or contours. This is one of the most important of the laws of organization. The pattern at (1), for example, is almost always seen as a smooth sine wave superimposed on a square wave. This is in opposition to the law of closedness, which would cause the perception of something like (2). Can you now explain why the number 4 is more effectively concealed at (3) than at (5), even though there are more extraneous lines to confuse you at (5)? How does this law contribute to the reading the map at (6)?

The patterns shown in Figures 62 and 63 are all ambiguous. By changing the patterns in various ways, we can discover how to make one or the other alternatives easier to see. These stimuli therefore lend themselves to a systematic study of the stimulus determinants of shape and form, and the Gestaltists' demonstrations constitute such a study, albeit an informal one.

A number of "laws" of organization have emerged from the study of such ambiguous stimuli—although they really shouldn't be termed "laws," at this stage in our uncertainty about them.

Some of these laws, such as those of *area, proximity,* and *closedness* (Figures 62*A*, *B*, and *C*) are amenable to measurement and to being stated in quantitative terms. Can the other laws of organization, such as *symmetry* and *good continuation* (Figures 62*D* and *E*), also be treated quantitatively and objectively?

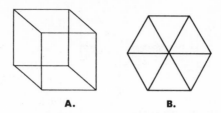

A.   **B.**

FIGURE 63. Tridimensionality as a function of organizational simplicity. Patterns (A) and (B) are equally accurate (or inaccurate) drawings of a wire cube, yet one is easy to see as a tridimensional cube (A), while the other remains a flat pattern (B). Why this difference? In order to see (A) as a flat pattern, or to see (B) as a tridimensional one, you have to break the good continuation of the lines, to make the figure less simple; that is, you see one as tridimensional, the other as flat, depending on which way a *simpler* organization is achieved (Kopfermann, 1930; Hochberg and McAlister, 1953). This is a powerful principle, if we can find some objective way of measuring simplicity.

Simplicity and the minimum principle as psychophysical "laws" of combination. If we examine the examples in Figure 62, a pattern seems to emerge. In each case, we perceive what seems to be the simplest or the most uniform of the alternative possibilities. A more obvious example of this principle is shown in Figure 63. Both patterns are equally good views of the same cube. Why does *A* appear in three dimensions while *B* does not?—because *A* is *simpler* in three dimensions and *B* is *simpler* as a flat pattern. A pattern thus seems to appear flat if it is simpler (in some sense that we still have to define) to see it that way; conversely, it appears to be tridimensional if that is "simpler" to perceive.

Let us now return to Leonardo da Vinci's depth cues, with which we started the whole problem of combining perceptual parts into the objects and events of the perceived world (pp. 52ff). How do the pictorial depth cues fit this law of simplicity, this Minimum Principle?

Looking at Figure 64, we can see that many of the depth cues[5] might be explained as a special case of the Minimum Principle in operation. In response to the relative size cue at (*A1*), isn't it simpler

[5] Two cues that do not fit the Minimum Principle are *illumination direction* (Figure 27C) and *familiar size* (Figure 27Y; Figure 56). There is evidence of some innate component in the former, in that Hershberger (1970) has shown that chicks raised in cages illuminated from below nevertheless responded to photographs of dents shaded below and above as being convex and concave, respectively, as though the chicks, like humans, assume the source of illumination to be overhead. But it is hard to imagine how familiar size can be anything other than a learned cue, and the fact that it is at all effective (Chapter 4C) means that we cannot hope to explain depth perception completely in terms of either higher-order stimulus variables or the Minimum Principle without reference to cues based on past experience.

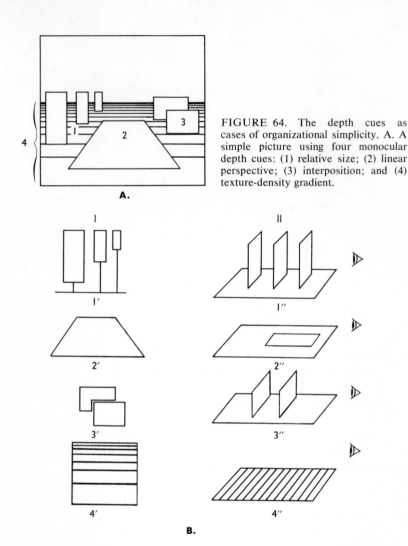

FIGURE 64. The depth cues as cases of organizational simplicity. A. A simple picture using four monocular depth cues: (1) relative size; (2) linear perspective; (3) interposition; and (4) texture-density gradient.

A.

B.

B. Compare each cue as a flat pattern in an upright plane (column I) and as the tridimensional arrangment it represents (column II). Which seems simpler in each case, the arrangement in (I) or (II)? If organizational simplicity were an innate operating characteristic of the nervous system, what would this figure imply about depth perception?

to see three equal rectangles at different distances (*B,1''*) than three unequal ones at the same distance (*B,1'*)? In response to the linear perspective cue at (*2*), isn't it simpler to see an equal-sided square flat in the plane of the ground (*2''*) rather than an upright trapezoid (*2'*)? In response to the interposition cue at (*3*), isn't it simpler to see two squares, one before the other (*3''*), rather than an inverted *L* and a rectangle in the same plane (*3'*)? If we were willing to accept the Minimum Principle as being an innate characteristic of the nervous system, then at least some of the monocular depth cues, as consequences of the Minimum Principle, may be innate as well.

This "law of simplicity" looks like a very powerful principle *if* we can be sure that it really is a principle at all. There are two serious difficulties with it:

1. How can we define "simplicity" objectively? So far, we have been appealing to intuition. Without some way of deciding *how* simple each alternative is, we really have no way of predicting in advance which way an ambiguous picture will appear (or whether it will be ambiguous). The situation is a little like the difficulty in applying Helmholtz's principle that we perceive what is most likely (Chapter 4C).

2. The demonstration in Figure 64 really cuts both ways: If the depth cues may all be expressions of the Minimum Principle, the latter — and all of the laws of organization that it summarizes — may merely be a reflection of our experiences with objects in space. That is, *the "laws" of organization in Figure 62 may really only be good cues as to which part of the optic array represents an object's surface, and which is farther away.* We will take a more specific look later on at how we can (and indeed, why we should) think of the determinants of organization as "local depth cues."

First, let us see what we can do about providing objective, quantitative formulations of the Minimum Principle, and how far that principle can take us.

The psychophysics of form and motion: Information and redundancy as stimulus measures of organization. Can we decide, objectively, which shape is the simplest of any set of alternatives? How can we measure simplicity? Let us look at Figure 65*A* page 142).

Information and redundancy in the psychophysics of static shape. In this figure several patterns are arranged in order of their increasing complexity in two dimensions. What physical variables increase from one shape to the next?

Suppose that you had to tell someone how to construct each pattern. In each case, the amount of information that you would have to give that person would increase from left to right within each row of patterns. How can we measure this information? We could make many kinds of physical measurements that would differ from one shape to the next and would also seem to be plausibly related to simplicity of organization. The problem remains this, however: to discover *which* of all the possible measures of shape complexity best predicts the actual likelihood that each of the alternative forms will be perceived.

In order to answer this question, we need a special set of tools. We have to find some kind of stimulus pattern that produces two clearly different alternative perceptual organizations, and that will permit the complexity of one of the alternatives to be systematically varied, while the complexity of the other alternative is kept constant. In this way, we will be able to study the psychophysical relationship between some measure of the complexity of each alternative form, on the one hand, and the strength of the tendency to see that form, on the other. The kinds of reversible-perspective pictures shown in Figure 65*A* provide us with just such material for studying the psy-

(Text continues on page 146)

FIGURE 65. Measuring simplicity: information and organization. So far, we have relied on intuition in order to decide which of two organizations is simpler. The objective and quantitative measurement of organizational simplicity is a most challenging problem since it seems to be the key to many other problems. Its study, however, is just beginning.

A. The different views of each object in (1) through (4) are arranged in order of increasing tridimensionality in each row. According to the hypothesis of Figure 63, this means that the two-dimensional alternatives must be getting less simple and more complex as we read from left to right in each row. What measurable physical characteristics of the patterns in (1) through (4) increase as we move from left to right in each row?

B. The number of interior angles, the average number of different angles, and the number of continuous lines, can be combined to provide a fair measure of complexity. In the graph, the horizontal axis shows the complexity measures for each of the 2D (two-dimensional) patterns in (A); the vertical axis shows the apparent tridimensionality of the same patterns, as they were judged by scores of observers (Hochberg and Brooks, 1960).

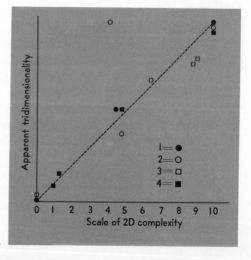

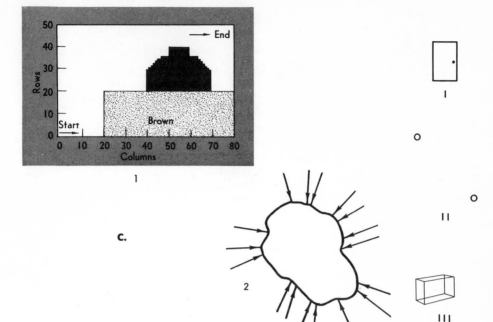

C.

1

2

C. Two closely related measures of figural simplicity were proposed and used by Fred Attneave (1954): One method requires subjects to guess whether each successive *square* in a sheet of graph paper is black, white, or brown. They are given no advance information about what the correct pattern (1) looks like, only whether they are right or wrong on each guess. Subjects made only 13 to 26 errors for the entire sheet of 4,000 squares—immensely less than they would have made had they been guessing at random on each square. Where did their knowledge come from?

Having discovered one part of the figure, a subject could then make some pretty good guesses about the remainder, since areas are compact, lines and slopes are regular, and the shape is symmetrical: that is, (1) is a "good" or simple figure. Thus, one measure of simplicity is the predictability of the whole from the part—that is, the degree to which, by knowing some of the parts of the figure, a subject can correctly guess the rest of the parts. Some parts of any shape are usually highly predictable, like the continuation of a straight line; these are called *redundant,* or uninformative. Other parts are not predictable, and it is these unpredictable segments that provide the information that is needed if the shape is to be identified or reproduced. (2) is one of a number of outline shapes that subjects were asked to reproduce as closely as possible, using only ten dots to represent each shape. The small arrows point to the places at which subjects most frequently choose to place the dots: the strategic bends and curves where the contour is most different from a simple, straight predictable line.

Other things equal, the fewer the bends or angles (and the fewer the lines), the simpler and the more predictable the shape. This kind of measure of simplicity was designed for problems of shape identification or communication, so that it seems to be a little removed from the problem of figural organization as such. However, we have seen in B that a very closely related measure of simplicity did appear when we attempted to predict the relative frequency-of-appearance of alternative figural organizations.

Figure 65 (continued)

143

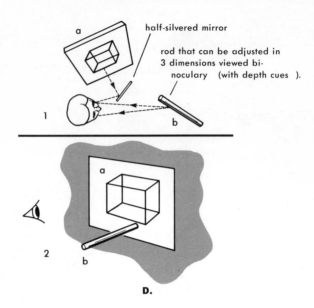

Figure 65 (continued)

D. The arrangement used by Attneave and Frost (1969) to study how the angles and side lengths of an outline cube affect its apparent three-dimensionality. Viewed from above (*1*): The subject sees the picture of the cube only with his left eye (as reflected in the half-silvered mirror); he sees the rod (*b*) with both eyes, so he has binocular information about how the rod is slanted toward him in three dimensions. What he sees (*2*) is a monocular view of the cube (*a*) and a binocular view of the rod (*b*). His task is to line up the rod with each side of the cube, in turn. Since he views the rod binocularly, he is sure of its location and arrangement in tridimensional space, and this in turn tells us how he perceives the tridimensional arrangement of any part of the cube with which he has aligned the rod. By varying the angles and lengths of the cube's sides, and observing how that affected the three-dimensional appearance of the cube, Attneave and Frost concluded that subjects perceived just that three-dimensional arrangement in which the angles between the sides and their lengths, were most uniform as a three-dimensional object. (This does not mean, however, that drawings in correct perspective are necessarily better ones: see p. 196).

FIGURE 66. Shape and motion. A1. Five different shapes, or a door of constant shape swinging through the third dimension? When these patterns are viewed successively, as in a motion picture, the constant shape of the door and its path through space are equally and overwhelmingly compelling.

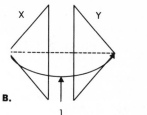

B.

I

B. If *X* alternates with *Y*, we could see two different shapes in different places at successive intervals in time, or we could see a single constant triangle, turning over through the third dimension, as shown by the solid path (1); this latter alternative predominates.

O

O

II

1

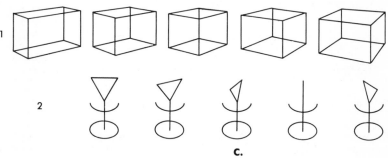

2

III

C.

IV

C. Each view of the cube at (1) is ambiguous, in that each can be seen as either a flat pattern or as a tridimensional cube. Each of the triangles at (2) is, individually, different but quite flat-appearing. However, if these are the successive views of a rotating object, one *could* still see a succession of changing flat patterns, but it is much simpler to see a single rotating tridimensional object, of constant shape, and this is what one sees (Wallach, O'Connell, & Neisser, 1953).

D. Flip the right-hand pages, from 143 to p. 151, as shown, looking at the marginal figures (I) (III), and (IV).

V

D.

chophysics of form, since the flat, two-dimensional shape varies from one figure to the next, while the solid three-dimensional form remains the same for each member in the series. Thus, each pattern in Figure 65*A* can be described either as an arrangement of flat shapes or as a three-dimensional object. The simpler any 2D arrangement, the more we should tend to see that picture in 2D; conversely, the more complex the 2D arrangement, the more we tend to see it as 3D (since the 3D form must be the same and, therefore, of identical simplicity, for all views of any object). As the *number of angles,* the *number of continuous lines,* and the *average number of different angles* increase in each pattern, the tendency to see the flat arrangement decreases and the apparent tridimensionality of the form increases, although there are almost certainly other factors as well that we have not yet found.

In all of these patterns, the sides are parallel, which makes the 3D alternative inconsistant with linear perspective in every case: If the object in Figure 65*A* really were a cube (that is, with equal sides and angles), then its near face would have to be larger, in the picture plane, than its far face. Using the procedure described in Figure 65*D,* Attneave and Frost showed that subjects seemed to perceive just that set of 3D arrangements which would make all of the angles, line lengths, and slopes in the perceived object most equal to each other.

Such data may be a first step toward discovering and using objective measures of the minimum principle, and toward bringing the Gestalt laws into quantitative and measurable form. And that would in turn make possible a psychophysics of shape and form, in which we would be able to use objective measures of the stimulus patterns to predict how those patterns will be perceived.

We will discuss some serious problems with this approach later on (Figure 69). First, however, let us see how far we might pursue the application of the Minimum Principle, in these terms, to perceptual organization in general.

The psychophysics of form in motion. If the concealed bird in Figure 2 once moves, it snaps into visibility. The views of Figure 66 come to life and move compellingly into the third dimension as they follow each other in time. The door swings open in (*A*). In (*B*), if we alternate patterns *X* and *Y* in rapid succession, apparent motion occurs in the direction shown by the arrow, which flips through the third dimension.

We saw in Figure 65 that whether a stimulus pattern will appear flat or solid seems to depend on the relative simplicity of the alternative organizations. In Figure 66*B,* we can either see two different triangles successively or one triangle rotating in space, maintaining its sides and angles constant. In Figure 67, the movements of the two objects between three different end-points are simply not perceived; instead, the objects move toward and away from each other on a single path.

I

Apparently we perceive that arrangement of motions which involves the fewest changes and which allows objects to remain as constant and as rigid as possible. In Figure 66*A,* we perceive just those movements that will allow the door to remain a rectangle, that allow the triangle to retain the rigidity and identity of its parts, and so on. Given this tendency to see as few changes and as much constancy of lengths and objects' angles as possible, we are led to view Gibson's proposals in another way.

II

The monocular stationary view of any object is ambiguous, as we have seen in Figure 28. Many different objects (including pictures) can produce much the same image at the eye. On the other hand, each successive view of a rotating object presents new information to our visual system. How many different rigid objects — objects whose shape does not change — could produce at the eye the same sequence of views as those in Figure 66*A–C?*

III

In consequence, objects whose spatial forms may be ambiguous when they are stationary should, and, usually do, become vividly three-dimensional when they are rotated. This is what Wallach and his colleagues called the *kinetic depth effect.* Moreover, once having been endowed with spatial form by the kinetic depth effect, a pattern like that in Figure 66*C,2,* which previously had appeared to be flat when stationary, will subsequently appear tridimensional, a fact that would seem to be important to any theory of perceptual learning (Wallach, O'Connell, & Neisser, 1953).

IV

Note that we have worked our way back to the psychophysics of space, starting with a form of the Minimum Principle. We can bridge the span from static pictures to moving world with what appears to be a simple principle, although no attempt has yet been made to apply a single set of measures of information across the various examples, nor to apply more than the primitive quantitative tests that are summarized in Figure 65. But a qualitative account could be offered as follows:

V

A single view of an object may be ambiguous, but successive presentations reduce this ambiguity. Similarly, as

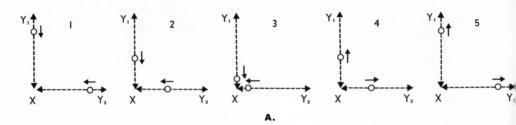

A.

FIGURE 67. The perception of alternative motion organizations. A. Two lights move at right angles to each other, repeatedly coming together at point (X), then retreating from that point along paths (Y_1) (Y_2). Flip the pages of the book from p. 143 to p. 151, looking at marginal figure (II). We do not perceive this motion, which is in reality what falls on the retina of our eye, any more than we perceive absolute light intensity or visual angle (Figures 37 and 38). Instead, the following set of motions are perceived predominantly:

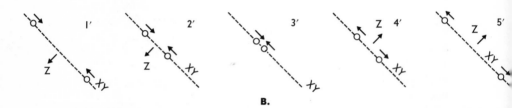

B.

B. The lights appear to approach and retreat from each other along the diagonal (XY); the diagonal path itself moves up and down along the direction (Z), although this is not very noticeable (Johansson, 1950). Flip the pages of the book to visualize the resultant motion. The simplest relative motion is what we see, within the framework of the shared or common motion (Z), which may not even be perceived at all. Johansson has recently shown (1973, 1974) that these same analyses also seem to apply to the perception of "biological motion" (the movements of spots of light attached to the joints of people who are walking or dancing; such complex movements are almost immediately organized by the viewer into the appropriate perceived actions by unseen actors; see Figure 83A).

we start to assemble a number of different objects into a single static scene, one spatial arrangement becomes more economical than any of the alternatives (if the assembling is done correctly). In Figure 27B, the relative size difference between boys *1* and *2*, the convergence of the lines, the interposition of cards *4* and *5*, the texture-density gradient — all of these are *individually* simpler if they are seen in three-dimensions, but if the scene as a whole is perceived as a consistent three-dimensional layout, the collective economics of the "cues" should reinforce each other.

If we now add the effects of the *observer's* motion, as he is free to change his viewpoint, the informational economy of seeing only one spatial arrangement — the true or veridical arrangement — becomes overwhelmingly greater than that of any other.

D. The Limits of Perceptual Psychophysics:
Local Depth Cues and Perceptual Inference

I

We do not yet know how well we can actually use these rich sources of potential visual information about the world. The importance of self-initiated visual feedback cues is strongly supported by the fact that the kitten who was confined in the cart shown in Figure 36D did not "learn to see" as adequately as its free-moving partner, but this does not mean that we take full advantage of these higher-order variables. In "rich, normal" environments, an observer can use self-produced motion parallax to arrive at very precise distance judgments, but the same parallax often fails to work well in "laboratory conditions" (Eriksson, 1974). And even in a normal environment, we probably don't use all of the information. Perform this simple experiment. Choose a long, straight street or highway, and while you walk a steady pace along it make the following judgment: Do the sides of the street converge toward the horizon, or do they appear to stretch away from you in a completely parallel arrangement? If they appear to converge at all, what does this imply about your use of the available information?

II

When we took up the problems of space perception in Chapter 3, we started with the puzzle of explaining how we see the world so correctly, with so little information on which to base our perceptions. The problem has now reversed. Considering how much stimulus information there appears to be *potentially* available to an observer, we must wonder why his perceptions of space are not always perfectly correct. When we consider the reasons why erroneous perceptions of the world can occur even with motion perspective in a textured environment, we must form a picture of the perceptual process that is very different from the one that we have outlined in the bulk of this chapter. It will be much more like the *perceptual inference* of Helmholtz and Brunswik with which we closed the previous chapter, except that it doesn't start with elementary point receptors and their point sensations.

III

IV

V

THE LIMITS OF THE SINGLE GLANCE:
WHAT WE LEARN FROM INCONSISTENT
OBJECTS AND SCENES

A *gradient* may extend over a large extent, but its individual elements of texture may be small. The *Minimum Principle* refers to an entire object or even a scene, but the stimulus pattern to which it applies may consist of small details. *Because our visual acuity is high only in the small area of the fovea, we can pick up detailed information only from a small part of a texture-density gradient, or from a small part of an object in each glance. To obtain detailed information from another part of the surface or object, we must shift our fovea to it, and of course in so doing, we lose our detailed view of the first part.*

These obvious facts would be unimportant either if (1) detailed vision were unnecessary to pick up the information in question (and if there were no other reasons why looking at any region with your fovea were important); or (2) the storage of detailed information from one glance to the next were so good that we could normally ignore the limitations of the momentary glance. We will see that neither of these conditions is true either for the higher-order spatial psychophysics of moving surfaces, or for applying the Minimum Principle to object perception.

The Ames "window". Figure 68*A* shows the shape of a flat, trapezoidal surface viewed from in front. It is mounted on a rotating shaft so that it revolves as shown in *A* by the solid arrows. Viewed monocularly from a distance of about ten feet or more, oscillation is perceived instead of rotation: it appears to swing back and forth, as shown from above by the dotted arrows. Why does this happen? The static monocular depth cues of linear perspective and relative size have overcome the motion perspective of the surface's movement. Far from being automatically informative, in fact, motion perspective is sufficiently unprecise to the extent that parts of rotating shapes may appear to detach themselves and rotate opposite their actual direction, and opposite the apparent direction of rotation of the other parts (Gillam, 1972); whether or not this will occur appears to reflect the "law" of closure or *enclosedness* (Figure 62*C;* Gillam, 1975).

These experiments tell us that threshold factors *are* important to the use of motion perspective in perceiving surfaces' slants, distances, and movements: If the viewer stands closer to the rotating trapezoid, the difference between the proximal stimulus movements of the receding edge (*2*) and the approaching edge (*1*), in Figure 68*B,* become large enough in his retinal image to overcome the static depth cues, and the true rotation is now perceived. So we know that the details that convey movement perspective must be discernible before the movement perspective information can be used. This in turn suggests that the difference in acuity between fovea and periphery is also probably important in the viewer's ability

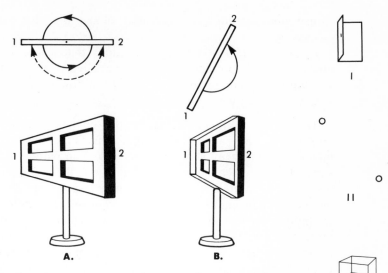

FIGURE 68. *The rotating trapezoid: perceptual coupling and unconscious inference.*

A. The Ames Window is a trapezoid (usually painted to look like a window seen in perspective) mounted on a shaft that rotates as shown by the solid arrows in the top view at (*A*). Note that it is shown in the frontal-parallel plane, meaning that edges (1) and (2) are then at the same distance. When the trapezoid rotates in the direction shown by the solid arrow, it appears to oscillate back and forth, instead, in the direction shown by the dotted arrow (Ittelson, 1952). Why does this happen?

B. At a point in its rotation when edge (*2*) is actually further away from the viewer than edge (1), the convergence of the horizontal edges, and the relative sizes of (1) and (2) are what the *static* stimulus at the eye would be if edge (2) were nearer. Therefore, after passing through the point at which (*1*) and (2) are equal, the direction of rotation appears to reverse. The static monocular depth cues of *linear perspective* and *relative size* (see p. 53) have overcome the motion parallax produced by the direction of the surface's movement. Other depth cues will also work in this way (Canestrari and Farne, 1969). Perceived size and perceived distance (or perceived direction of movement) thus appear to be *coupled* to each other in a way that is not explained by the higher-order information in the stimulation (Figures 57-59).

Perceived size also varies with perceived distance when figures like Figure 63A reverse: Whichever side looks nearer also looks slightly smaller, according to the logic of *unconscious inference* (see Figures 43-45 and adjacent text). The effect is weak (it can be increased somewhat by elongating the figure: Sanford, 1897; Hochberg, 1972b). Similar couplings were also found between perceived lightness and perceived illumination (Figure 54) and between perceived distance and familiar size (Figure 56 and text), but the perceptual couplings found in the rotating trapezoid and in reversible figures are particularly difficult to explain in terms of stimulus information alone: In the latter case, *the stimulus itself remains unchanged* when depth appears to reverse and size appears to change. These facts support a cognitive theory of perception but as we see in Figure 69, "unconscious inference" is too general to be an adequate explanation.

to use motion-produced information of the kind that we have been discussing.

Let us consider some demonstrations that *where* we look at an object can be important to *how* we perceive it, demonstrations that will tell us something about the matter of how we store our successive glimpses as well.

Impossible objects. Consider the objects pictured in Figures 69*A* and *B*. They appear 3D rather than flat. If we apply the Minimum Principle, they should appear 2D. The pattern is, admittedly, somewhat complicated as a 2D figure; but there should be no contest: it is *impossible* as a 3D object unless we see the continuous line (*x*) as changing its function from representing one dihedral angle to another somewhere along its length. When you look at the left side, the frame faces one direction; when you look at the right side, it faces another. Its apparent spatial orientation depends on which parts of the pattern fall on the fovea. When the two sides are close together, and both fall within the area of detailed vision, the figure collapses into 2D (Figure 69*D*).

Is this fact, that the corners appear to act independently of each other in Figures 69*A* and *B*, a mere curiosity specific to such inconsistent figures? And isn't it possible that we haven't applied the Minimum Principle correctly? No: The same phenomena can be demonstrated with completely consistent figures in which there should be no question of how to apply the Minimum Principle: Figure 69*E* appears to be oriented as in Figure 69*G*, as long as you look at point (*1*); if you look at point (*2*), perspective reversal will occur after a few moments, and the orientation will shift between those of *F* and *G*.

These figures tell us two things: Like Figure 68, they tell us that threshold factors (and hence whether we are looking at something with our fovea or with our periphery) do affect our ability to pick up the available information for the operations of the higher-order variables and the Minimum Principle. Additionally, Figures 69*A*, *B*, and *H* suggest that we do not store from one glance to the next all of the information about spatial arrangements.

Why have these limitations not been evident all along? Because objects and surfaces are usually consistent from one point to the next, and the information that is picked up at one point doesn't contradict that at another without some clearly noticeable change. It is only stimuli like these (in which *strong perspective has been put into conflict with weak parallax, or in which good continuation has been put into conflict with the local depth cues*) that show us that the consistency we normally perceive is supplied by the world and not by our perceptual systems.

Local depth cues, global features, and perceptual storage. Our peripheral vision may tell us that Figures 69*A* and *B* are each single objects, but the individual corners act as depth cues only for the small region we are looking at foveally. Although you can see with foveal vision that each 6 is not a 9 in Figures 69*H* and *I*, the entire pattern that the 6s form is not *perceived* (although it may be figured out with a considerable effort) until the differences are made evident to peripheral vision as well: We do not store all of the information picked up by the fovea from one glance to the next so completely that we can ignore the extremely limited nature of each one.

We will discuss research to this point in the next chapter. For now, let us see what we can conclude about the issues of this chapter.

PERCEPTUAL INFERENCE AND THE
MINIMUM PRINCIPLE

In Figure 56, we saw that the Minimum Principle could explain the monocular depth cues as well as the Gestaltists' laws of organization; in Figure 69, we see that local depth cues rather than any overall Minimum Principle determine how an object is perceived. Which of these is right?

Something like the Minimum Principle might work for any of the three following reasons, only one of which is inconsistent with Figure 69.

Possible bases of the Minimum Principle. 1. Perhaps our visual systems are so organized that we perceive the simplest object or scene that would fit the overall proximal stimulus. This is what we discussed in Figures 64 and 65, and it is clearly inconsistent with Figure 69.

2. Perhaps we remember only a part of what we see, from one glance to the next, and we look at only part of what there is to see; consequently, what is simplest is what has the best chance of being seen and remembered. We will consider this in the next chapter.

3. Perhaps we perceive just that arrangement of edges and objects that is most likely to produce a set of sensory patterns. This is, of course, Helmholtz's proposal. Why would it result in something like the Minimum Principle?

The Minimum Principle was proposed to summarize situations like those in Figures 62 through 65. Consider Figure 63, however. *Figure 63B may look flat because it is extremely unlikely that one would view a 3D object (like 63A) from the one position out of so many others that would produce just this pattern* (see Hochberg,

(*Text continues on page 155*)

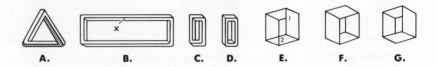

A.   B.   C. D.   E.   F.   G.

FIGURE 69. *Objects in the mind's eye: Our perceptions are constructed from successive glances.*

A. "Impossible pictures," like this one by Penrose and Penrose (1958), portray objects that could not exist as they are shown. Their very considerable theoretical importance is made more clear in Figures *B–G.* Neither (*A*), (*B*), nor (*C*) should look solid, according to the Minimum Principle of Figure 65, because they are neither simpler nor more consistent as whole 3D objects than they are as flat patterns. The shape at (*C*) looks flatter than (*B*), though it is no less possible, which suggests that the inconsistency within the figure is more tolerable at (*B*) because the opposite ends are not visible at once within a single glance; that (*C*) isn't flatter merely because of its proportions is shown by (*D*). This independence between parts of objects that are not seen foveally within a single glance can also be shown in the same figures that were used to demonstrate the Minimum Principle: Figure (*E*) has the same 3D structure as (*G*) as long as you keep your gaze fixed on point (*1*) within the pattern; if you fixate point (*2*) in Figure (*E*) instead of point (*1*), perspective reversal between the orientations of (*F*) and (*G*) will begin after a while: As long as point (*1*) is not in foveal vision, it does not determine which way you perceive the object. The various features that contribute to objects like those in Figures 63 and 65 must contribute to the three-dimensional perceptual organization one glance at a time.

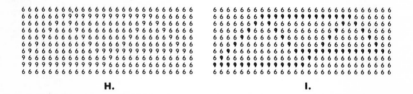

H.   I.

H, I. Peripheral vision is also important to the organization of perceived objects and shapes: There is the same form, delineated by 9s among the 6s, in (*H*) as in (*I*). Trace it out with your eye to make sure. Does it ever become sufficiently 3D for the perspective to reverse, as it will if you look at (*I*) for a few moments?

J. These same considerations apply to shape and figure-ground organization. It is not hard to perceive the head of a white and dark bird at the same time in the pattern at (*J*) (adapted from M. Escher, 1960). Is this compatible with the assertion (see Figures 47 and 61) that you can see only one side of a contour as figure?

The demonstrations on this page are incompatible with a holistic approach like *Gestalt* theory (Figures 62, 63, 65), and the inconsistent pictures in A–E, above, show that perceptual structure does not simply reflect physical structure as we might expect from an uncritical application of the doctrine of unconscious inference (Figure 60). Some theory like Hebb's (Figures 49, 50), which attempts to explain how we combine the peripheral and foveal information from successive glances, and to include attentional and cognitive factors in the account of the perceptual process, seems the most plausible line to pursue next. We consider such factors in the next chapter.

J.

1974).[6] Similarly for the law of good continuation and for most of the determinants of organization; let us then consider Helmholtz's rule, as applied in this fashion.

Perceptual inference: Its rules and limits. Perceptual inference does better, in a general way, than the Minimum Principle, now that we have surveyed this wide range of phenomena. It explains most of the same demonstrations and facts, as we have just seen; it explains the properties of figure and ground which, strangely enough, neither the original Gestalt theory nor its "information-theory" successor could do; and it is not necessarily embarrassed by the phenomena like those in Figures 68 and 69.

But to say that we perform such perceptual inference accomplishes little. We cannot know what the results of such a process will be unless we know explicitly the "rules of inference" that are being followed and the limits of the domain to which they apply. As we have seen, an uncritical application of "familiarity" will not work (pp. 73, 77, 85); some of the most "obvious" examples of inference are almost certainly accomplished by specific sensory processes, and are not "inferential" at all (pp. 107-116); and we obviously have severe limits on what we take into account in solving our perceptual problems (Figure 69). Before we can go much further with the Helmholtz-Brunswik proposal, we shall have to separate the various domains of space and time better than we have done so far.

This assessment does not mean that the facts and theories of this chapter are useless: The Gestaltists' rules, the Minimum Principle, the higher-order variables of color and space—all can predict quite well how objects and scenes will appear under many circumstances. But it requires a deeper understanding to know *when and why these rules will not work;* and more important, to know how perception contributes to, and draws upon, the wider range of cognitive processes in which perceptual processes are embedded. To approach such understanding, we will have to inquire how the moment-by-moment sensory contributions are combined over time, and that we will consider in Chapter 6.

Summary

A higher-order variable is a measured relationship between individual measures. In this chapter we look briefly at possible sensory receptor mechanisms that are sensitive to such higher-order features,

[6] It is not an accident that simplicity and probability are related; that is what made information theory applicable to problems of perceptual organization in the first place. See Fig. 60B; Attneave, 1959; and Garner, 1962.

PERCEPTION 156

and we considered how the use of higher-order variables of stimulation might solve many of the problems of sensory analysis that arose in the previous chapter—particularly, problems of color- and size-constancy and of the organization of form and motion. For example, ratios of the light energy of adjacent regions in the optic array will predict the colors we see (and explain the phenomena of constancy and of contrast) far better than will measures of each region considered separately.

Another simple higher-order variable is a *gradient,* which is the rate at which some measured property changes uniformly from one end of some region to the other. Surfaces at some slant to the line-of-sight produce characteristic gradients of texture-density in the optic array, providing a higher-order variable of stimulation that automatically takes distance into account and, thereby, providing a possible explanation of size-constancy in particular and distance-perception in general.

The organization of form remains a somewhat more difficult problem. Gestalt theorists used ambiguous patterns (which lend themselves to the study of what causes one form or motion rather than another to be perceived) to derive numerous "laws" of organization. Most of these can be summarized under the "law" of simplicity ("we see what is simplest to see")—a law whose application obviously depends on our being able to measure simplicity. Since in recent years first steps have been made toward the objective measurement of simplicity, predictive laws of shape perception and of motion perception seem as possible to achieve as do those of color and size perception.

Whether by early perceptual learning or by inborn arrangement, our nervous systems seem to choose those ways of seeing the world that keep perceived surfaces and objects as simple and constant as possible, and this fact offers a very different picture of space perception than that of Chapter 4: Earlier, the eyes seemed to provide only ambiguous information about the world of space and motion; now, when we consider the higher-order variables produced in the optic array by the observer's own movements, the available visual stimulation is potentially quite unambiguous.

This promise—that higher-order variables of stimulation will explain our perceptions of physical space as simply as other variables predict our perceptions of colors—should not suggest, however, that surfaces are the elements for building all perception (including, for example, the perception of social qualities and events).

These explanations have application to the search for complex physiological structures, to the discovery of the dynamic features of the moving observer that guide him through space, and to the principles that make still pictures more or less intelligible.

We must pick up our information, over time, by momentary glances. Close consideration of examples of what this implies makes it plausible to view the Gestalt laws as cues to what parts of the visual field belong to the same object or surface. The study of momentary glances also directs us to the problems of sequential attention and of how we combine our successive glances, which we shall address, with particular emphasis on reading text and perceiving motion pictures, in the next chapter.

MORE ADVANCED READING

BECK, J. *Surface color perception.* Ithaca: Cornell University Press, 1972. Chapter 8: Surface textures and qualities.

CORNSWEET, T. N. *Visual perception.* New York: Academic Press, 1970. Chapter 11: The psychophysiology of brightness, 1. Spatial interaction in the visual system, 268–310; Chapter 12. The psychophysiology of brightness, 2. Modulation transfer function, 311–364.

GIBSON, J. J. *The perception of the visual world.* Boston: Houghton Mifflin, 1950.

GIBSON, J. J. *The senses considered as perceptual systems.* Boston: Houghton Mifflin, 1956.

HABER, R. N., and HERSHENSON, M. *The psychology of visual perception.* New York: Holt, Rinehart and Winston, 1973. Chapter 12: Two major points of view on the perception of space, 279–293; Chapter 13: Spatial information available to the perceiver, 295–325.

KAUFMAN, L. *Sight and mind.* New York: Oxford University Press, 1974. Chapter 12: Analysis of pattern and form, 463–499; Chapter 13: Analysis of pattern, 500–525.

KLING, J. A. and RIGGS, L. A. (Eds.) *Woodworth and Schlosberg's Experimental Psychology,* New York: Holt, Rinehart and Winston, 1971. Chapters 12 and 13, by J. Hochberg: Perception, 1. Color and shape, 395–474; Perception, 2. Space and movement, 475–550.

LINDSAY, P. and NORMAN, D. *Human information processing.* New York: Academic Press, 1972. Chapter 1: Human perception, 1–49; Chapter 2: Neural information processing, 51–113.

SCHARF, B. (Ed.) *Experimental sensory psychology.* Glenview, Illinois: Scott, Foresman, 1975. Chapter 7, by L. Ganz: Vision, 216–263.

How Do We Combine
Successive Sensory Input?

chapter six

The problem of how to combine successive sensory input is central and pervasive: In vision, in audition, in exploratory touch. In vision, we know that the eye explores the world by means of discrete saccades, each of which normally provides detailed vision of only a small part of the field of view. In hearing, most but not all of the information that we obtain comes in parcels of syllables, words, and sentences. And our sense of touch is most effective when we explore an object actively by stroking its surface rather than by pressing it all at once against the skin (Gibson, 1962). We learn about the world and communicate with each other by obtaining successive *samples* of sensory information.

So far, we have not discussed how we deal with perception *over* time. Until we face this issue, we have no way of stepping beyond the very unnatural momentary stimulus display, a situation that is totally unrepresentative of the normal conditions of perception.

Let us first outline the components of the problem, then discuss what we know about them (mostly from the study of verbal material), and finally consider how those components are combined in such sequential perceptual activities as reading and listening, looking at still pictures, or watching motion pictures. By the very nature of such activities, we will have to consider as well two aspects of perception that we have so far managed to ignore almost entirely — *attention,* and the perceiver's intentions, or perceptual *purpose.*

A. *Fovea, Periphery, and Saccadic Eye Movements*: A General Statement of the Problem

Remember that details are seen only in the center of vision, the fovea. To obtain detailed vision of the different parts of an object or scene, the eye must explore it by a succession of fixations. These can be made at a rate of about four or five per second, the eye moving very rapidly between the fixations (pauses). So even though the visual field is spread over a wide two-dimensional space, details are picked up *serially,* not simultaneously.

Thus, in the first second or so that we look at the picture in Figure 70*A,* the fovea obtains about four to five separate glances. In Figure 70*B,* we show approximately where the first five foveal fixations would fall; in Figure 70*C,* we show what the successive glances would add up to if they were merely superimposed — if the eye merely summed the light falling on it. Similarly, in Figure 70*D,* the marks under the line of type show where the reader's fixations would be likely to fall; in Figure 70*E,* we have merely added the glances.

Of course, we don't perceive that way at all. How do we combine our successive glances into what appears to be a spatially laid-out

(Text continues on page 160)

FIGURE 70. *The problem of successive glances.*
A. The first five fixations made by a typical viewer (after Buswell, 1935).

A.

(Figure 70 continues)

B.

C.

Now is the time for all good men to come to

D.

Now is thNoiwesftheallrgeddmodlrgtoocbmerntdo come to

E.

B. What he sees clearly in those fixations. *C.* The first four retinal images superimposed. *D.* The first four glances at a line of text. *E.* The first four retinal images, superimposed. (These examples are elaborated from those of Gibson, 1950.)

scene? What guides the glances that we take? And what motivates and sustains our looking behavior?

RETINAL AND EXTRA-RETINAL SIGNALS: INFORMATION ABOUT EYE DIRECTION

As a first step, of course, we must know where our eye was directed during each glance. As we saw in Chapter 2, the viewer has both nonvisual and visual information about how his eye has moved. It is tempting to think that this solves the problem: If the viewer subtracts the amount of his eye movement from the amount that his retinal image has moved, and there is no movement of the image left over, he perceives that the scene that he is looking at has not changed.

This explanation of how we combine our successive glances probably contains some truth. But it really only faces up to a small part of the problem:

WHY KNOWING THE EYE'S DIRECTION DOESN'T SOLVE THE PROBLEM

Knowing how our eyes have moved is neither sufficient nor necessary to enable us to keep track of the succession of glances.

We can demonstrate the first point right here: Move your eyes across the symbols in line *A* from left to right. At each fixation point, you see only one symbol clearly. By the time you reached the eighth symbol, your clear sight of the first symbols is about two seconds old, and you can no longer remember their order: Consider Line *B*. Is it the same as Line *A?*

LINE A   e   a   e   e   a   e   a   a   e   a

Now, compare Line *C* and Line *D*: Are they the same? You knew your eyes'

LINE B   e   a   e   e   a   a   e   a   e   a

locations equally well in both cases, but the contents of the glances were

LINE C   p   e   r   c   e   p   t   i   o   n

probably not equally remembered in Lines *A* and *B* as compared to Lines *C* and *D*.

LINE D   p   e   r   p   e   c   t   i   o   n

Let's look at the opposite side of the coin: You do not need to know where your eye is directed, in each case, to know how to assemble the successive views you receive, as a couple of minutes in front of the TV set will convince you: For the past fifty years, motion pictures have not been made by setting up a camera and recording what goes on before it. Instead, the filmmaker splices together different views, or *shots,* to convey to the viewer a scene vastly larger than the motion picture or TV screen on which it is displayed. Most of what you see in motion pictures has never existed anywhere but in the mind's eye of the viewers and the filmmaker.

What these examples tell us is that the viewer must have some "mental structure" into which the individual glances are entered. This sounds vague now, but we will be able to make it a little less so by the end of the chapter.

In order to do that, we will have to introduce a new set of terms and concepts that come from a relatively new discipline variously called "information processing" and "cognitive psychology." We will define a number of terms very briefly; then we will use these and others in discussing the perceptual activities themselves.

B. The Terms and Components of "Information-Processing" Analysis

The way we respond to the flow of stimulation from the world can be divided into several logical components. We will introduce them briefly here, and then use them in talking about reading and listening. The reader should be cautioned, however, that some distinctions have been ignored in the interests of brevity; moreover, such a division into components is itself really a theoretical commitment: Thus, Gibson has long insisted that we should consider the stimulus-field-over-time, or the four-dimensional array of stimulation; and if followed systematically, such an approach would develop a very different kind of analysis than the one given in this chapter.

The momentary sample.   In *vision,* this means, basically, the sensory contents of the single glance, which normally is a fixation of at least 1/5 second in duration. In *audition,* the durations of the samples are less distinctly bounded. In both cases, what is sampled is a relatively small section of a larger object, scene or continuously changing event.

Extraction, comparison, and encoding.   The momentary glance provides a patterned flash of color, texture, a movement. Does it contain some letter—say, a *T?* To decide, you must compare the pattern to some criterion (e.g., to decide that it is not an *F*); and by encoding the shape as a *T,* other information in the flash—color, brightness, precise shape—may be discarded.

Storage: Short-term and long-term memory.   The encoded information must be stored in *short-term* (immediate) *memory,* until the perceiver can report it, combine it with the information from the next glance, or transfer it to *long-term memory.* (Students of learning often attribute different characteristics to short-term and long-term memory; that distinction is not implied in our present usage.) The *span of immediate memory*—its storage capacity—is limited to approximately 5 to 9 *independent items,* or *chunks* (Miller's "magic number," 7±2): The number 031-742-6859 is probably beyond your immediate memory span, whereas the number 1492-00-1776, consisting of only three independent items, or chunks, is not. That is because each of the numbers in 1492 and 1776 is not independent but has an assigned place in a learned pattern—a *schema*—of numbers (Warren and Hess, 1975). ("Schema" and "chunk" are roughly equivalent terms, and most of the time we will use them interchangeably.)

Combining the successive samples. We have been discussing individual, independent glances. This is a somewhat misleading idea of the perceptual process: In normal perception, as when a viewer looks at the different parts of some object, the samples he receives are not independent glances. They are not independent because the physical world has consistencies, or *structure* (see p. 63 in Chapter 4), so that each glance provides for some anticipation of the next, and the schema whose features are to be tested on any glance is often already in immediate memory from the preceding glances.

This is an abstract and somewhat forbidding set of terms, but their meaning will become more apparent as we apply them to perceptual activities.

C. Reading and Listening

Reading is the best-studied of the perceptual activities that involve the combination of successive glances, and forms the basis of most research on the momentary glance. *Listening* is the best source of research on selective attention, which we shall take up shortly. Both of these abilities illuminate each other and are worth studying for what they reveal about the perceptual process in general, as well as for their own sakes. But we should note first that reading text and listening to speech are fundamentally different from all the perceptual activities that we have considered.

THE ARBITRARY NATURE OF LANGUAGE:
NONICONIC AND ICONIC SYMBOLS

Until now, the stimuli we have considered were all determined directly or indirectly by the nature of our physical environment—by our perceptual ecology. For example, *linear perspective* and the *size-*

distance relationship were not inventions of artists or psychologists—they were discoveries. All organisms that share our visual ecology must encounter these aspects of the world thousands of times each day. It is even reasonable to debate, as we did in Chapters 4-D and 5-D, whether our mechanisms for responding to these aspects of the world are innate; and if they are learned at all, they must be very well learned indeed. Even pictures, though they are man-made and symbolic are not arbitrary, but share stimulus features with the scenes that they represent. Considered as symbols in a strict sense, pictures are symbols of a special kind—they are *iconic* symbols, which work by virtue of the features shared with the objects and scenes they represent.

Reading text and listening to speech, however, involve what are essentially arbitrary pairings of almost totally man-made stimuli and responses; the relationship between words and their meaning is unquestionably learned. And although a great deal of practice goes into learning to read, the amount of practice that we get in perceiving objects (and the features that they share with pictures) is incomparably greater.

Accordingly, when we attempt to learn about perception in general by studying reading and listening, we must be very cautious: The perception of objects and events might not be at all like the perception of verbal material. Nevertheless, the processes of purposive looking and listening, selective attention, and of the integration of successive glances (and sounds) may be most clearly revealed by studies of reading and listening; and we will later see that these studies do in fact appear to help us understand the perception of pictures and motion pictures. So it is worthwhile to proceed, but with these reservations in mind.

READING: A SKETCH OF THE GENERAL FACTS

As an information-gathering behavior, reading rests on the two earlier skills that are usually very well developed before the child ever comes to the reading task: First, active looking around at the world; and second, active listening to speech. Let us first mention a few of the more salient and well-established facts about reading, and then consider their general explanation in terms of the more fundamental skills that underlie reading behavior. (For recent surveys, see Kavanagh and Mattingly, 1972; Gibson and Levin, 1975; and Singer and Ruddel, 1976.)

Reading rate and its determinants. Reading speed varies

widely, and it clearly depends on the reader's purpose or intention, and on the nature of the text, as well as on his ability: An average speed for an average reader might be about 200 words per minute; a skilled reader, reading for speed, may achieve 500 words per minute or more. But the same skilled reader, detecting spelling errors or reading a legal document, may drop to 100 words per minute or less.

Reading, of course, proceeds by means of eye movements which "scan" the text in a series of *fixations*. The eye movements themselves are very quick saccades, taking about 1/20th of a second; most of the reading time is therefore spent on the fixations, in which the eye pauses for about 1/4 of a second at a particular point in the text. The good reader makes fewer and briefer fixations on each line of type (although 1/5 to 1/4 of a second is as brief as fixations generally go, since it takes about that time to prepare to execute an eye movement); the poor reader makes more and longer fixations, and makes more "regressive" eye movements (i.e., he returns his eye more often to text that he has already passed).

How does the good reader manage with fewer and shorter fixations, and why does his advantage drop when he looks for errors? The following results from *tachistoscopic* experiments (in which the visual material is shown to the viewer for a brief time, like the fixations between saccades) will help us answer these questions and develop further the information-processing analysis of the components of perception.

The momentary glance: The tachistoscopic experiment. In the tachistoscopic experiment, some visual material is flashed before the subject for a brief duration. The duration is usually kept too short to permit eye movements to be made; remember, it takes about 1/4 of a second to decide to move your eye and do so. By increasing the duration, a threshold can be measured: How long an exposure is needed for the viewer to recognize the display?

The determinants of recognition: familiarity, attention, and set. With a single brief exposure, the viewer can identify about five unrelated letters; but he can recognize much longer, familiar words or even phrases. In learning to read, the reader has indeed "learned to see more in a single glance." And it is not only familiarity that increases what he can see: If he is asked to attend to some part or aspect of the display—say, to the upper left or to the colors of the letters—he will do better at those, even if the instructions about what he should attend to come *after* the tachistoscopic display. Finally, if the viewer is *set* to expect a particular *kind* of material, he will see it better at a shorter exposure.

There are two questions here: First, what sets the limits for recognizing unfamiliar material? Second, how are those limits overcome by familiarity and affected by attention and set?

A classic experiment by Sperling (1960) answers the first question and anticipates a great deal of what has followed in cognitive psychology.

The partial report experiment. If the viewer is shown a matrix of letters and numbers, like that in Figure 71A, for a brief exposure, he can identify only about four or five of them. But immediately after he is shown the matrix, he can report almost any item in any row, chosen at random, that the experimenter instructs him to (using a prearranged musical tone to signal which row he should report). As the time between the exposure and the signal increases, the percentage of correct answers decreases until, at about 500 msec. (1/2 second), the viewer is performing back at the level of four or five items (Figure 71A,3). Thus, even though the physical exposure was very short, a persistent image (or *icon,* as it has been called [Neisser, 1967]; see Figure 14B) lasts long enough for the subject to direct his attention to the location he is told to report.

(Text continues on page 168)

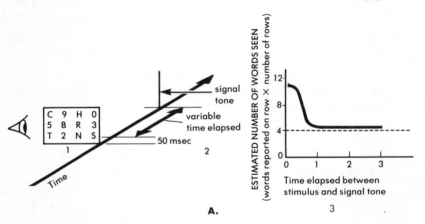

A.

FIGURE 71. *Information-processing experiments.*
    A. The partial report experiment. (1.) A matrix of letters and numbers is presented very briefly (50 msec.). The subject can recall only about 4 numbers (the dotted line in the graph at [3]). This is a fairly general limit. (2.) If some very short time after the brief presentation at (1), a signal tells the subject which of the rows he should report, he can do so almost perfectly regardless of which row is signaled, indicating that the entire matrix is within his *sensory* capacity. (3.) If the signal is delayed, performance rapidly declines to the original level (the dotted line) (Sperling, 1960, 1963). As the perceptual limits are not sensory, they must lie in the next stages (the *encoding, storage,* or *retrieval* stages). The tone signal in this experiment told the viewer which row to encode first. By the time that was done, the image had faded sufficiently that he no longer had any stimulus information to encode. Practice and attention affect what subjects can report with a single exposure by affecting the order and form of the encoding (Harris & Haber, 1963).

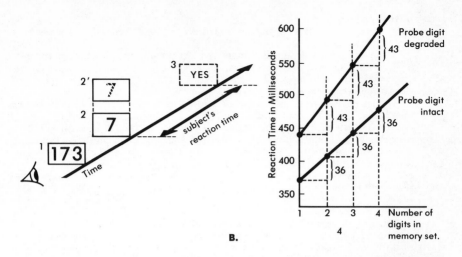

B.

B. The comparison process: STM and LTM. A subject is given a set of numbers to remember (*1*), shown an individual number (the *probe digit* [*2*]), and asked to answer as quickly as possible whether the probe was a member of set (*1*). The more numbers there are in set (*1*), the longer it takes the subject to respond—the longer his reaction time. The reaction time increases with each additional digit in the memory set, suggesting that the probe is being compared with each member of the set before the subject responds (*4*). If the probe is visually degraded (*2'*), at least under some conditions reaction time increases by approximately *43* msec. for a one-digit memory set, by *86* msec, for a two-digit memory set, and so on, suggesting that the probe digit is compared with each member of the set in a form that is slowed down by the degradation, and that the comparisons are therefore made between "visual representations" (Sternberg, 1969). Although there is a great temptation to think of *encoding* as a process of translating visual presentations into their names and storing them in that ver-

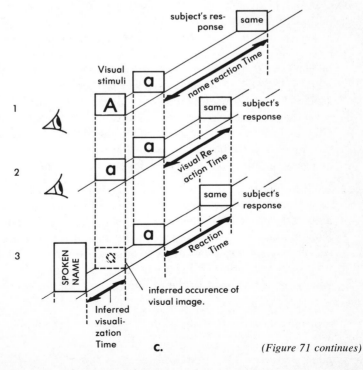

C.

(Figure 71 continues)

(Figure 71 continued)
bal or acoustic form, this experiment is evidence of visual encoding, and we will see other evidence to this point.

These experiments use small memory sets within the limits of what is called *short-term memory* (STM). With larger sets, subjects would have to draw on *long-term memory* (LTM), and they would have to retrieve the items from LTM to make the comparison, which should take longer.

C. Retrieving an item for comparison. How long does it take to retrieve an item from LTM? An estimate might be made as follows: (Posner *et al.,* 1969) If a subject is given two letters, one after the other, and has to decide whether or not they are the same, his reaction time is faster when both letters are visually identical (2) than when they have the same names but different shapes (1). If the first of the letters is not actually shown to the subject, but it is told to him and he is given an additional 1/2 second in which to visualize it, his reaction time to the second letters is the same as it is when both letters are presented and are visually identical. This suggests that it takes approximately 1/2 second to retrieve the visual image from LTM and get it ready to compare to the second letter.

This kind of inquiry, and the general set of assumptions that it shares, is usually called the *information-processing* approach. Note that no assumption is made about whether the "images" that are used in these explanations have any counterparts in conscious experience: This kind of analysis is not, therefore, a return to the structuralist experiments of Figure 26.

This experiment tells us that the limits on what can be perceived in a single glance are not only sensory limits; in addition, *it takes time to encode the sensory input into some more permanent form, and what the viewer has not encoded during the time that the effects of the single glance persist is lost to him, since in tachistoscopic experiments he gets only that one look.*

How then do attention and familiarity overcome those limits? Figure 71*A,3* suggests that the effect of the signal, in the experiment outlined there, is to lead the subject to encode one row first before it has a chance to "fade." In fact, Harris & Haber (1963) and Haber (1964) have shown that subjects perceive those aspects of a brief, tachistoscopic display that they have been instructed to attend to, more fully and at shorter exposures, because they encode those aspects first, and when they get to report aloud the unencoded material is no longer available for them to refer to. That would account for the effects of attention. As to the effects of familiarity, we will see that the answer must lie in the way that words, as opposed to meaningless and unfamiliar strings of letters, are encoded or stored.

Encoding the momentary glance. How do you recognize a letter or a word? Consider first a letter: It seems like an immediate and automatic process to identify a *V,* but when you are told that it is Roman numeral, you have to shift gears and identify it from another set of possibilities. That raises two issues: the nature of the *criterion* by which you identify the item, and the nature of the process by which you compare it to the criterion.

The test: templates, features, and legibility. Assume that the subject is required to make a single decision: Is the following letter a *t?*

T

One way to decide would be to compare the pattern to a *template,* or a stencil, like fitting a piece of a jigsaw puzzle into its place: if it fits well enough, it is accepted, but if too much of the template and the letter fail to coincide, it is rejected. The peculiar numbers that are printed on bank checks are designed to be read by machines that use such templates. Because we can recognize letters in various sizes, type faces, and orientations, our visual systems would have to apply some rather complicated standardizing operations to them before comparing them to the templates, but templates are implausible for other reasons: What we recognize as being the same letters can differ more from each other, overall, than resemble each other, and it is clear from the collection of letters below that some features are more important than others.

CGK CGK CGK CGK **CGK** CGK
CGK CGK CGK **CGK** CGK CGK

Most psychologists today accept something like a *feature analysis* rather than template matching for the test stage. E. J. Gibson (1969) has classified the letters of the alphabet in terms of whether they have horizontal, vertical, right-diagonal, or left-diagonal lines; whether they have closed or open curves, whether they are symmetrical, and so forth. Gibson and her colleagues have shown that the greater the number of features that two letters have in common, the more likely that they will be confused (Gibson *et al.,* 1963).

Note that features are not just small templates, to be fitted together in different arrangements. They can be quite large in size and might include such characteristics as word length, whether the word has ascenders and descenders, and so forth: The skilled reader may learn the characteristic features by which he can recognize frequently occurring letter groups and even words. Letter group features and word features do exist. In fact, because UPPER-CASE TEXT obliterates the group features that are provided by the ascenders and descenders in lower-case text, it is—other things equal— harder to read (see Tinker, 1963, for a discussion of the factors that affect the legibility of labels, text, etc.). It is unfortunate therefore that so much recent research on reading has been performed exclusively with capital letters.

Here, then, is one point at which familiarity might affect encoding: Because he can recognize features of entire letter groups, the skilled reader might extract stimulus information in larger units. This does not mean that the individual letters are "lost," as had once been assumed, when they are embedded in familiar words. In fact, subjects can detect letters *faster* when they are included in familiar words than in nonwords (Reicher, 1969; Krueger, 1970, 1975; Wheeler, 1970; Estes, 1975). Nor does the fact that these large-scale stimulus features, such as characteristic word shapes and letter groups, are theoretically available to the reader to use, mean that subjects *necessarily* use them (Smith *et al.,* 1969; Thompson and Massaro, 1973; Massaro, 1973), let alone that they use them so exclusively that the individual letters cannot be read. One of the reasons that we cannot be sure about such matters is that most of the research has been done with single words, and it is not clear that we use the same methods to read single words as when they are in context. During the next five years, we can expect to gain a great deal of information about the features that are used in the course of normal reading by means of studies like those of McConkie and Rayner, described on p. 175.

The comparison process: scanning immediate memory. In order to identify an item in the momentary glance, it must be compared to some schema or chunk in immediate memory. The more alternatives the subject has, the longer it takes him to decide. In fact, by showing subjects a set of from one to four digits (the *memory set*), then showing them a single digit (the *probe digit,* in Figure 71*B*), and asking them to decide as quickly as possible whether that digit had been in the first set, Sternberg (1969) found that each additional digit in the memory set increased the decision time by 30 msec.

Note that the subject appears to compare the probe digit to all of the members of the memory set—i.e., the search is *exhaustive*. Note also that the process is *serial,* in that one item in immediate memory is compared to the probe digit before going on to the next, if we accept the evidence of the curves in Figure 71*B*. *This does not mean that words are actually processed serially, one letter at a time, when we read them:* There is ample evidence for *parallel processing,* both in terms of being able to recognize and search for more than one letter at a time (Neisser, 1967), and in terms of being able to respond to features that are characteristic of entire letter groups or words (Eriksen & Spencer, 1969; Neisser, 1964; Travers, 1974) or of an entire category of symbols like digits as distinguished from numbers (Egeth *et al.,* 1972; Jonides & Gleitman, 1972). However, it is also very difficult to rule out the logical possibility that a very rapid scanning process (within the nervous system, and not involving actual eye movements) underlies word recognition (Townsend, 1972; Gough, 1972)—a process so rapid (about 10 msec. per letter) that, if it occurs at all, we can ignore it on the time scale at which the reading process proceeds.

Each digit in this experiment is, of course, itself a familiar unit, and we don't know the features by which the sensory sample—the probe digit—was compared with each set of digits in immediate memory. It does seem reasonable to conclude that at least under some conditions the comparison is made in *visual* terms—i.e., that the viewer does not encode the probe digit into verbal form, and then compare that to the set that he is holding in immediate memory (even though he rehearses that set by saying it to himself while waiting for the probe digit!): We know that, because when the probe digits were degraded, as in Figure 71*B2'*, reaction times increased for each member of the set that was in immediate memory, suggesting that each such comparison took longer to make because of the visual degradation of the probe. If the probe digit had been transformed out of its visual form right after having been seen, any additional time that was required to overcome the effects of the visual degradation would be added just that once to the reaction time of the subject, and not increase the reaction time as the memory set was increased. That is, the two slopes in Figure 71*B,4* should have been parallel, which they are not. This study is a good example of the new purposes for which the classic concept of images is now used and the kinds of operation that measure and define it; contrast this with the example in Figure 26 for a different measure and, therefore, a different definition. We do not know as yet whether these different procedures tap a common or even related process.

All the members of the set to which the probe digit was being compared were already in immediate memory. If the set had contained too many indedendent digits—say, more than seven—and therefore exceeded the span of immediate memory, the subject would have had to retrieve items from his long-term memory. And that would surely have taken much longer than 30 msec. How much longer, is hard to say. Our best estimate may be on the order of 500 msec. (1/2 second), which comes from the experiments by Posner *et. al.* that are summarized in Figure 71*C*. But we can't really name any specific time with confidence because it depends on how closely words are related to each other in the subject's long-term memory, and on the degree to which they have been "primed"—that is, gotten into readiness—by preceding events (Beller, 1971; Rosch, 1975; Collins & Loftus, 1975).

And that offers two additional points at which familiarity, attention, and set can affect the perception of the momentary glance: First, by increasing the likelihood that material is brought into short-term memory from long-term storage; and second, by increasing the likelihood that the material can be held in short-term storage while the sensory sample is tested.

Let us consider these two points in the context of discussing immediate and long-term memory.

Short-term and long-term memory. The previous accounts of why and how familiarity, attention, and expectation affect the momentary glance were all open to question. The two mechanisms that we will now consider are both massive ones that are very easy to demonstrate. Moreover, they must be of central importance when we come to combine the successive glances.

The first is the likelihood that a word or phrase will be brought into short-term memory in the first place. The effects of *set* — of what the viewer expects to see — are known to affect tachistoscopic recognition. Thresholds are lower and judgment is quicker when the word is one that the subject expects to see. This is true in part because he needs less information in order to decide what the word is; and in fact, if we tell the viewer that the word will be one of a small set of alternatives, he has a better chance of guessing correctly *by chance alone* than if he was told nothing: This is true because by telling the subject what the alternatives are, we have put *constraints* — limits — on what he should expect, and this is of course what information is: an input which reduces the alternatives that the subject can expect to occur (Chapter 5C). Now, if in addition the viewer also gets *some* information from the stimulus — say, the word's length or its initial letter — he can make do with a very short exposure. Consider: Is the following word "cat" or "elephant"?

CXX

If no explicit set is given the viewer, he forms his own, based on the experimental context, on whatever partial information he gets from the brief exposure (Bricker & Chapanis, 1953), and on familiarity: other things equal, we expect to see or hear frequently used words more than infrequent words, and we are more ready to use them ourselves. Familiar words are more accessible from long-term memory, therefore, and more available to use in encoding the briefly seen stimulus.

In fact, even if *no word at all* is shown in the momentary presentation, the response that viewers make to these blank presentations still reflects the frequency of word usage (Goldiamond & Hawkins, 1958).

This is very much like what we called *response bias* in Chapter 2, but we are not talking about any response that we can actually observe; moreover, the effects of familiarity cannot merely be a matter of guessing, since subjects can detect letters in, and differences between, familiar words faster than with nonwords (p. 170).

Finally, and probably most important: As independent items, you can store from five to nine letters in immediate memory; as a word — say, "antidisestablishmentarianism" — you can store and test many more letters. Or, more accurately, you can store the "label" for the word from which you can regenerate the letters when they are needed. In fact, the same kinds of effects of familiarity that are found in tachistoscopic presentations are obtained when the exposures are long enough to read all of the letters individually, (Baddeley, 1964); and in that case the effects can only be due to the greater ease of storing familiar material.

Let us now see how the results of the tachistoscopic experiments fit in to the normal reading process. Neither the reader's expectation of what will come next nor his familiarity with words and phrases can show their full effects when we study only a single momentary glance. When we consider how the successive glances are combined in the course of active reading, most of the information-processing components that we have been discussing will fit into place, but the process will look very different.

COMBINING SUCCESSIVE GLANCES: ACTIVE READING

The beginning reader may often have to spell out the text that he is trying to "decode," letter by letter and word by word, a procedure that requires small, repetitive eye movements. This is very different from the way in which we normally use our eyes to scan the world and requires a sounding-out procedure that is very different from the ways in which we normally speak and listen. This activity is quite onerous, and if the student doesn't give up on the whole enterprise, he must follow a different method as soon as he can and whenever he is able to (i.e., when he is not reading very unfamiliar material or looking for spelling errors.)

By what methods can he avoid the necessity of letter-by-letter fixation and decoding?

Although reading normally depends on eye movements, and although the way in which the reader moves his eyes reveals his reading ability (and the difficulty of the text), the eye movements themselves are merely instrumental actions. Until recently, the main method we had for investigating how eye movements are used in active reading was to interfere with the text in various ways and observe how each kind of interference affected reading. The good reader can overcome remarkable changes in text, that require him to make eye movements very different from those he normally uses: With a little practice, he can take in his stride the alternation of left-to-right and right-left flow of text (Kolers, 1968), or keep his eyes relatively still, and read the text as it moves behind a window (Bouma & De Voogd, 1974). But interference with the features that allow the reader to use his peripheral vision to guide his eye movements and inform him about the kinds and lengths of the word outside his fovea, affects both his reading ability (Smith *et al.,* 1969; Hochberg, 1970; Fisher, 1975) and eye movements (Fisher, 1976). Here is an example, adapted from a procedure used by Fisher (1975).

ThIsiSaNeXaMpLeOftHeKiNdOfiNtErFeRaNcEwItHtExTtHaT
MaKeSwOrDfOrMAnDwOrDlEnGtHUn-
AvAiLaBlETotHerEaDeRaNd
fOrCeaLeTtErbYlEtTeRdEcOdInGpRoCeSs(After Fisher, 1975).

These findings argue strongly (but not conclusively) that the reader uses at least some information from his peripheral vision to guide his reading behavior; that such information is very limited; and that the eye movements are often directed to places about which the reader has specific questions—as shown by the fact that the eye often returns to words that were misunderstood or mispronounced when reading aloud (Geyer, 1968). It would seem, therefore, that there are two interacting systems that affect our reading behavior: *peripheral search guidance* (or better, *parafoveal* search guidance since, as we will see, most of the work is done by regions very near the fovea), and *cognitive search guidance* (Hochberg, 1970b; Hochberg and Brooks, 1970). More direct means of study are needed, however, before such hypothetical processes can be accepted, sharpened, and understood.

A procedure that has recently been perfected for studying how the reader picks up information during the actual course of reading is a good way of illustrating the previous points about the reading process. McConkie and Rayner programmed a computer to display text to a reader while his eye movements were being monitored. The letters (and spaces) in the text could be replaced by *x*s (or by other letters), but a "window" of intact text remained in the immediate neighborhood of the point at which his eye was directed at any moment. Whenever the subject moved his eye to a new point, the window moved with it (that is, the xs were deleted, and the letters of the text were restored at the place to which the eye had moved). If the window was too small, the subject could detect the xs, and also the fact that they changed when he moved his eye; therefore it was possible, by adjusting the window size, to determine how far out from the center of the fixation point the subject was actually picking up letters and other graphic information (McConkie and Rayner, 1975; Rayner, 1975). Let us use that paradigm to illustrate the difference between eye movements of good readers and poor readers. Here is a line of text:

A. The Psychology Department at Columbia University in the City of New York

The first four fixations, about ¼ second per glance, might look like this for a good reader:

B. The Psychxxxxx Xxxxxxxxxxxxxxxxxxxxxxxxxxxxxxxxxxxxxxxxxxxxxxxxxxxxxxxxxx

C. Xxx Xxxxxxxxxy Deparxxxxx xx Xxxxxxxxxxxxxxxxxxxxxxxxxxxxxxxxxxxxxxxxxxxxxx

D. xxxxxxxxxxxxxx Xxxxxxxxxt at Colxxxxx Xxxxxxxxxxxxxxxxxxxxxxxxxxxxxxxxxxxxx

E. xxxxxxxxxxxxxxxxxxxxxxxxxxxxxxxxxxxxxxx Xxxxxxxxty in the Xxxx xxxxxxxxxxx

The first four fixations of a poor reader, perhaps 1 second per glance, might be:

F. The Psycxxxxxx Xxxxxxxxxxxxxxxxxxxxxxxxxxxxxxxxxxxxxxxxxxxxxxxxxxxxxxxxxxx

G. Xxx Xxychologx Xxxxxxxxxxxxxxxxxxxxxxxxxxxxxxxxxxxxxxxxxxxxxxxxxxxxxxxxxxx

H. Xxx Xxxxxxlogy Depxxxxxxx xx xxxxxxxxxxxxxxxxxxxxxxxxxxxxxxxxxxxxxxxxxxxxxx

I. Xxx Xsychlolgx Xxxxxxxxxx xxxxxxxxxxxxxxxxxxxxxxxxxxxxxxxxxxxxxxxxxxxxxxxxx

Note that the reader's fixation has *regressed* on line *(I)* to a point that had already been passed. The differences between good and poor readers are clear: Good readers make fewer and briefer fixations and fewer regressions than poor ones. This finding has led to attempts to improve readers by training them to move their eyes better. By itself, this really can't help.

As measured during the actual course of reading (with the ingenious method described above, and simulated roughly on lines *B* to *I*), McConkie and Rayner found that the reader picks up useful information about approximately 4 letters to each side of the fixation point on each glance and, in addition, can make out the general shapes and lengths of words for another 10 and 12 letters, respectively, around the fixation point. This amounts to some 16 letters per second, or 1,000 letters per minute, not counting the other information he gets—far more than he could retain in short-term memory as independent items, even in the first second, regardless of whether or not the individual letters are ever identifiable (p. 170). Those 1,000 letters per minute are the same as approximately 200 words per minute, which is—probably not by coincidence—about normal speaking rate. The contents of the successive glances clearly must be encoded in some more economical form if the reader is to retain them. Moreover, *since the good reader makes a saccade every 1/4 second, there probably isn't enough time for him to consult his long-term memory to determine the contents of each momentary glance, as he would have to do if those contents were completely unrelated to each other.*

What the good reader is doing, instead, is to fit the most likely word or phrase he can to what he sees, given the information he has about the text and its subject matter. How is he able to do this?

Most text and speech is *redundant;* you need not actually see (or hear) all of it to know what is being said. One measure of redundancy is the *Cloze Test,* in which the reader has to fill in deleted letters. In the following sentence,

The quick brown fox jumped over the lazy dog

we have dropped 47 percent of the letters (compare this to the partially deleted objects in Figure 74), with little loss of legibility. Because text is redundant, the skilled reader has been *set* by the preceding text to anticipate the content of each fixation he makes. His fixations can therefore be brief. It also means that he can complete a word, phrase, or even a sentence without actually fixating each letter (or even each word). So we can see why, if the text is normally redundant (e.g., if it is not a legal contract or a mathematical proof), and if he is not looking for spelling errors, the good reader needs fewer and briefer fixations than the poor reader: He encodes the text in larger units (Hochberg, 1970b, 1976; Haber and Haber, 1977).

We can see, too, why speed-reading courses are initially of some help: They encourage this active questioning procedure. But it is also clear that even with the best of intentions, the reader's speed will always be limited by the text's redundancy and by his ability to take advantage of it—through his knowledge of the subject matter and the size of the units he can encode.

What kind of units are encoded? The better reader also has a larger *Eye-Voice Span.* This is the number of words by which the voice lags behind the eye when the subject reads aloud. It is not a mechanical delay as in a word-by-word proceeding: The eye moves ahead, returns to mark time or check on some error that may have been made, while the voice completes *speech plans* that the reader formulated earlier (Geyer, 1968): If the light is abruptly turned off, the good reader can nevertheless continue until he reaches the end of a meaningful unit of discourse (Levin *et al.,* 1968).

In reading aloud, then, the good reader is not decoding printed words into spoken words one at a time: He seems to be executing a "speech plan" that he has formulated in advance. When he is reading aloud, those plans have to be carried out, which slows down his reading rate; in silent reading, only the "labels" of the redundant speech plans (those the reader knows he can fill in, if he has to — see Chapter 6B) are evoked. Most readers *subvocalize* somewhat (that is, they energize their speech-producing muscles without actually speaking aloud). In fact, the normal reader seems always "primed" to speak the printed word that he sees, regardless of his more general intentions. For example, in the *Stroop Test,* if the viewer is shown a word printed in red ink, and he is asked its color, it will take him longer to say "red" if the word itself is "green" or any word other than a row of X's. (Stroop, 1935; Warren, 1972).

According to this picture of the reading process, then, the skilled reader is set for most of his glances before he receives them, so that his long-term memory is primed; and within each speech plan, he is testing a chunk that is already in short-term memory: He does not combine successive samples by adding each to the preceding one. Instead, he moves his eyes to test and fill out his expectations, and to formulate new ones.

We should examine these plans and expectations more directly; and we can do that best in the *shadowing experiment,* which is a research procedure (very much like the Eye-Voice Span experiment) that is used in the study of active listening.

ACTIVE LISTENING TO SPEECH

The shadowing experiment and selective attention. In the *shadowing experiment,* the subject tries to repeat as simultaneously as possible what he hears a speaker saying. When the listener is exposed to two or more speakers (say, a man and a woman) and is instructed to shadow one of the speakers (say, the woman), the shadowing procedure assures us that he is *attending* to the intended speaker, or *channel,* and allows us to monitor how well he is doing. When questioned about what each speaker is saying, we find that, in general, the listener knows only what was said by the attended speaker (Cherry, 1953).

Selective attention has been demonstrated, then. How do we explain it?

The filter model. Selective attention might act like a filter to screen out the nonattended channel (Broadbent, 1958; Treisman, 1969). The analogy here is to the filter that screens out the high-frequency noise on a hi-fi set. But there are too many phenomena that simply do not fit this analogy. The most striking example is aptly called the "cocktail party phenomenon": When the listener's own name is uttered, he hears it even if it is on the nonattended channel (Moray, 1959). As Deutsch and Deutsch (1963) pointed out, it is clear that selection between the channels must be made *after* the sounds have been processed for meaning and not at the level of some simple physical criterion. We shall examine other objections to the filter model when we discuss an alternative later on.

The schema-testing model of listening: Analysis-by-synthesis and the encoding of speech plans. Before we consider a very different model of the attentional process, we should discuss briefly the nature of speech perception in general. First, let us consider the smallest sounds into which speech is analyzed, called *phonemes,* and how they are produced and perceived.

Speech sounds can be analyzed into *sound spectrographs,* which are graphs of the intensities of air pressure at the different frequencies the ear can detect (Figure 24). These pressure waves are normally produced, of course, by the vocal organs of the speaker. They can also be produced in a precisely controlled fashion by drawing a sound spectrograph and converting it back into synthetic speech sounds and sequences. We might consider speech to be a sequence of such phonemes, and the perception of speech to be the perception of phonemes and the order in which they occur. This is much too simple an explanation on both counts, and we must consider briefly why that is so.

First, as to the perception of the phonemes themselves. Liberman and his colleagues (1967), using synthetic speech sounds made as described above, showed that subjects' abilities to discriminate between two different phonemes depend not on the physical differences between the phonemes, but on the degree of differences between the movements speakers used to produce those sounds. Everyday examples are easy to find: because the Japanese language makes no distinction between our "L" and "R" sounds, Japanese speakers have great difficulty in hearing the sounds as different when either they or someone else utters them; hence, their characteristic accent when speaking English.

It is as though we perceive the speech sounds by attempting to match them—a process called *analysis-by-synthesis*. An extreme form of this theory would be that we perceive speech by silently moving our own voice box and tongue in response to the physical stimulus of sound waves, and we identify the sounds by noting the disposition of our vocal apparatus. This is not plausible for several reasons (see Neisser, 1967; Lindsay & Norman, 1972). Less specific as a theory but more plausible is that we perceive the speech parts for which we have *speech plans,* speech plans being behavior programs that we know (more or less) how to execute. We will return to this point in a moment.

At its lowest level, the perception of speech probably does not involve the discrimination of physically identifiable phonemes, one after another. What about the perception of the order in which they appear? The vocalized sounds that our ears receive arrive in a very rapid stream, far too many for us to remember as independent sounds after the first second or so of listening. The duration of the individual sounds in spoken English ranges from 80 to 100 milliseconds (Efron, 1967), so that we might receive 10 to 12 sounds per second, or 600 to 7,200 different sounds and pauses in a minute of listening.*

How, then, do we perceive a unit of meaningful speech—a word,

---

* In fact, if even a few brief *unrelated* sounds (specifically; a hiss, a buzz, a tone, and a vowel, each 200 msec. in duration) are presented in some repetitive order, the listener cannot tell the order in which the sounds occur even when he knows in advance what the individual sounds are (Warren *et al.,* 1969, 1970), whereas he has no difficulty in perceiving the order of short sequences of digits spoken at the same rate. As Bregman and his colleagues have shown (1971, 1973, 1976), the inability to perceive the order of unrelated sounds probably rests on a phenomenon called *primary auditory stream segregation:* Sounds that share certain properties (e.g., that are all high tones *vs.* low tones) are perceived in separate groups or substreams when they are presented in an intermixed sequence. (The results—and perhaps the basic process—of this phenomenon are similar to the phenomena of static grouping (Figure 62) and dynamic grouping (Figure 67) that we saw to be important in the visual perception of objects and surfaces.) Listeners cannot compare precisely the time and order of occurrence of sounds in different substreams. Making the transitions between the mixed high and low tones gradual and continuous ("ramped") rather than abrupt, reduced the listeners' tendency to group sounds into high and low substreams and enabled them to perceive the order of the sounds. Like "ramped" sounds, speech sounds are not discrete. Except for Swiss yodelers, who deliberately try to produce two independent melodies from a single voice box, human beings do not use their vocal apparatus to produce abrupt transitions between sounds. The phonemes dissolve into each other (Liberman, 1970), and this enables the listener to group the ordered sounds into a single stream.

This research tells us something about how we encode speech sounds into a single ordered stream, but it still leaves us with the problem of how we encode so many sounds, in view of the rapid rate at which they enter our listening memory.

clause, or phrase—when all we have identified as stimuli, up to this point, is a sequence of speech sounds so rapid that they would soon overflow our ability to store them as independent items?

The problem is a recurrent one in perception. The solution here is to look for higher units to which we can respond—i.e., to entire strings of speech sounds rather than individual 80 to 100 msec. bursts of noise. We have seen, however, that our perceptions of those fragmentary sounds are closer to our speech plans for producing them than to any simple physical descriptions of them. It seems reasonable therefore to extend the concept of analysis-by-synthesis to the perception of entire strings of phonemes—to the perception of entire syllables, words, or even very familiar phrases. This proposal, which is essentially the position taken by Neisser in 1967, is one that I consider to be the heart of an extremely powerful analysis of perception and cognition (and most of the rest of psychology as well). It permits the gathering together of the various separate theoretical strands that we have examined, and seems to apply to many practical as well as theoretical problems. We will remain within its general orientation throughout the remainder of this book. But the reader should be cautioned that this approach, which we will spell out in a moment, appears comprehensive and powerful only because it is still very sketchily worked out in detail and implication. For example, it is not at all clear to what extent the concept of short-term storage, as outlined earlier in this chapter, will remain compatible with the concept of generative plans when both approaches are spelled out in detail. And the reader should bear in mind that counterarguments and opposing evidence (some of which we shall mention) can be raised against all the applications of this theoretical approach in the following pages. Nevertheless, I think that the story is convincing and ties together enough different phenomena and lines of inquiry to use without further apology. Just remember that it is only one theoretical approach.

On speech plans, TOTES and other perceptuomotor sequences. Although the idea of speech plans may sound somewhat obscure, skilled actions are in fact usually *preplanned* sequences of behavior. When a typist rattles off a string of letters or a pianist executes a virtuoso arpeggio, there is not enough time between the finger movements for a nerve impulse to ascend to the brain from the finger that has just executed its movement, and for another impulse to descend and command the muscle of the next finger to move. The skilled pianist and the typist must be executing *programs,* or *plans,* which consist of entire strings of action that are stored under appropriate labels and that can be called up as units (there obviously is a close relationship between the concepts of plans, chunks, and schemas).

Miller, Galanter, and Pribram (1960) have presented a persuasive and extremely influential discussion of the pervasiveness of plans and their nature, to which the reader is urged to refer. The heart of their proposal is the TOTE (which is an acronym for Test–Operate–Test–Exit), the unit of purposive, planned, sequential behavior. With some goal or desired state, the first stage is to test whether the desired state already obtains. If it does not, the second stage is to perform some action; the third is to test whether the desired state now obtains and, if it does, to "exit" — to go on to the next goal in the plan, if there is one.

Three features of this scheme are important at this stage in our study of perception. First, it is *hierarchical* — that is, a part or detail at one level of analysis becomes a unit with its own parts at the next. For example, if the goal is to have a sunlit, cheery room, the action may be to raise the roller blind; if the goal is to raise the blind, the first action may be to pull down sharply on the pull-cord until the ratchet releases; if the goal is to pull down on the cord, the first step is to grasp the pull-cord. . . etc. The nature of perceptual organization is also clearly hierarchical: The face is a unit at one level, the eye at another, the pupil in the eye at a still lower level. What is a part at one level is a whole at another. (A particularly interesting discussion of this is found in Palmer, 1975.)

The second point is that perception, expectation (or "internal representation" or "image" of the desired state), intention, and action are all intertwined in this analysis. The *tests* consist of comparison of the existing state of affairs (roughly, perceptions) with the desired state of affairs — i.e., with a particular representation of the world that is selected by the organism's goals or intentions. What will make this most interesting to us is that *normal perception is itself a sequential perceptuomotor process, directed at identifying some aspect of the environment at some hierarchical level.*

The third point is that there are limits to how far down the analysis can go. In the execution of rapid, habitual actions, the sequences of behavior are preplanned and run off as an indivisible unit. As a lower limit in looking, for example, we cannot subdivide a saccade nor alter it substantially once our visual systems have "decided" to execute it. Hebb's *phase sequences* (Figure 50) provide a plausible way of approaching such sensorimotor organizations.

That is, when drawing on well-practised skills, the person can only test periodically whether his presequenced actions (like speaking, executing saccadic eye movements, typing, and so on) have had their expected and desired effects: even if the TOTE is not a necessary way to analyze behavior in general, it certainly applies to those actions that cannot be continuously monitored and appears to be characteristic of efficient and well-practiced skills (see Pew, 1974; Schmidt, 1975). And speech is certainly a well-practiced skill.

Speech plans are not executed in a vacuum: The speaker must listen to his own utterances (at least from time to time) as his plan unfolds to know how much of the phrase he has completed and whether he is speaking correctly. In fact, if we interfere with how the speaker hears his own voice by means of *delayed audio feedback* (a procedure in which what the speaker says is recorded and fed back to him about 1/2 second later) his speaking deteriorates to an astonishing extent (see also Figure 59*e*). So the speaker himself must have speech plans for saying the words (and even for saying frequently used clauses and phrases) that he is prepared to generate as a single skilled sequence, and to test by listening to them. And with these speech plans he can encode the speech of the person he is listening to, clause by clause and phrase by phrase, rather than phoneme by phoneme.

This gives us a radically different alternative to the filter theory.

An alternative to the filter theory: Attention as plan-matching and schema-testing. Let us now return to the shadowing experiment: When the subject is instructed to shadow one channel rather than another, the individual speech sounds come so rapidly that he can't listen to each one, recognize it, and repeat it. Instead, he must anticipate what will be said next, test those expectations, and if they are correct, formulate new expectations. He can thus keep ahead (*and fill in*), without attempting to listen actively to each phoneme. Since the rate is so rapid that he can do this for only one channel, and since the individual phonemes of the other channel exceed his span of immediate memory, he cannot remember what was said on the other channel.

This alternative to the "filter model" of attention is very similar to one developed by Ulric Neisser as part of his general approach to cognitive psychology (1967). It has several attractive features when applied to problems of perception (Hochberg, 1968, 1970a):

It brings us a view of perception that builds intention and attention right into the heart of the perceptual process: *Perception is the active prediction and sensory testing of expected objects and events,* so that by its very nature perception is selective—by electing to test one possible expectation, it rules out many others. No additional mechanism is needed to explain how we fail to hear what we do not attend to.

It very economically explains a number of facts about the shadowing experiments. For example, if the two message channels are not redundant and internally predictable (for example, if they are both strings of nonsense syllables or tones), the relative advantage of the shadowed channel disappears; whereas the advantage of the shadowed channel will be obtained with the same kinds of stimuli if they are arranged in some relationship that enables the listener to anticipate their occurrence (Treisman and Geffen, 1967; Moray *et al.,* In press). A listener who is asked to report meaningful categories (like plural nouns) fails to detect them when they are presented on the nonattended channel, but hears meaningless intrusions like a buzzer in the rejected as well as in the attended channel (Treisman and Geffen, 1967).

At the beginning of this section, it was said that Sperling's experiments (taken with those of Harris and Haber) contained the essentials of all that followed: presented with an array of numbers too large to recall after one brief presentation, a subject can recall the number that lies in any of the locations he is directed to attend. This effect of selective attention is due neither to an increase in sensory sensitivity in that location nor to a decrease in the sensitivities of the other locations (which would be equivalent to an auditory filter explanation of selective listening) because the effect can be obtained when the location is indicated to the subject *after* the array of numbers has been presented.

In fact, Shiffrin *et al.* (1976) demonstrated that there is no difference between cueing the subject (telling which location to report) before or after the array is presented for as many as forty-nine spatial locations (here the viewer had to detect whether a dot had been present or absent in a given location). Supporting the view that the effects of selective attention are due to limitations on what the subject can encode and remember, and not selection at the sensory level, Shiffrin and his colleagues (Shiffrin, 1975) showed that there is no difference between the condition in which the subject receives information simultaneously on two or more channels (the two ears, different skin locations, different sense modalities, etc.) and so has to "share attention" between them, and a successive condition in which the subject could attend to each stimulus in turn.

With these facts in mind, it is clear that the study of perception must be very much the study of what we can encode and store in short-term memory, and so far we have seen that most of the research to this point has been performed only with dots or alphanumeric symbols. We shall turn to other kinds of stimuli in the next section, but first, an additional note of caution:

We must remember that the case for both the specific explanation of selective listening and the general model of perceiving/attending of which it is a part is still very far from established. But this approach explains in a general way a number of phenomena over a wide range of perceptual problems in shadowing, in reading, and as we will see, in the perception of still pictures and motion pictures. It also connects up very well with theories of thinking and problem-solving, and with social perception and esthetics, as we shall see in the appropriate places.

D. Active Looking at Objects and Pictures

In the course of considering how we combine momentary sensory samples while reading and listening, we have also sketched a cognitive approach to sequential perception that is very different from the classical theories we discussed in the preceding three chapters. Since that cognitive approach was developed in connection with the perception of verbal material, and it is quite conceivable that such noniconic symbols follow their own laws, we must now try to apply this new approach to the perception of objects, events, and iconic symbols (that is, pictures).

Let us now return to the problem of how we combine our successive views.

CHUNKING AND SELECTIVE ATTENTION IN SCENES AND PICTURES

A few glances at a normal scene will tell you enough about where things are for you to feel that you know the layout. But that is because you have a pretty good idea of what you will find there, once you know what kind of scene it is, and even some idea of where you will find what. Thus, you can find a particular object faster when it is in a normal, appropriate scene than when it is in a jumbled or inappropriate one (Biederman, 1972). Because there is so much redundancy in familiar environments, and because we normally are not concerned with the detailed structure of their contents, once we have identified them, our perceptions of scenes and objects seem to be immediate and indivisible. This apparent immediacy and unity is misleading as is revealed when we ask the viewer detailed questions about scenes that contain more independent things than he can encode in immediate memory.

This is beautifully demonstrated in a remarkable study by Chase and Simon (1973) on the perception of chessboard arrangements: To a novice, the spatial layout of chessmen in a game consists of a large number of independent perceptual items: pieces of different color and shape at different places in space. Yet chess masters appear to grasp the situation in an instant: They can reproduce an arrangement of pieces on a chessboard after a brief (five-second) look at it (DeGroot, 1966; Jongman, 1973). How do they do it?

Chase and Simon had players of different abilities copy chessboard arrangements while the way that they glanced at the board that they were copying—the stimulus board—was recorded on videotape. They also had the players reproduce the chess arrangements after a five-second inspection; when the subjects made a long pause between setting up one group of pieces and starting to set up another group, this pause was assumed to mark their transition from one unit, or chunk, in their memory of the stimulus board to another. A comparison of the speed and patterns with which the pieces were set up after each glance back at the stimulus board in the first task (the perceptual task), with the pauses between moves that they made during the memory task, showed the following: (1) Subjects encoded one chunk per glance. (2) The number of chunks, even for a master, was well within the expected limit for memory, 7 ± 2. (3) Encoding speed and chunk size varied with ability: Better players encoded more pieces at a time and did it faster. (4) The master's chunks were not only patterns of adjacent pieces: He sometimes treated as a single unit configurations of chessmen that were related to each other only by the fact that they were converging in attack on some vulnerable piece. (5) *The master's superiority disappeared when arrangements of chessmen on the stimulus board were random,* and not actual chess positions. This is just what we found in the perception of verbal material. The chess master has acquired encoding structures, or schemas, into which the sensory information of each momentary glance can be tested and encoded.

In using layouts of chessmen on a board, we are still using arbitrary arrangements of elements that are more like reading text than perceiving natural scenes, of course. Let us consider what the structures by which we encode more natural scenes and objects might be like.

The structure of objects and scenes. It is relatively easy to imagine how we might test and encode numbers, letters, and words—noniconic symbols—because we have the concept of "speech plans" or other kinds of actions to call on. It is less evident how we might test, encode, and store our successive momentary glances at the world and at iconic symbols (pictures).

To do that, we will have to return to the nature of *images,* a topic we left behind in Chapter 3. As we saw then, the classical definition of perception included images as essential components: Percepts were *sensations plus the set of memory images that they evoked.* It was the images that were thought to be responsible for the integration of successive glances, both by providing a storage function and by providing for anticipation of what the next moment would bring.

For several decades, the very concept of images was discarded from psychology—for several reasons. Some of the reasons were ideological rather than scientific in nature, stemming from the strong but philosophically primitive behaviorism that dominated much of the midcentury. But some of the reasons were good ones: For example, introspection failed to observe any imaginal content in the perception of objects and events, as we saw in Chapter 3, and it failed as well in attempts to study the imaginal basis of thought (which was presumed to be entirely composed of imagery).

But images were not brought into the classical theory *only* because they appeared to be facts of introspective experience, and therefore we cannot discard them simply because we have doubts about their reliability in that regard: They also seemed to be needed to explain many of our abilities that appear to depend on mental structures, and that may still be true.

"Mental structures" are useful theoretical conceptions in psychology for several quite different purposes. In the study of perception, they must guide and encode the individual glances (that is, they locate the features that will identify an object, and provide a test of the feature); and they must store the information thus obtained. We should distinguish at least two kinds of storage: First, the short-term storage that enables us to combine our momentary glances. Second, there is long-term storage.

After the object or event is gone, we are still able to say things about it as though we were making observations of it: How many windows are there in the library tower? Doesn't Aunt Mary look like Cousin William around the eyes? What would this statue (or street) look like from above? Can I find a shortcut between Church Street and Park Row? *Note that it is not the subjective experience of "having an image" that is at issue: It is the ability to make what-*

ever new observations are called for, to retrieve new comparisons from the remembered (but absent) object or scene.[1] (cf. Kosslyn, 1975.)

We mention these more general functions because of the recurrent belief that all of them are served by the same kind of mental structure, namely images, and that those may be thought of as mental reconstructions of physical things: "representations" that the subject can lift down from a shelf in memory and look at.

In some respects, in fact, the ways in which subjects use mental structures do indeed resemble the ways in which people manipulate objects and retrieve information from them in the physical world. Let us first consider a few examples of this to show the kind of power that can be gained by using images (or other sorts of mental structure) as a tool to explain and predict subjects' performances; we will subsequently consider examples of why we must be very cautious in ascribing the properties of physical objects and space to subjects' mental structures.

Mental rotation, mental space and cognitive maps. In a particularly striking series of experiments, Shepard and his colleagues have shown that when subjects have to decide whether two objects are the same (Figure 72A), the time it takes them to do so is proportional to the angle between the two objects: The viewers behave *as though* they mentally rotate one of the objects at a constant rate until both are at the same orientation, before they can decide (Shepard and Metzler, 1971; Cooper and Shepard, 1973). The rate of mental rotation is the same, whether the objects have to be rotated in the two-dimensional plane of the page or into three dimensions. It is tempting to think that the subjects are observing mental objects moving through a medium of mental space. There are other phenomena that seem to have similar implications. For example, stroboscopic movement occurs, as we noted in Chapter 4C, between stationary, successively presented stimuli if the stimuli are presented with the right timing and spatial separation. If the distances separating the two successive stimuli are increased, longer intervals must elapse between them in order for the viewer to obtain convincing perceptions of movement. With the *retinal* separation held constant, but the *apparent* separation varied only by the depth cues (in accordance with the size/distance relationship we discussed in Chapter 4), Attneave and Block (1973) and Corbin (1942) found the timing needed

---

[1] Very close to this last point is *thinking,* which is the manipulation of mental structure: Will this stick reach that banana? There is a long history of work in problem-solving that is usually thought of as "visual thinking"—that is, surrogate visual actions that are not actually carried out.

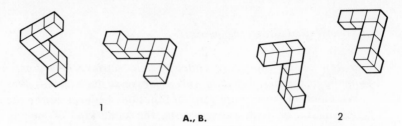

A., B.

1   2

FIGURE 72. *Events in "mental space."*

  A. Mental rotation. The time that it takes subjects to decide whether two shapes like the pair in (*1*) are the same or different increases according to a remarkably regular function of the angle between them, as though the subjects actually rotated one of the shapes in "mental space." This is true equally of rotation in the frontal plane (*1*) or into depth (*2*). Note that the pair of objects shown in *A,2* differs according to the degrees of rotation into depth. Judgment time increases as the angle increases, with the same function for rotation into depth (*2*) and rotation in the flat plane of the picture (*1*). (Reproduced with permission from Shepard and Judd, 1976).

  B. Apparent movement through mental space. There is strong evidence for the existence of sensory mechanisms that respond directly to movement in the retinal image (Chapter 5 B). In contrast, there is also evidence of a more "cognitive" class of apparent movement — *apparent motion between locations in apparent space* instead of displacement in the optic array (Attneave and Block, 1973; Rock and Ebenholtz, 1966; Corbin, 1942). Most recently, Shepard and Judd (1976) showed that the time intervals needed to get the clearest stroboscopic movement between successive views of a rotating object, like those in (*1*) and (*2*), is a function of the angle between them *in represented three-dimensional space* — again, as though the events occur in mental space, not between locations in the retinal image.

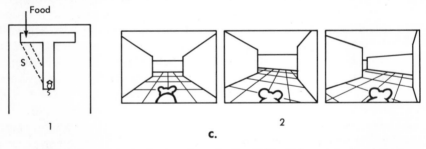

1   2

C.

  C. Mental maps and stimulus vistas. In the 1940s, Tolman introduced the term *cognitive map* to deal with the facts of *place learning.* If an animal has learned that food is on the left in the T-maze shown at (*1*), it has not only learned to turn left at the choice point: it will take a shortcut (indicated by the dotted lines), given the opportunity to do so (Tolman, 1948). It is *as though* the sequence of views (*2*) that are generated by the animal's locomotion, could be viewed from above, like the map at (*1*), so that the shortcut becomes directly evident to the animal. Notice that this is very close to the rotation tasks of (*A*), above. It seems clear that people (if not animals) *can* generate, rotate, and use maps in this fashion: observe yourself the next time you follow a road map, especially if the map is oriented at some angle to the way in which the car is pointed. However, we shall see (Figure 79) that this is by no means an automatic and perfect process.

to get the clearest apparent movement depended on the apparent separation, not on the retinal separation. As with the mental rotation task, there seems to be some sense in which one can say that stroboscopic motion occurs in mental space; in fact, Shepard and Judd (1976) found that the times that would produce the most convincing apparent rotation between pairs of views like those in Figure 72*A,* were a linear function of the *represented* angle between the objects – that is, were proportional to the amount that the objects would have to be rotated into depth (*2*), not their separation in the picture plane and in the retinal image.

Here, as in Helmholtz's *unconscious inference principle,* we have something that we might call *perceptual causation* at work: The way we perceive the objects' spatial arrangements appears to determine how we perceive their movements. Whether or not we are comfortable with this kind of explanation on philosophical grounds (see p. 106n), we cannot use mental space as an explanation in this way unless we know its supposed characteristics; Figure 69 is enough to assure us that perceived space and physical space do not in general have the same attributes, and we cannot simply explain perceptual phenomena by assuming that objects exist and events occur in a "space" in our minds that is just like the space in the physical world. (See Hochberg, 1956; Pylyshyn, 1973, for discussions about the purposes and nature of such definitions.)

The mental rotation task – rotating an object into depth in the mind's eye, in order to find out what it will look like from a different vantage point – is also, of course, very similar to the way you use a map, and maps as mental structures have a long history in psychology.

In the forties, Tolman and his colleagues demonstrated that rats who had learned to run an alley maze (Figure 72*C,1*) could, when given an opportunity, take a shortcut (S in Figure 72*C,1*), as though they had assembled their successive views of the tunnel into a *cognitive map,* which they could view from above to detect the shortcut.

We have seen three kinds of phenomena in which the mental structure the subject uses to perform perceptual tasks seems to have the same properties as the physical world it represents. Let us now see why we cannot take this to be a general principle.

Why mental structures are not, after all, models of the physical world: Mental structure is not physically consistent, nor do remembered objects serve to replace physically present ones. Two points are sufficient to remind us that encoded objects do not act in the same way as physical objects: To the first point, simply recall the "impossible objects" of the last chapter (Figure 69, *A–C*) and the way in which their parts could reverse their apparent orientations independently (*F, G*). To the second point, note that although you can search out and find alternative shapes in reversible pictures (like those in Figure 63) while you are actually looking at them, you cannot do it from memory (Reed and Johnsen, 1975): The pictures have already been encoded, and the sensory tests that would permit you to encode the other "reading" if the picture were still present, cannot be performed in its absence. An image of an object — say, the image of one of those pictures — is not the object itself and cannot take its place (see Pylyshyn, 1973).

If images are not mental replicas of physical objects, what then? Let us see how the concepts of *features* and *schemas,* which we have discussed in connection with the testing and encoding of linguistic material, would be used in the perception of more pictorial stimuli.

Features of objects and scenes. Regardless of whether they agree that the perceptual process involves the use of mental structure, most psychologists now believe that recognition entails some kind of analysis by features. In some cases, what this might mean has been reasonably well spelled out. Features may be quite large and abstract (even, perhaps, the spatial frequencies that we mentioned on p. 111), or they may be relatively concrete and local, like those listed for letter recognition on p. 169, like the vocabulary of object parts in Figure 73*B,* and like the local depth cues in Figure 73*A.* In some cases, our ideas about what features are relevant to the perception of objects or events are still quite vague. For example, in what seems to be an extremely promising line of thought, Kevin Lynch, a city planner, developed what amounts to a set of features to characterize how people think about and navigate in their cities (e.g., "landmarks," "paths," "nodes"; Lynch, 1960). Something like these should be useful both to analyze cognitive maps and, perhaps, to encode objects and forms as well (Hochberg and Gellman, 1977). So far, however, all we really have is Lynch's intriguing terminology.

We shall see that the concept of the perceptual *schema,* and its close relatives, is in a similar state of partial development.

The idea of the schema. Since Head, a physiologist, first used the term to refer to the context that embeds all experience, the term schema has been used in a variety of definitions by many psychologists, including Bartlett, Woodworth, Oldfield, Piaget, Vernon, and many others. (For recent reviews of the term, see Anderson, 1975; Posner, 1973; and Reed, 1973). In use, the concept is not always well defined; what's worse, it comes surrounded by many related concepts that are themselves not well defined. But the concept is necessary. For our purposes, *the schema is the structure by which we encode (and can generate or reconstruct) more information than we can retain from individual items.* Any individual object is recognized first by identifying its schema, and then by noting a small num-

(Text continues on page 192)

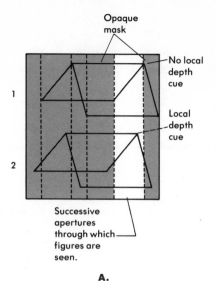

FIGURE 73. *The features of objects and scenes.*

A. If patterns like those in (*1*) and (*2*) are viewed through an aperture that reveals adjacent parts successively, the pattern is recognizable in both cases; but it looks three dimensional only in (*2*) because the "slices" in (*1*) were taken so as to subdivide the *local depth cues* provided by the corners and intersections (Hochberg, 1968). Referring back to Fig. 65A will show some of the forms that can be constructed using these local depth cues. Such features can be discriminated from each other faster than can the individual lines of which they are composed (Pomerantz *et al.* In press), supporting the suggestion that they function as perceptual elements (Hochberg, 1968).

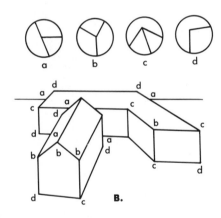

B. If computers are to deal with the real world, they must be programmed (or be able to program themselves) to distinguish one object from another. Features that might provide reasonable bases for such programming are shown at (*1*). At (*a*), our old friend the cue of interposition (Figure 27) indicates that one object occludes another; at (*b*) and at (*c*) are indicators that two or more adjacent surfaces belong to the same object; (*d*) most likely divides two surfaces. At (*2*), a set of objects assembled from these features (adapted from Guzman, 1969).

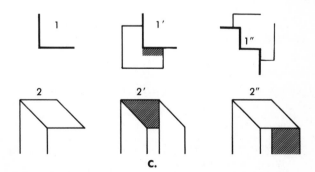

C. Features like those in (*A*) and (*B*) *must,* of course, be ambiguous by the logic of Figure 28. At 1′ and 1″, two different "readings" of (*1*); at 2′ and 2″, two different readings of (*2*).

ber of features that identify the object more specifically and set it off from other examples of the schema to which it belongs (Woodworth, 1938; Attneave, 1957).

There is indeed some research to show that we can use "schemas-plus-corrections" in this way to identify patterns like those in Figure 60*A,B*. Figure 74*A,2* shows a *prototype* (a), or "central schema" from which the distorted versions, or *examples* (*b, c*) were derived. If all the examples derived from a single prototype belong to one category, and if subjects have to learn to identify the category that each new example belongs to, they do this better if they have first been trained with the prototype patterns—presumably because they have then learned the schema which, with a few corrections, will allow them to encode and to identify the examples in each category.

But where does the subject get his schemas from when they are not provided by the kindly experimenter? How would this work in the real world? The following results speak to this point: When subjects were given *only* examples (*b* and *c* in Figure 74*A,2*) to memorize, they were later able to place the prototypes, which they had never seen before, in their proper categories; they did so with the prototypes better than with the examples that they actually had been given to memorize; and in fact they thought that the prototypes that they had never been shown before were patterns from the list (i.e., examples) that they had been given to study (Posner and Keele,

(*Text continues on page 194*)

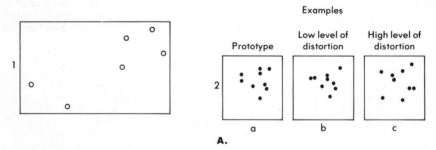

A.

FIGURE 74. *Schemas and prototypes, completion contours and canonical forms.*
    A. At (*I*) is an unfamiliar pattern of six dots that you would probably have trouble remembering. If you turn it upside down, you will probably be able to recognize it as the constellation, the Big Dipper, especially if you connect the dots as we have done in (A1') on the next page. Now, the pattern becomes easy to remember: As the Big Dipper, with a mental note that it is inverted. Using arbitrary patterns like those in Figure 60*A*2, Attneave (1957) showed that subjects could learn them faster if the subjects were first shown the simpler schemas from which the patterns' had been derived. Moreover, subjects who had experience *only* with examples (2*b*, 2*c*) that had been generated by random variations of a *prototype* like (2*a*) thought that they had seen the prototype before when they were shown it (Posner and Keele, 1968, 1970), which demonstrates that they abstracted (or inferred) the prototype from the examples they had seen.

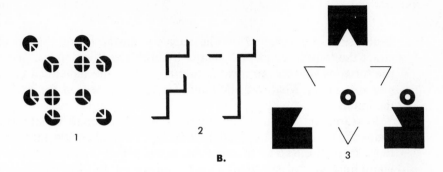

B.

B. Completion phenomena. Something like schemas also appear to operate with more realistic pictorial stimuli and in more perceptual situations: In the completion phenomena in B, we can either see individual patches (like the "stars" in *A1*) or the object that could most probably produce the particular collection of features (*1*), shadows (*2*), or interruptions and discontinuities (*3*) that we have been given. When we *do* perceive the object, it is bounded by clear "subjective contours"—the figure-ground phenomenon, here divested of the brightness contours that normally accompany these schematic objects' edges. In these examples, it is particularly easy to distinguish between the overall form (which must be supplied by the viewer) and the local features and fragments to which it is fitted. See also Figure 73. Figure (*1*) is adapted from Bradley and Petry, 1975; (*2*) is from Coren (1972) and (*3*) is a figure by Kanizsa (1955) modified by Coren (1972).

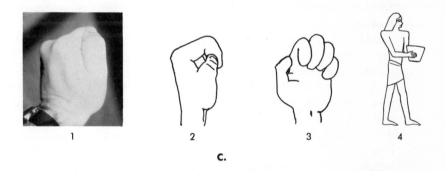

C.

C. Beyond pictorial "fidelity". In Chapters 3 and 4, we saw that one way a picture could represent a scene or object was to provide the eye with the same pattern of light. But pictures can differ greatly from their objects and still "work." In fact, Ryan and Schwartz (1956) showed that cartoons may be perceived faster than photographs of the same objects. Figures *C1* and *C2,* respectively, are a photograph and a line drawing that show, in exaggerated form, the differences in representation that were used in the Ryan and Schwartz study. Figure *C3* is a drawing of the hand which, while clearly incorrect anatomically, provides an even more immediately comprehensible view of the hand's position in *C1* and *C2.* Figure *C4* is, of course, a stylized Egyptian drawing in which feet, arms, shoulders, and profile are each shown from their own most characteristic viewpoint.

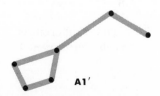

A1'

1968, 1970; Posner, 1975). The subjects appear to be able to abstract the "visual concepts" shared by each set of examples, and to use those as schemas to identify and remember the individual examples (by adding whatever additional features are needed for each of the latter).

Research on schemas and features has been done mostly with simple patterns like those in Figure 74*A* and schematic faces like those in Figure 81*B* in the next chapter (Reed, 1972), and there are many fundamental questions as yet unanswered. But the terminology seems applicable to the perception of more natural objects and pictures, as we shall now show.

Explaining picture perception in terms of feature analysis: An alternative to Gestalt theory. First let us reconsider what a picture (including a caricature) is; then we will consider an alternative to the Gestaltists' explanations of their own examples.

In Figure 27 (Chapter 4) we saw how a *high-fidelity* picture could be constructed to act as a *surrogate* for a real scene or object by producing the same proximal stimulation at the eye. In Figure 61 (Chapter 5), we saw that outline drawings, which do not produce the same stimulation at the eye as the objects they represent, are nevertheless comprehensible without special training. In fact, as we shall see (Figure 74*C*), outline cartoons are perceived faster than photographs of the same objects. Why should a low-fidelity pattern of lines communicate as well or better than a high-fidelity photograph?

As we saw in Chapter 5, the chief elements of the physical world that must be portrayed in a picture are surfaces and their features: edges, corners, bulges (Figure 58). Now, there are many different ways that each of these can be detected in the visual field: by texture-density changes, by motion parallax, by binocular stereopsis, separately and in various combinations. What these different stimulus patterns have in common is that they are all generated by the same underlying visual concept—a prototypical edge, corner, or bulge. We can plausibly regard these underlying visual concepts (or "deep structures") as prototypes by which the viewer can encode the important aspects of the environment; the prototypes can in turn serve as features by which the viewer can test and encode larger schemas such as objects constructed from them, and which they serve to distinguish. What may help in learning the prototype in each case is that most of the examples will also be accompanied by a brightness difference: Under natural lighting conditions, there is almost always a difference in brightness wherever there is an edge or a corner between surfaces. Luminance differences produce contours (Figure 53*D*), and so do outlines drawn in pencil or ink. Therefore, an outline may quite naturally indicate an object's edges and corners; this is especially true in peripheral vision, where the eye's poor acuity may mask other factors (like the texture of paper) which would show that both sides of the outline are in fact in the same plane when looked at with the fovea (Hochberg, 1962, 1972). By itself, of course, the outline is ambiguous; it doesn't reveal which side of itself is nearer (the *figure,* Figure 61), and which side is farther (the background). The viewer can therefore fit quite different schemas to an outline and encode it in two or more quite different ways (Hochberg, 1970, 1974). Indeed, the viewer is not obliged to see a single line, or a very simple line drawing, as a picture: he can see it simply as a mark on paper or as an object, or he can try to see it as a picture — that is, to fit an object to it (see Kennedy, 1974).

Some features, when drawn in outline, however, are less ambiguous than others. As the pictures in Figure 69 show, very considerable inconsistencies in pictures can go unnoticed if they are not detectible within a single glance. Pictures, then, have a "loose-jointedness" that permits the artist to use the most characteristic view of the different parts of an object he is portraying, even though that view violates the rules of optics. It has long been noticed that artists usually do not draw circles and rectangles as foreshortened as they really appear in strict perspective (Pirenne, 1970); and in fact, viewers consider objects drawn in parallel perspective (like those of Figures 63*A,* 69*G*) both more realistic and more accurate than those drawn in correct, converging perspective (Hagen and Elliott, 1976).

A cartoon (in fact, any work of art) often combines the least ambiguous and most characteristic features, even though in reality they could not all be simultaneously visible (Figure 74*C,4*). Drawing an object in its *canonical form* (the form that best displays its characteristic features) is something like Attneave's procedure described in Figure 74*A,* — that is, the canonical form provides a prototype that the viewer can use for encoding and storing objects when he comes across them. In this sense, art may affect our perceptions, a fact demonstrated by the use of diagrams in training manuals and political cartoons in newspapers.

It is possible to assemble a set of features that fits more than one object-schema equally well, as shown in Figures 73*A,C* and 74*B*. In each case, you can deliberately fit one of the alternative objects to the lines on paper and make the other alternative imperceptible — *not because you have filtered it out but because you have encoded the first object.* In Figure 51*C*, we saw that subjects who had been exposed to one or the other alternative of the young girl/old woman double portrait tended to see only that alternative when shown the ambiguous figure (Leeper, 1935); our present interpretation is that this occurs simply because the ambiguous figure contains no features that contradict either of the schemas the viewer might choose (Hochberg, 1970a). Furthermore, Chastain and Burnham (1975) have shown, using a related ambiguous pattern, that forcing the viewer to begin his first view with a part more characteristic of one alternative than the other determines which of the two he perceives.

Note that the examples in Figures 73*A, C,* and Figure 74*B* were originally used by Gestalt psychologists as examples of brain-field organization (compare them with their counterparts in Figures 63 and 64 in Chapter 4). They now demonstrate the assumptions about edges and angles that our perceptual system uses to encode the objects and spatial relationships in the world around us. From this viewpoint, the "laws of organization" are not the expression of underlying brain physiology, as the Gestaltists believed. They are characteristic features of objects, the "visual language" of objects into which the individual glances are encoded.

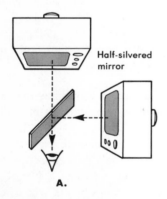

Half-silvered mirror

A.

B.

FIGURE 75. *Selective attention to visual events.* Using the setup shown at (*A*), two different videotape recordings of people playing games are superimposed in the subject's field of view (*B*). When they try to follow one event, subjects cannot describe the other (Neisser and Becklen, 1975), a phenomenon directly analogous to that of *shadowing* discussed on p. 177. The two sets of shapes and movements are *equally present in stimulation,* and fall equally on the eye, but *only the set that the viewer intends to perceive is encoded and stored.*

For example, the "law of good continuation" is simply a version of the depth cue of *interposition* (Figure 27). It follows the Helmholtz-Brunswik rule that we see the most probable object that will fit our sensory information; it is very unlikely that the observer views two objects lying at different distances from him from just the one position that will cause their edges to line up (Hochberg, 1974). In fact, our ability to detect nonalignment is extremely acute. It is the absence of this feature, interposition (Figure 73 *B,C*), that makes reversible pictures reversible. In general, most of the Gestalt laws of organization can be readily interpreted as features that most probably identify objects.

So far, it seems as reasonable to talk about object and scene perception in these terms—encoding, expectation, feature, and schema—as in the language of brain fields and organization. But the real advantage is obtained when we find that the effects of attention, which are essentially unassimilable mysteries in classical theories of organization, are readily explained in these new terms, in much the same way that we dealt with selective attention to verbal material.

Selective attention to alternative events. In the course of discussing ambiguous figures, we have proposed that the effects of attention might arise directly as a result of choosing one or another of two mutually exclusive schemas with which to encode the momentary glance; but those accounts were really quite speculative, and it would be good to have a procedure more directly analogous to the selective listening experiments that we first used (p. 177) to demonstrate attention as encoding. The experiment outlined in Figure 75 provides just that.

Videotape recordings were made of people playing games that could readily be described by observers. Pairs of these recordings were then displayed to subjects *simultaneously,* superimposed one on the other by the procedure shown in Figure 75*A*. When subjects were asked to attend to one action, they were unable to report on the other—a finding directly analogous to the results of the selective listening experiment, but obtained in circumstances that are even more amenable to explanation in terms of an encoding theory of attention, and even more resistant to a filter theory (Neisser and Becklen, 1975).

Of course, this still does not *prove* that the same kind of process is at work when we build up our perceptions of an object or a scene by successive glances, but we shall see evidence to this point when we return to motion-picture cutting, later on.

COMBINING THE SUCCESSIVE GLANCES

We saw at the beginning of this chapter that the combination of successive glances entails three problems: How do we assign the contents of each glance to its correct "address" in the scene or object, instead of merely superimposing it over another glance? What guides the glances that we take? And what motivates and sustains our eye movements? We can now, with different degrees of success and confidence, begin to answer these questions.

Separating and assigning the glances. There really are two questions here: The first, concerns the persistence of vision: Why doesn't our view from the preceding glance intrude into the next one? The second is How do we know where one view fits with respect to the other?

In answer to the first question, there *is,* some intrusion, of course, as when you glance from a bright light to a dim corner of the room, and the afterimage of the light is clearly visible. But there is also the masking effect of the second field of view on the first (see p. 111, Chapter 5), and in addition there may be a specific mechanism to keep the glances separate: When the patterns of dots in Figure 76*A* and *B* are superimposed, a nonsense syllable (*VOH,* in this case) can be detected. If *A* and *B* are presented successively, the percent of correct recognition of such syllables gives us an ingenious measure of the degree to which the glances have or have not been kept separate. If the two halves are shown concurrently for 25 msec., and one half is 5 msec. longer, subjects recognize about 75 percent of the nonsense syllables when the two views end simultaneously; they recognize only about 48 percent when they begin but do not end together. That is, even though (*A*) and (*B*) are on together for the same length of time in both cases, turning one off while the other is still on decreases the detection of (*C*). This suggests that an "off" response helps keep the glances from merely being added to each other. The same procedure could be used to study other possible sources of separation such as the rapid blur that must accompany the saccade itself, brief though it is; Gibson has proposed this as a source of information about the direction of the successive views.[2]

In addition to keeping the glances separated, of course, we must

[2] In a recent experiment by Festinger and Holtzman (1977) a computer–operated display was controlled by the viewer's own eye movements in such a way that the experimenter could modify or eliminate the blur that accompanied any saccade. Although the blur could be shown to have some effects on the apparent directions and amounts of displacement between successive views, the effects were complex, and saccadic blur alone could not account for those appearances.

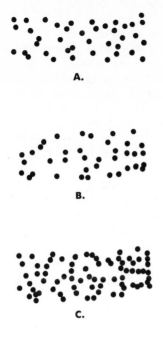

A.

B.

C.

FIGURE 76. *Superimposition of successive views.* "Persistence of vision" cannot explain motion pictures: it can only cause successive views to merge. To measure the determinants and limits of such superimposition, Eriksen and Collins (1967) presented successive views like (*A*) and (*B*) which, individually, contain no recognizable letters. Simultaneously presented, as in (*C*), the two views form a nonsense word, and subjects' recognition of such words when the separate views are presented successively provides a powerful measure of the first view's persistence. There is some evidence from such research that the visual system uses an "off" response, when (*A*) ceases as a signal, to cut short its contribution (Eriksen and Collins, 1967; Cohene and Bechtoldt, 1975); see text.

have some basis for deciding their relative locations. To the degree that the viewer knows in advance where he is moving his eye—what he is bringing to the fovea to test with his detailed vision—the question disappears: He knows where each glance fits because he knows what part of the field of view he wants to learn about. This presupposes that eye movements are in fact made to specifically chosen points in the field of view and are not executed according to some arbitrary search pattern. Let us consider that point.

What guides our glances? Many eye movement studies, dating back to Buswell (1935), have shown that the eye does not move to random places in the scene: The fixations are directed toward those parts of the display (usually a picture) that are most likely to contain informative or important detail.[3]

[3] What defines "informative"? There probably are stimulus features which, when seen in peripheral vision, promise to be informative, and which attract the eye under almost all circumstances. Advertising studies have been directed to discovering them. But all of the studies on which the statement in the text is based (Brooks, 1961; Hochberg and Brooks, 1962; Mackworth and Morandi, 1967; Pollack and Spence, 1968; Antes, 1974) use subjects' judgments as to which parts of the scenes are most informative; however, this is prediction of subjects' responses from subjects' responses, and prediction from stimulus measures would be more useful. Moreover, in all such studies, viewers knew their eye movements were recorded and—perhaps—suspected that they should be fixating important-seeming things. This remains an essential field of inquiry. Recent research on meaningful (Loftus, 1976) and configurational (Brooks and Hochberg, 1976) determinants of fixation have shown that prediction from stimulus measures is in fact possible.

Back in Figure 70, we showed that the five most frequent first fixations included most of the informative parts of the picture. There is
not much left to look at after the first second or so. The time course
of looking behavior reflects that fact.

The course and maintenance of looking. When subjects are
first shown realistic paintings, their initial saccades are large and
their fixations are brief; these are followed by smaller saccades and
longer fixations (Antes, 1974). Viewers seem to make large exploratory movements first, directing their gaze to the most informative
regions of the scene; subsequent glances are made toward details in
the neighborhood of the earlier fixations, and eye movements appear
to decline after viewers have found out as much about the scene as
the task requires.

There are two ways to keep viewers visually interested, to keep
up their active looking. One is to increase the information content of
the picture; we will return to this point when we discuss the perceptual nature of visual art in Chapter 7. The other is to change the
picture as soon as their looking rate starts to decline. This is what is
done in motion pictures—in cinema and TV—and we will discuss
that too in the course of considering those media.

As long as we have to measure viewers' eye movements and infer
their sequence of glances, the study of how successive sensory samples are combined must be both indirect and technical. Let us now
consider the perception of motion pictures, in which the filmmaker
determines directly what the sequence of views will be. In order for
motion pictures to be comprehensible, the filmmaker must correctly
judge the viewers' ability to combine the sequence meaningfully.

THE PERCEPTUAL BASES OF MOTION PICTURES

Motion pictures and television offer a wealth of direct applications
of perceptual principles. The analysis of films does for the perception of successive events what the analysis of pictorial depth
cues, from Da Vinci on, did for the perception of space and distance.

What is a motion picture? The motion picture is a sequence of
still pictures shown at the rate of 24 per second in cinema and 30
per second on television. By taking the pictures at slow rates and
projecting them at normal rates, events that are normally too slow to
perceive, like the growth of plants, are made perceptible; and conversely, taking pictures at very fast rates and projecting them slowly
("slow motion") allows us to see movements that are normally too

rapid to perceive. Filmmakers are free to manipulate time and space in other ways, of course: They can assemble views in sequences quite different from those in which the views occurred; they can move the scene instead of the camera, or vice versa; and, above all, by juxtaposing views in time they can construct scenes and spatial layouts that exist nowhere outside of the mind of the viewer and the filmmaker. It is this feature that makes film central to the point we are pursuing in this Chapter. If small, progressive changes are made from one picture to the next, as in Figure 79C, the perceptual system responds as though smoothly moving stimuli had confronted it. This is usually called *stroboscopic motion* (see Chapter 4-C). It is still sometimes wrongly attributed to "persistence of vision"; it is, of course, nothing of the sort. Persistence of vision could produce only superimposition of successive views as in Figures 70, 75, and 76. There are also more abrupt, discontinuous changes, as when the scene shifts from New York to London with no intervening views. We will consider these two kinds of transition separately.

Continuous transitions. The camera may approach some object in a *dolly shot* (Figure 77A); it may move at an angle to the scene in a *tracking shot* (Figure 77B); it may swivel from side to side in a *pan* (Figure 77D); or, finally, by changing the camera lens' focal length, the image smoothly magnifies or diminishes in a *zoom* (Figure 77C). The dolly is superficially like the zoom, and the tracking shot is superficially like the pan. But there is a very real and important difference between actually moving the camera through the scene (Figure 77A and B) and keeping it in its place while merely changing its view (Figure 77C and D). In the former, what Gibson has called "motion perspective" (Figure 59C) offers the viewer information about the tridimensional spatial layout. Such motion perspective supplies a powerful depth cue that is impossible in still pictures.[4] In the latter, even though they look superficially like the first two, motion perspective is absent, and so is the experience of depth.

Despite these differences, all of these continuous transformations do have one thing in common: They contain visual information about the location of one view with respect to another. And for that reason they do not take us to the heart of the problem of combining successive views, for continuous transformations are not the main-

(Text continues on page 204)

[4] In order to take advantage of this factor, the filmmaker must keep his camera moving as much as possible, and this requires careful physical preparation (such as building a smooth path for the camera to travel on) and planning (such as not running out of space to move in and preparing the viewer to expect and accept such movement).

FIGURE 77. Motion picture transitions *(explanatory caption on page 204.)*

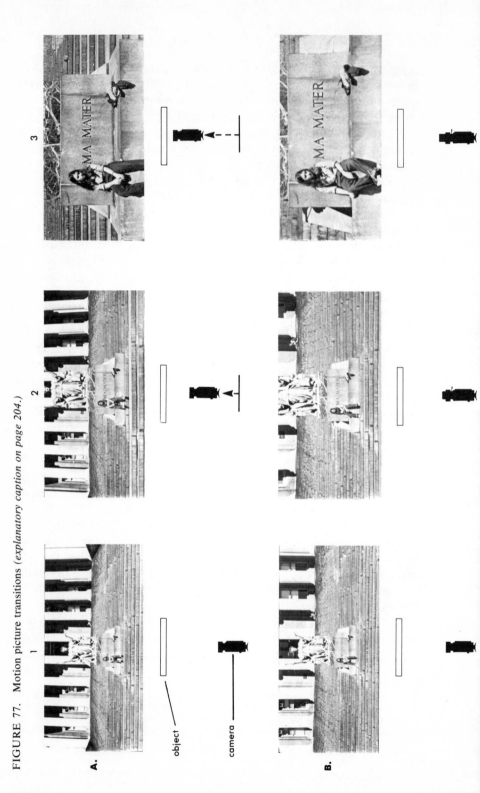

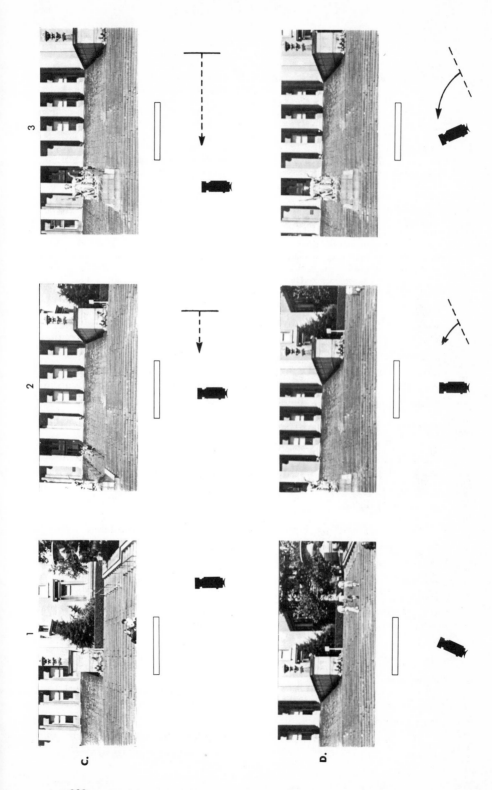

FIGURE 77. *Motion picture transitions.*

Continuous changes. The scene may move on the screen because the camera changes its view in any (or all) of four ways, as the following examples show. In each example, we show the first (1), middle (2), and last (3) shots of a sequence of views.

(A) The camera approaches the object (*dolly shot*). (B) The focal length of the lens is changed (*zoom*). (C) It moves from right to left (*tracking shot*). (D) The camera swivels to the left, but its center of rotation remains fixed in space (*pan*). Notice that (A) and (C) are not the same as (B) and (D) respectively: (A) and (C) contain *motion-perspective information* about the layout of three-dimensional space, whereas (B) and (D) do not. (If anything, they contain motion-perspective information that everything is in one flat plane.)

Cuts. The filmmaker can change abruptly from one view to another; if he eliminates the transitions, then (*1*), (*2*), and (*3*) in (*A*) and (*B*) are *long shots, medium shots,* and *close-ups,* respectively. He can cut from one direction to another within the same scene with more overlap between the views (as between (*1*) and (*2*) or (*2*) and (*3*), in (*C*) and (*D*)), or with less overlap (between (*1*) and (*3*) in (*C*) and (*D*)). Or he can make abrupt transitions between one time and place and another far removed from it. Some cuts, therefore, are similar to the successive views we receive when we make a normal saccadic eye movement, and some are very different. From Hochberg and Brooks (In press (a)).

stay of filmmaking. Filmmakers rarely present a motion picture in which the camera's viewpoint remains uninterrupted for more than twenty seconds: Since Porter assembled *The Great Train Robbery* from fragments (or *shots*) of pre-existing film, motion pictures have relied heavily on combining shots taken from different viewpoints into a single sequence of visual events.

Discontinuous transitions: "cuts". In the case of continuous transition between two views, the movement on the screen as the camera turns from one to the other can provide information about their relative location. Such information is not available in discontinuous transitions, or *cuts. How, then, do we know how these shots fit together?*

When and why are cuts comprehensible? The filmmaker's repertory includes a variety of discontinuous transitions, or *cuts.* In many cuts, the successive views overlap. The filmmaker can, for example, change camera directions abruptly, as between *1* and *2* in Figure 77*C* or 77*D*. Overlapping cuts usually provide information about their relative positions, (for example, in Figure 77*C* it is clear that what is shown in shot 2 lies to the left of what is shown in shot 1) and it is possible that some simulate the successive glances of saccadic eye movements. The filmmaker can also change lenses to move abruptly from a *long shot* [1] in Figure 77*A* or 77*B* to a *medium shot* (2) to a *close-up* (3). It is possible (though implausible) that such cuts simulate rapid approach and retreat, and that is why we understand them.

It is more plausible that they simulate *the expansion or contraction of the field to which the viewer is prepared to attend.* That is, the viewer is given a wide or a narrow view that either enables him to make a general survey of the scene or confines his successive glances to one small region.

But film can also be constructed from cuts that do not overlap at all between successive views (for example, Figure 78*A,1*). How does the viewer comprehend these transitions? Some of them (like "flashbacks") obviously are arbitrary conventions that were devised and established by filmmakers. In general, however, comprehending a

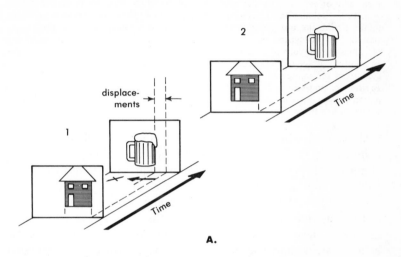

A.

FIGURE 78. *"Bad cuts" and their perceptual implications.*
   A. In a discontinuous cut, apparent movement may occur between quite different objects, as shown by the arrow marked x between the two successive objects in sequence (*1*). This can be disturbing to the viewer (Vorkapich, 1972), and filmmakers often try to avoid the jump by aligning successive views of different objects, as in (*2*).

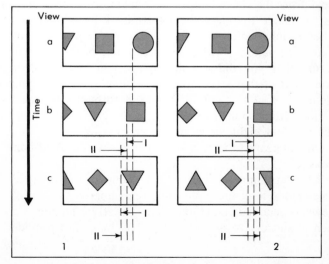

B.   *(Figure 78 continues)*

(Figure 78 continued)

B. The phenomenon in *A,1* may be only an annoyance to the filmmaker, but it is a serious matter to the perception psychologist. At *(B,1)* we have a succession of views in which the apparent movement from one view to the next (shown by the vector marked *I*) is to the left; the objects in the scene are actually being displaced to the right (the arrow marked *II*). At fast rates of presentation (one or more views per second), subjects see only a strong movement to the left; at very slow rates (more than 2 seconds per view) they can perceive the actual direction of displacement (the views in sequence [*B,2*] of course, appear to move to the right over the whole range of speeds) (Hochberg and Brooks, 1974). What makes this phenomenon possible is that *apparent movement does not depend on the detailed shape of the displaced object.* There is a great deal of evidence to this point (Saucer, 1954; Kolers and Pomerantz, 1971; Navon, 1976; Sekuler and Levinson, 1977). This kind of sensory movement seems to be totally unlike the transformations that Gibson and Johansson have proposed as the general basis for visual perception (Chapter 5) and equally unlike the cognitive kind of "apparent movement in apparent space" of Attneave and of Shepard (Figure 72). In addition, it seems very likely that different sensory mechanisms underlie the perception of the movements of more and less detailed stimulus features (Saucer, 1954; Breitmeyer and Ganz, 1976; Petersik and Pantle, 1976). These various kinds of apparent movement will have to be disentangled before we can assess their respective contributions to perception.

rapid sequence of views draws on our normal visual encoding abilities, abilities more usually employed in integrating our successive glimpses of the world; these rapid sequences therefore provide a valuable tool for understanding those abilities. Let us consider a very abstract example of nonoverlapping cutting (Hochberg, 1968).

Imagine that you are being shown the sequence of pictures in Figure 79*A.* These views might be the hands of a clock or the corners of a square jumping around behind the aperture in an irregular sequence. But if you first see the long shot shown at *B,* you perceive the sequence at *A* to be an orderly procession around the corners of a cross. The long shot has enabled you to perceive the direction of motion, and to separate figure from ground (i.e., the surface of the cross from the space behind it). This information is *not* in the stimulus: It must therefore be determined by a mental structure, or schema, into which you fit the successive views, and thus confirm your anticipation of what features come next. And when something occurs that you did *not* anticipate, you incorporate it in its most likely part of that structure: For example, in the sequence shown in Figure 79*A,* it is clear in frames 8 through 10 that the view has jumped from point *h* to point *k* in the cross (at *B*), when you know that the first eight views fit the schema of a cross—that is, the sequence appears to take a short cut across the right-hand arm of the cross.

What has happened is this: The sequence of unrelated right angles, which is too long and rapid to be remembered as a set of independent views, is encoded and stored as the orderly sampling of a single object seen in successive partial views. The long shot provides the viewer

(Text continues on page 208)

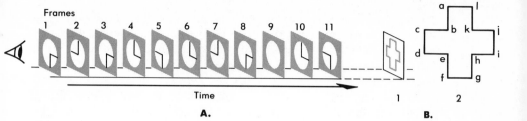

Frames

Time

A.

B.

FIGURE 79. *The schematic maps that integrate our successive glances.*

   A. A sequence of right angles projected one after another on the same screen. Are they the hands of a clock? Or the corners of a square, jumping around erratically behind the circular aperture? The sequence is much too long to remember, like one of the letter strings *A* or *B* on p. 161.

   B. A long shot of a cross (*1*), the corners of which are shown sequentially in (*A*). If the camera zooms in for close-ups of the corners starting with (*a*), as they are labeled at (*2*), and then proceeds with the sequence at (*A*), the sequence now becomes comprehensible, like the letter string *C* on p. 161. The viewer then recognizes that the sequence has taken a shortcut from *h* to *k* on the cross. Compare this to (*1*) in Figure 72*C*. The viewer, in a sense, is following a map given him by the long shot.

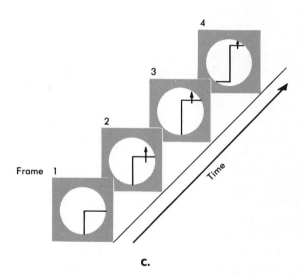

C.

   C. In normal viewing (and often in motion pictures, as well), we are never given a long shot and must therefore build our own maps. Adults do not require long shots if there is sufficient overlap between successive views, or if they have some expectation of the direction of the next view, or if the views are connected by continuous motion (Hochberg, 1968; Murphy, 1973). Children do not do as well, however, and the younger they are the less able they are to recognize overall shapes presented in this fashion (Girgus, 1972, 1973, 1976), for reasons not yet understood.

with a schematic map that allows him to anticipate views (and to incorporate those that he has not anticipated) and store them afterward. The fact that the viewer can "take a shortcut" from *h* to *k* indicates that he is following a map; this is essentially the criterion for *cognitive maps* in learning theory and problem-solving research (see Figure 72*C;* Levine, and Jankovic, 1977).

If this description of what is going on in motion-picture cutting sounds familiar, it should: It is very much the same set of processes that we described in connection with reading and selective listening, except in this case the structures are visual, not verbal.

The task of the filmmaker therefore is to make the viewer pose a visual question, and then answer it for him. In that way, the viewer knows where each view fits, often even before he receives it. The use of long shots, medium shots, and close-ups is not arbitrary, nor are they introduced merely for artistic variety. They are important tools in this visual question-and-answer process. It is of more than artistic interest, therefore, to discover what makes cuts succeed or fail.

Bad cuts, smooth cuts, and good cuts.   Bad cuts occur for two reasons: first, because of certain mechanical factors in sequential vision; second, because the viewer has not actually asked and answered the visual question himself. (See Reisz and Millar, 1968.)

The mechanical sources of incomprehensibility. As we saw in our discussion of stroboscopic motion in Chapter 3, contours that fall near each other in successive views evoke a strong experience of movement or displacement; this is so, *regardless of the overall shapes of the objects* (Orlansky, 1940; Navon, 1976; Kolers *et al*, 1971, 1972, 1976). In cuts, therefore, motion may appear between an object in one view and *an entirely different object* in another view (Figure 78*A,1*) that just happens to fall near the place occupied by the object in the first view. This "accidental" motion may be in any direction at all; if it is opposite the direction intended by the filmmaker, it may take the viewer longer to comprehend the sequence.

To avoid such "jumps" and assure smooth transitions, the main objects in successive views are often made congruent, even though they may be otherwise unrelated. Notice how the two shapes in Figures *78A,2* are presented successively in the same place so that no apparent motion occurs between them. But this may really do more harm than good if it delays the viewer's realization that a change in scene has occurred. Since the apparent motion is momentary and does not long outlast the transition itself, it can be compensated for by allowing each shot to remain on the screen until it is comprehended, before making the next cut. In Figure 78B,1 the objects appear to move to the left (the arrow marked I) at a rapid cutting rate, whereas they appear to be displaced to the right (arrow II) at a slow cutting rate. And the sequence in Figure 78B,2 appears to move to the right (pan to the left) at all cutting rates, because the mechanical apparent motion has been made to serve, rather than oppose, comprehensibility.

In general, the time needed to comprehend a cut depends on how well the viewer has been prepared to expect the sequence, and how rapidly each view can be perceived (that is, how graphically comprehensible it is—see Figure 74). Although the filmmaker's skill is still the basis for good cutting, the principles that we have surveyed in this chapter promise to supplement that skill. As a very rough set of limits, from 1/2 second to 3 seconds per shot are needed to build a comprehensible sequence, depending on the factors we have mentioned.[5]

Why use cuts? One reason, already mentioned, is to present a scene, piecemeal, that does not really exist in any one place, or that is too large to display simultaneously in adequate detail. (This is particularly important in TV because the lack of detail requires many close-ups; TV scenes must be assembled from many more small pictures than motion pictures.)

Cuts also direct the flow of the viewer's visual thought; they can call his attention to something by presenting a close-up of it. This approach to the study of thinking and problem-solving remains unexplored: The two classical Russian film theorists, Eisenstein (1949) and Pudovkin (1958) had conflicting (and only tentative) prescriptions about how films affect the thought processes of the viewers. To Pudovkin, ideas were assembled from the sequential presentation of their elements; to Eisenstein, new ideas emerge from the conflict

---

[5] If the next shot has already been "primed" and is in immediate memory, the limits are purely sensory—say, two frames, or about 80 msec. Otherwise, about 500 msec. are needed for overcoming any accidental motion (e.g., as in Figure 78), plus from 500 to 1,000 msec. to access long-term memory (see the experiment in Figure 71C). It should also take some variable amount of time in order to adjust to any change in the camera's viewpoint (remember the "mental rotation" experiment in Figure 72A, B), and that time is probably decreased if the change in viewpoint matches what the viewer has been led to expect (Cooper, 1976) and if there are clear landmarks that help the viewer identify the successive shots and the relationship between them (Hochberg and Gellman, 1977).

between views already presented. These are not just practical issues for filmmakers, but are of potentially major theoretical importance for psychologists, and have yet to be studied scientifically.

Eisenstein and Pudovkin agreed (as have many of their successors) about the *emotional* effects of cuts. Because each cut creates a momentary arousal in the viewer, the pace and rhythm of cutting is presumably mirrored in the viewer's physiological state; by simulating the pattern of responses that would occur in some emotion, cuts can lead the viewer to experience that emotion. Thus, by filming a scene in an uneven, accelerating rhythm, similar to a heartbeat during fear, the filmmaker can presumably lead the viewer to experience the same emotion. Although we know of no actual study of the efficacy of this procedure, it stands very close to the research of Schachter and his associates, and to *attribution theory,* in social psychology, which we discuss in the next chapter.

A third reason for using cuts is to maintain interest, or *visual momentum* (Hochberg and Brooks, In press (b)): people do not normally take more than a few "interested" glances at a scene or object. If a relatively simple scene remains in view for more than a very few seconds, it "goes dead" visually. (The problem is particularly noticeable in TV close-ups, where "talking heads" are so hard to avoid; the problem is helped somewhat by switching from one camera view to another of the same speaker, as when the anchorman on a news program swivels to face alternate cameras every few seconds.) By cutting to another shot before the viewer becomes fatigued, visual interest is maintained in a way that cannot be done in a single view (Spottiswoode, 1962; Brooks and Hochberg, 1976).

In fact, cutting helps the motion picture achieve a unique economy of presentation: In real life (and even on the stage), many actions are extremely redundant. Just think of how many individual movements and how much time it takes to get an actor out the door and off the stage, and compare it with how simply it can be done in a single cut. In effect, the filmmaker enables the viewer to "skim" a long series of events by presenting only the essential features. This suggests that we have means of encoding visual events — *schematic events* — similar to the schematic objects and speech plans that we have already discussed in this chapter; that events can be encoded is, in fact, the assumption of Heider's approach to interpersonal perception, which we shall discuss in the next chapter.

For now, let us note that the various purposes of cuts make cutting a rich and complex problem for the filmmaker; and an awareness of the perceptual components and of their quantitative bounds can be as helpful to the filmmaker as they are to the perception psychologist.

Summary

When we come to consider how we combine our successive glances, we find that we must place the problems of perception in a broader cognitive setting. The issues that then arise—the nature of encoding, storage, and the schemas in which sensory information is organized—are best explored by studying the acts of reading and listening to speech, and the perception of still pictures and movies. In connection with these activities, we have developed further the idea (introduced at various stages in the previous two chapters) that perception is by its nature purposive and attentive, and that selective attention is merely another name for testing one set of perceptual anticipations about the world or one schematic solution to a sensory problem, rather than some other one.

In the next chapter, we will survey the immensely important but sparsely investigated areas of social perception, applying what we have learned in this chapter to the perception of people, their ways of expressing themselves, and their relationships.

MORE ADVANCED READING

ANDERSON, B. *Cognitive psychology*. New York: Academic Press, 1975. Chapter 2: Primary perception, 25–69; Chapter 3: Secondary perception, 71–108.

GOMBRICH, E. H. HOCHBERG, J., and BLACK, M. *Art, perception and reality*. Baltimore: The Johns Hopkins University Press, 1972. Chapter 2, by J. Hochberg: The representation of things and people, 47–94.

HABER, R. N., and HERSHENSON, M. *The psychology of visual perception*. New York: Holt, Rinehart and Winston, 1973. Section 2: Perception as information processing, 153–273.

KAHNEMAN, D. *Attention and effort*. Englewood Cliffs, N.J.: Prentice-Hall, 1973.

KAUFMAN, L. *Sight and mind*. New York: Oxford University Press, 1974. Chapter 14: Information processing and attention, 526–539.

LINDSAY, P., and NORMAN, D. *Human information processing*. New York: Academic Press, 1972. Chapter 2: Theories of pattern recognition, 115–148; Chapter 9: Transient memories, 329–372.

NEISSER, U. *Cognitive psychology*. New York: Appleton-Century-Crofts, 1967.

NEISSER, U. *Cognition and reality*. San Francisco: W. H. Freeman, 1976.

POSNER, M. *Cognition: An introduction*. Glenview, Illinois: Scott, Foresman, 1973. Chapter 3: Abstraction and iconic concepts, 44–60.

SCHIFFMAN, H. *Sensation and perception*. New York: Wiley, 1976. Chapter 6: Complex Auditory Phenomena 11; Sound as Information.

Social Perception
and Communication

chapter seven

The unifying aim of all the questions considered in the previous chapters has been to discover how we perceive and portray the world of physical objects and events; some incidental consideration has been given to the perception of linguistic events (speech and text) where they would help to answer those questions. These problems are still important, but they can no longer be considered fundamental to all other perceptual questions. It is easier, of course, to experiment with points and lines and colors than with, say, facial expressions during social interactions; and it is easier to describe what we have done in the former experiments because we have excellent standardized instruments to measure size and color, and only recently have any instruments that measure facial expression been developed. It is not necessary, however, to understand the perception of points, colors, and surfaces in order to understand the perception of facial expressions.

One recurring objection to studying most of the phenomena of social perception is that they are so clearly the result of learning. The same argument would have to be made about the perception of physical objects and events, however. In his discussion of space perception, Berkeley maintained that, "As we see distance so we see magnitude. And we see both in the same way that we see shame or anger in the looks of man. . . . Without . . . experience we should no more have taken blushing for a sign of shame than of gladness." This proposition was widely accepted in the eighteenth and nineteenth centuries, but it did not prevent the active investigation of distance and magnitude then, and it should not prevent the study of the perception of shame or anger now. Though their effectiveness may be the result of learning, the stimuli of social perception are themselves used as tools to predict and control human behavior, including learning: Most of the things people covet and work for, in societies above the subsistence level, and most of their recreational activities (i.e., watching TV, movies, plays, going to various social gatherings) involve the perception of other people or being perceived by them. The great problems of human motivation are implicated in this area of study, and the research prospect is all the more exciting in that there is so little real information available. Centuries of preoccupation with the perception of the physical world have left the area of social perception open to exploration.

The main difficulty, however, is deciding what *direction* the study of social perception should take. As long as our studies were centered on discovering the fundamental elements and laws of physical perception, the more complex questions of social perception could be deferred to the future. That rainbow of complexity and promise is now before us, however; and the problem of what we should study has become serious, considering the immense range of perceptual phenomena, none more "fundamental" than any other. Initially, therefore, we should bear in mind the potential of social perception research, and consider the ethical questions of where it might lead and what uses it might be put to.

THE FIELDS OF "SOCIAL PERCEPTION": WHAT THEY ARE

Three general areas of research have usually been included in social perception. Closest to the traditional perceptual problems is the study of how social variables (such as motivation and deprivation) affect the perception of physical properties (such as lightness thresholds and color discrimination). The second area is the perception of people and their physical and social properties; these have been studied for very diverse reasons, and at present can be only imperfectly represented by a short summary. The third, is the perception of social events and relationships. This research is potentially of the greatest importance to psychology and to the social sciences in general.

In addition to these traditional areas, we shall briefly discuss a fourth: visual esthetic interest. We include esthetics in this chapter because the subject matter of so much visual art is social, and because a work of art (including the popular forms, architecture, and the entertainment media), like many social relationships and events, is *perceptually rewarding;* a work of art is ostensibly looked at for its own sake, not for some further goal.

A warning that was set forth in the introduction to this book will bear repetition here: As we progress through the topics of this chapter, their importance for daily life and for the other social sciences increases. And the financial rewards for being able to claim expertise also increases. But the sparseness and unreliability of the data, and the speculative nature of their interpretation, tend to increase as fast or faster.

A. Social Effects on Psychophysical Measures

In discussing sensory psychophysics we noted that the observer's expectations, interest, and motivation might affect his sensory thresholds. Social psychologists first turned to using these "errors" for their own purposes about forty years ago. This was followed by a tremendous surge of interest during the post-World War II drive to bring psychology out of the laboratory and into the area of improving human society. The available perceptual laboratory methods were geared for the study of color and space, and therefore the initial studies of social perception used these methods. Social relevance was introduced to psychophysical measures by means of two related approaches: socially produced distortions of psychophysical correspondence and socially altered recognition thresholds.

DISTORTIONS OF PSYCHOPHYSICAL CORRESPONDENCE

Social variables include all those effects of past experience—interest, reward, punishment, expectation, and so forth—which are most likely different for people from different social backgrounds. Two examples would be familiarity with coins of different denomination or words of varying vulgarity. Social variables have been shown to influence how subjects judge physical dimensions such as the size of coins or the colors of patches of paper that are briefly presented and then have to be judged from memory. These effects, however, are small. Indeed, after more than two decades of research in this area, it is not clear that there are any reliable effects of this sort in *perception* — i.e., in subjects' actual experience of objects they are looking at, as distinct from their willingness to guess one way or another.

Because most of these effects are smaller than the JND of the sensory quality concerned, they may be merely *response biases*. A more interesting issue arises in the various attempts to demonstrate the *Whorfian* hypothesis: that our thought processes and perceptions depend on our language. There is really very little evidence that linguistic structure affects our perceptions of the physical properties of objects that we are actually looking at, however. Colors that are easier to name are in fact remembered better (Brown and Lenneberg, 1954), but there is no evidence that they are actually perceived differently. Moreover, the ways in which preverbal infants categorize colors (as estimated by the way in which they direct their gaze from one color to another, in an extremely interesting procedure employed by Bornstein *et al.,* 1976) are essentially identical to the ways in which adults categorize or group colors. The structure of language does seem to affect how we encode and remember things, especially if those things are words or ambiguous pictures (Chapter 6). But there is little evidence that our perceptions of physical properties are, under normal conditions, significantly affected by linguistic structure: The structure of the physical world is far more ubiquitous and powerful than that of language.

What made this research appear promising was that it used the available psychophysical apparatus and methods for social-psychological research. A second approach that also used simple psychophysical equipment and techniques still retains some popularity and deserves separate consideration.

RECOGNITION THRESHOLDS OF SOCIAL STIMULI:
SUBLIMINAL PERCEPTION AND PERCEPTUAL DEFENSE

If we *impoverish* the conditions of seeing, either by making a slide projection too dim, too brief, or too blurry, we can then gradually improve the visibility and find its threshold by determining how much light or how long an exposure is needed to see it. In general, different social stimuli (say, different kinds of words) have different thresholds. These effects were particularly interesting to clinical psychologists and advertisers because they seemed to support Sigmund Freud's theories about the unconscious determinants of behavior.

Consider a case in which taboo or threatening words (of which there were many more when these experiments were done in the forties and fifties than there are today) are shown to have a higher threshold—i.e., they require a longer exposure to recognize—than nonthreatening words. There seems to be a significant paradox here.

Don't the viewers first have to correctly recognize these words in order to perceive them as a potential threat and only then defend themselves by raising their thresholds? And doesn't this in turn imply the existence of *two* observers within each viewer, one that recognizes taboo words and raises barriers against them and the other—the self we are aware of—that sees only what the unconscious observer permits him to see?

The idea that "preperceptual observation," or "subception" occurs at an unconscious level of the personality achieved public notoriety about a decade ago when commercial proposals were made to use *subliminal* (i.e., below threshold or unnoticeable) advertising. It was assumed that viewers would be particularly vulnerable to subliminal advertising because they could not recognize the source of what was entering their memory and therefore could not examine the content critically. Less diabolically, it was proposed that emotionally charged words and symbols be inserted between the successive frames of movies and TV shows to heighten their dramatic value.

Unfortunately for both the unconscious observer theory and the flamboyant commercial ventures that were to be based on the efficacy of subliminal phenomena, the effects are neither significant nor well corroborated. In fact, it never did make sense to conceive of a "threshold" or barrier separating the conscious from the unconscious parts of the personality. By definition, a perceptual threshold is what an individual can correctly identify 50 percent of the time; we have seen that many factors such as attention, motivation, and familiarity influence the recognition process (see Erdelyi, 1974), not just the "unconscious." In fact, there is very little in perceptual processing that *is* conscious in that it can be meaningfully contrasted with an "unconscious."

Even if these phenomena were significant and reliable, how would they help us understand social perception? Although real-life situations may be confused, ambiguous, and subject to quite different interpretations, they are not generally poorly lit, limited to hundredth-of-a-second glances, nor viewed by observers with advanced, uncorrected myopia. Nevertheless, these are the conditions under which most threshold experiments are conducted. Generalizing from such research to normal social situations is like assuming that one kind of perceptual difficulty is equivalent to any other—that our perceptual system tackles the problem of deciding whether an attractive stranger is merely being coy or genuinely dislikes us in just the same way it identifies a blurry word.

If we want to study the thresholds of social perception, we would first have to identify which stimulus variables—the curve of an eyebrow, the hesitation in a greeting, the degree of nonconformity in dress—determine the social perception in question. And to know what those variables are, we would have to know much more about how we perceive social qualities and personal relationships than we do now.

Compared to simple shapes, sizes, and colors, people and social events are difficult to manipulate experimentally, difficult to measure, and difficult to describe with precision. In recent years, however, techniques have been developed to surmount these problems, and a small body of research now exists.

B. The Perception of People
And Their Physical and Social Properties

THE PROBLEM OF LIKENESS AND RECOGNITION:
PEOPLE, PORTRAITS, AND CARICATURES

Let us sidestep the general question of how we recognize that a given object is human and start with the question of how we recognize a particular person.

The recognizability of faces. It is possible to recognize a great many people after only a very brief look at them and to recognize familiar people from just a small section of their faces (although young children do not do well at this; see Goldstein and Chance, 1964).

How do we recognize faces? Do we see them as whole configurations as in template matching? (See Chapter 6A) This seems very unlikely. Although simple transformations such as inversion and reversal of light and dark as in photographic negative, which do not alter form in any way, impair the recognizability of faces and facial expressions (Hochberg and Galper, 1967; Galper, 1970; Sorce and Campos, 1974; Yin, 1969), we can generally recognize people we have seen only once in a photograph, even when they have changed their facial expressions, which constitutes a considerable change in form (Galper and Hochberg, 1971). As with the general problem of object recognition, we do not yet have a clear understanding of the processes that underlie face recognition. Subjects *can* make a feature-by-feature comparison if the task requires it (Bradshaw *et al.*, 1971), perhaps just as they make letter-by-letter comparisons between words when they have to (see p. 170); but the normal process seems to be one of comparing each face to a *schema* or *prototype* that represents a familiar type and then noting the features that distinguish the individual.[1] Congruent with that description of the process, we can recognize members of a familiar racial group better than those of an unfamiliar one (although ability at this latter skill improves with age and training) (Malpass *et al.*, 1969, 1973).

Encoding and storing faces according to a schema simply means that *we need not notice all of the differences among faces in order to tell them apart*. We can identify Moshe Dayan from his eyepatch alone, but only when we see him in the context of political leaders; in *Treasure Island* the mention of an eyepatch automatically signifies Old Pew. These examples suggest why just the few lines—or an eyepatch—make a caricature of a celebrity that is more instantly recognizable than a sharp, highly resolved photograph. The group of people to which any celebrity belongs is usually very small, and if the right feature is chosen to be caricatured, only one or two celebrities can possibly fit (Hochberg, 1972).

If we can recognize a person even though his facial expression has changed, then at least some of the features that distinguish him from others have remained unchanged. This obvious point also implies that we can recognize a facial expression for what it is—a temporary, changeable characteristic as opposed to a permanent attribute. Let us consider this point in more general terms.

The many things a face must communicate. Each person is a unique individual whom we should be able to recognize by looking at his or her face. But he or she is also a member of many other groups and categories, and these determine much of our behavior toward him or her. Some categories are more or less permanent: race, eye color, sex. Some are temporary states that can be revealed by facial expression, posture, gesture, and voice quality: attentiveness, anger, conciliation, withdrawal. Some categories are semipermanent

[1] Thus, using stylized faces like those in Figure 81*B*, Reed showed that when subjects were given a category-learning task similar to the one using dot patterns (see Figure 74*A*), they learned predominantly by forming schemas of the sets for which they had been given examples (1972).

and change very slowly: age, height, linguistic skills. We are forced to make some perceptual assumptions and hold some expectations about a person, or we cannot interact with him or her. What those assumptions are and what cues we base them on, forms a large part of the uncharted subject matter of social perception.

Some of the cues by which we categorize a person are *extrinsic:* e.g., uniforms that reveal official roles and status, or clothes, grooming, and cosmetics that signal mood or availability for one role or another. But many categories are indicated by the face alone, and students of social perception are confronted with the problem of how the same set of facial features conveys both personal identity and other permanent attributes and also temporary states of mind. What are the consequences of the fact that the face fills both stimulus functions?

THE STABLE ATTRIBUTES: TYPES AND TRAITS, PREJUDICES AND STEREOTYPES

For many human characteristics, there are corresponding *coupled behavioral attributes:* The larger adult is usually stronger than a smaller one; the infant lacks the skills and knowledge of the child. Thus, physical attributes provide cues to behavioral attributes, and therefore one might expect that people have learned to make such couplings in their perceptions just as they have learned to couple their perceptions of size with size cues. Furthermore, just as certain gross behavioral attributes are correlated with physical attributes, might it not also be true that less obvious behavioral attributes like amiability or honesty might be correlated with physical properties such as chubbiness or a steady gaze, respectively? In fact, there have been many attempts in the past to relate character (i.e., behavioral dispositions or *traits*) with recognizable facial or bodily characteristics. People generally believe that they can judge a person's character from his face. Let us consider this subject in more detail, because it contains some important facts in its own right, and also because it raises some serious questions in the study of social perception.

Facial cues to character traits and abilities. There have been a great many unrewarding attempts to link certain characteristics of facial structure and body type with behavioral traits such as honesty and dishonesty, stupidity and intelligence, friendliness and hostility, and so forth (Figure 80*A* and *B*). Most people consider themselves good judges of character, and the use of face-to-face interviews and

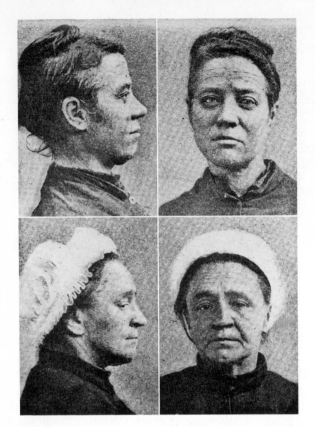

A.

FIGURE 80. Physiognomy, physique, and personality. Can personality and character be read in one's face or figure? Common sense suggests it, and many philosophers have thought so for centuries, and reasonably specific schemes have been presented tying face or body to temperament. At (A), two examples of the typical criminal face, according to Lombroso in 1896; at (B), the elementary body types and their traits of character, as described by Sheldon in 1940. Neither of these theories is at all widely accepted today.

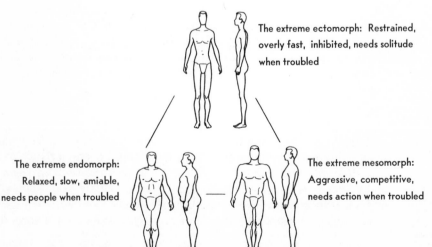

The extreme ectomorph: Restrained, overly fast, inhibited, needs solitude when troubled

The extreme endomorph: Relaxed, slow, amiable, needs people when troubled

The extreme mesomorph: Aggressive, competitive, needs action when troubled

B.

application photographs in personnel departments testifies to the widespread belief that a person's behavior can be predicted from his appearance.

First of all, we must ask how reliable and consistent are subjects' judgments of other peoples' traits. Right or wrong, if people agree and are consistent in their judgment over time, there is a definite social-perceptual phenomenon that can be measured and studied.

The prevalence and reliability of trait attribution. We have reasonably good measures for the cluster of abilities represented by IQ scores. How well can a person's IQ be judged from his face? The experiment summarized in Figure 81*A* revealed that although the judges misjudged the IQs of most of the persons they rated, they did agree with each other about which persons appeared to be intelligent and which did not. In other words, they responded consistently and reliably—if wrongly—to certain physical characteristics; and this would seem to mean that if we can discover what stimulus characteristics they responded to, we can predict and control social perception just as we can now *predict and control many factors in space and object perception.*

Physical appearance does more than affect the ratings that people receive; it also can alter the way in which their remarks are interpreted. When subjects were asked to decide what a person meant by some ambiguous remarks in a typewritten conversation—i.e., was the person asking for a bribe? offering reassurance? or making a neutral, indifferent comment?—it was found that changing the photograph of the person supposedly holding the conversation strongly affected the subjects' interpretations of the written remarks (Hochberg and Galper, 1974).

In addition to photographs, research in trait perception has used highly simplified drawings (Figures 81*B,* 84*C*), photographs combined with character descriptions, and even shopping lists. In this last case, Mason Haire, applying experimental techniques to market research, showed two groups of women identical shopping lists that differed only in that one included instant coffee, and asked them to describe the fictitious housewife who had made out the list. The women interpreted the inclusion of instant coffee as a trait of laziness, wastefulness, and poor planning, a distressing but useful finding to the makers of instant coffee at the time of the survey. While this experiment was more of an attitude survey than a study of perception, the same question—How does varying any given feature of a person affect how his character is judged?—can also be asked about facial features. Thus, Secord and his colleagues found that

(Text continues on page 224)

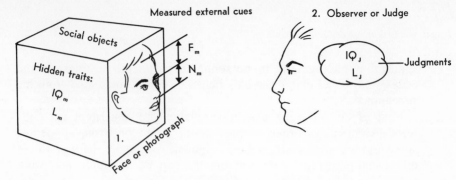

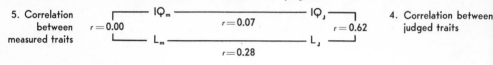

A.

FIGURE 81. Judging intelligence and other traits from pictures. The task of judging traits from faces is similar to that of judging distance from depth cues. (A.) Photographs of 46 soldiers (the social objects) (1) were rated by 25 judges (2) to obtain judgments of intelligence, IQ_j, likeability, L_j, and other traits (Brunswik, 1956). The actual measured IQ's of the soldiers, IQ_m, and their own judgments about each other's likeability, L_m, could then be compared with the observers' judgments of these qualities, and with measurements of each soldier's features, such as his height of forehead, F_m, or length of nose, N_m. The extent to which these measures and judgments agree with one another was measured by the *correlation coefficient, r,* in which a value of 1.00 means perfect agreement and 0.00 means no agreement whatsoever. At (3) we see that measured and judged IQ's did not correspond to any appreciable degree, but that we did obtain a *halo effect:* If observers rated a soldier as intelligent, they also tended to rate him as likeable, and vice versa, as indicated by the correlation between IQ_j and L_j at (4). This correlation is not veridical, since there is no corresponding agreement between IQ_m and L_m (5). The halo effect is a type of response bias that is particularly prevalent in social perception, and acts as a kind of prejudice that someone who is endowed with one good trait will also have other good traits — if there is no other basis for deciding about the latter.

B.

B. Because it is difficult to vary the features (the measured external cues, such as F_m and N_m in [A]) when using persons or their photographs as social objects, schematic drawings have been used instead to discover the contribution made by different spacing of facial features to judgments of intelligence, age, character, and so on (Brunswik and Reiter, 1937), and the effects of varying eye position on qualities such as cuteness (see Figure 84 C). This solution is limited, however, to those facial cues that can be readily manipulated and measured. A less restrictive procedure is illustrated at (C).

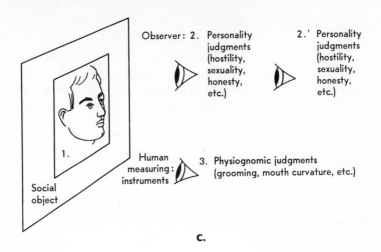

Observer: 2. Personality judgments (hostility, sexuality, honesty, etc.)

2.' Personality judgments (hostility, sexuality, honesty, etc.)

Human measuring: instruments

3. Physiognomic judgments (grooming, mouth curvature, etc.)

1.

Social object

C.

C. Faces differ from one another in ways that are difficult or impossible to measure in inches or millimeters, but we can still try to discover the specific stimulus features that are responsible for different perceptions of personality. Suppose that two different samples of observers, (2) and (2'), show close agreement in their judgments of a set of photographs (or of other social objects), (1); that is, those objects that one group considers to be high in hostility, are also judged high in hostility by the other group, and those judged to be low in honesty by one group, are also so judged by the other; in fact, correlation coefficients do range between 0.36 and 0.98 for a number of judged personality traits. This implies that there are features of the objects to which both groups of judges are responding in the same way, and it is then our task to discover what those features are. (Note how similar this problem is to the search for effective stimuli in form perception, p. 142; it is a procedure that arises whenever we start with a reliable set of perceptual responses first, and then wish to discover the particular stimuli producing them.) To discover the features that are responsible for the perceived traits, still another group of observers (3) may be employed; this time, however, they serve as human measuring instruments, since all we want from them is their judgment of such features as the relative grooming, mouth curvature, complexion, and so forth, for each social object—measures which would be extremely difficult if not impossible to obtain with purely physical instruments. By such procedures, we find that wearing glasses imparts apparent intelligence, dependability, and industriousness; lips that are relaxed, of more than average thickness, or heavily lipsticked, cause a woman to seem highly sexual; and so forth (Secord and Muthard, 1955).

D. The discovery of social attributes.

D.

thin lips are regarded as a sign of conscientiousness, thick lips of sensuality, high foreheads of intelligence, protruding eyes of excitability. By trial and error, caricaturists have discovered the same facts about each of these features. There is good evidence, therefore, that certain character traits are *reliably* attributed to certain facial features—that is, people agree about them. But how *valid* are these attributions?

The dubious validity of trait attributions. How does a facial characteristic become a cue for a personality trait in the first place? As we have seen, one popular hypothesis holds that there really are definite body-personality types and that certain genetically inherited physical characteristics are usually accompanied by specific behavioral characteristics. Our prejudices would then result simply from our having learned to associate a certain physique with a certain personality; and while these prejudices might be wrong in single instances, they would be right more often than not. This is essentially the Helmholtzian explanation of the constancies and illusions that we first met in Chapter 4C.

Plausible as this hypothesis may sound, "physiognomic" theories of personality no longer enjoy wide support (Figure 80*A* and *B*). Significantly, in the one case for which there are objective measures of a trait—IQ scores—the subjects did agree about which faces looked more intelligent, but their judgments did not agree with the objective measures—i.e., their judgments were reliable, but invalid.[2]

But people do judge others according to physical appearance and make assumptions about their traits. There must be some basis for these assumptions, and to discover what it is, we must consider some of the other social functions of the human face.

STATE, ATTRIBUTION, AND STANCE:
THE ELEMENTS OF INTERPERSONAL COMMUNICATION

The face, voice, and body posture are signals about an individual's temporary state, and it is therefore just as important to recognize the same expression on different faces as it is to recognize different expressions on the same face. What are these expressions, and what is there to express?

The two general classes of expression are the *emotions* (or, in

---

[2] When human beings are the stimulus objects, as they are in such experiments, it is most important to have an *ecological sample* that truly represents the population about which we wish to make generalizations. For example, how valid would the ratings in the experiment in Figure 81*A* be if half the sample of stimulus objects consisted of very intelligent scientists with high foreheads and thick glasses and the other half were idiots specially selected for their low foreheads?

milder forms, *moods*), which inform other people of an individual's internal state of arousal or excitation, and communicative *stances* and *gestures,* which are used more flexibly and are not intended to reflect a state of emotion.

Facial expressions as cues to emotional states. It was Darwin who first systematically studied the way in which emotions are expressed in the face. For social creatures, the evolutionary value of such display is obvious: One member of a group who responds to danger by contorting its facial features in a characteristic way can warn many others who do not see the danger directly. It would clearly be valuable for the survival of a species if the bases for producing and responding to facial warning signals were innate. Now, after decades of controversy, there is reasonably firm evidence that at least some emotional expressions are innate and universal (Ekman *et al.,* 1972; Izard, 1969, 1971). It is true that there are cultural differences in the manner of expressing emotions, but these seem to be due primarily to different degrees of inhibition in emotional display. For example, in one study Japanese subjects showed little or no emotion in public, but *when alone* exhibited the same facial expressions in response to emotion-producing motion pictures as did Americans (Ekman *et al.,* 1972).

It is not certain at this time how many innate emotional expressions there are, or which of them are readily recognized. We are also not sure of the total number of recognizably different expressions of emotion and mood (although one estimate is shown in Figure 82*A*) for two general reasons.

The first is a question of how the stimuli are chosen. Most research has used posed pictures (that is, actors instructed to look "happy" "angry," and so on), and the remainder has used pictures of people in what were chosen to be emotion-producing situations (e.g., Frijda *et al,* 1961). In both cases, the set of expressions is limited by the instructions to the actors or by the choice of the arousing situations, as much as by the expressive abilities of the pictured persons and the perceptual skills of the viewers. This has probably resulted in too low a number of recognizable expressions. As Gombrich pointed out (1956), artists can scarcely put down a scribble on paper without producing *some* expression, and cartoonists have developed a vocabulary of facial expressions by trial and error. Like depth cues, these are not arbitrary conventions invented by the artist; they are discoveries that *this* set of squiggles will have *that* effect on the artist—and therefore on other viewers as well (Figure 81*D*). The trial-and-error procedure has an advantage in that it is less confined by the preconceptions of the experimenter.

(Text continues on page 227)

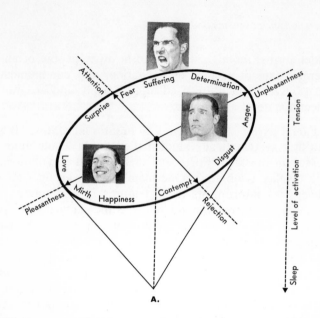

A.

FIGURE 82. Facial expressions of feelings and intentions. Since Leonardo da Vinci, various rules for conveying emotions by different facial contortions have been proposed (in unpleasant moods, the mouth turns downward, while in pleasant ones, it turns upward, and so forth). Although judges may not agree on the precise name to be given to any posed or unposed photograph of an emotional expression, they can place such photographs with considerable reliability on a three-dimensional scale (A), which runs from attention to rejection, pleasantness to unpleasantness, and sleep to tension (Schlosberg 1952). It appears, therefore, that any static emotional expression may be described completely in terms of its share of each of these three qualities, much as any patch of color can be described in terms of its hue, saturation, and brightness.

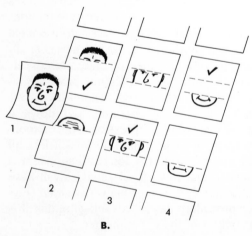

B. A procedure for measuring facial expressions of emotion. Models were photographed while they moved their facial muscles in each of the three areas of the face that can move independently. To specify the emotion displayed by any face that one is interested in measuring (1), each of the three areas is compared to the corresponding area in the *Facial Atlas* (2,3,4), described by Ekman and Friesen, 1975.

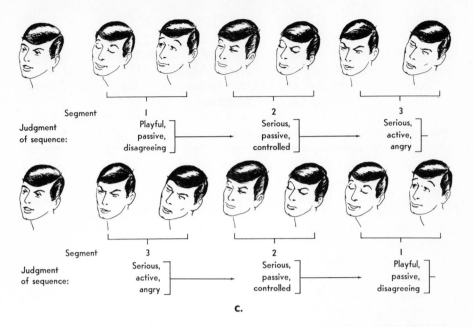

Segment	1	2	3
Judgment of sequence:	Playful, passive, disagreeing	Serious, passive, controlled	Serious, active, angry

Segment	3	2	1
Judgment of sequence:	Serious, active, angry	Serious, passive, controlled	Playful, passive, disagreeing

C.

C. In the social intercourse of real life, in the social communication of the stage and screen, and in the animated cartoon that cuts across all cultures to capture the interest of sophisticate and savage alike, we are confronted by continually changing expressions, not by static photographs. In order to analyze this flow of social communication, we shall need some appropriate unit of analysis. A bare start in this direction has been made by showing judges motion pictures of conversations, and allowing them to stop the action each time the actor's face changes from expressing one intention or feeling to another. That judges showed a very great deal of agreement at this task is promising with respect to the existence of such units. When drawings of the middle and end frames of each of these expressive segments were extracted from the movie (such as 1, 2, and 3, above) and combined into sequences in different orders, the social qualities of each segment remained the same regardless of the sequence in which it was embedded, which is promising with respect to the stability of these units. It still remains to be determined whether the three dimensions shown in (A) are as sufficient to describe the flow of expression as they are for static photographs.

A promising approach to the problems of generating expressions and measuring them is the Facial Affect Scoring Technique (FAST) developed by Ekman and his colleagues. Actors are photographed as they systematically use all of their facial muscles; their faces are divided into three areas; and those areas are compiled in an atlas. By combining these areas in different ways in composite pictures, one can generate all possible expressions (and some impossible ones); by comparing any person's face area by area to the relevant sections of the atlas, one can specify its expression (Figure 82B).

The second reason that we can't be sure how many different emotional expressions can be perceived is that the *perception* of expression—as distinguished from the tendency to *produce* expression—is very clearly dependent on cultural experience. Members of a culture that is schooled to avoid emotional expression are not only less able to interpret the expressions of members of other cultures, they are not very good at recognizing the expressions of members of their own culture (Argyle, 1975). The fact is, of course, that we can conceal our feelings by maintaining a "poker face"; by "acting" we can communicate feelings we do not really have; and in those cultures and subcultures that use them some emotional expressions serve merely as a base on which much more elaborate signal systems are built. This is not a uniquely human trait: apes and monkeys accompany their moods and actions by a continuous stream of changing expressions; each species has about thirteen expressions that are discernible to a human observer (Goodall, 1968).

Before we consider the use of expression for communication, we should consider what emotional expressions express.

The perception of one's own state.   Normally, we think of our emotions as direct experiences of our own internal state, not as signals to others. We are certain that we know our own feelings, moods, and intentions simply because they are our own. But this is the same introspective assumption that we have been repeatedly forced to discard throughout this book, and a good case can be made that we should discard it here as well.

William James argued (in 1890) that emotions are perceptual inferences that we make, based on the bodily signals we discern in ourselves and on the external situations we find ourselves in:

> We see the bear.
>> We perceive that we are running.
>> And that our heart is pounding.
>>> And, taking these all together, we perceive that we are afraid.

If this sounds far-fetched, ask yourself what else "feeling afraid" might mean. Consider, too, the influential approach in social psychology called *attribution theory,* and particularly the pioneering work by Schachter and his colleagues on the individual's perception of his or her own states.

There are two classic experiments that illustrate the proposal (which has essentially become the heart of attribution theory) that we perceive our own states and feelings in much the same way that we perceive those of others — i.e., by trying to account for our bodily symptoms in terms of what we can perceive about the situation in which they are occurring. In the first experiment, Schachter and Singer (1962) administered epinephrine to four groups of subjects (epinephrine is a drug that induces symptoms of many strong emotions, like a pounding heart and flushed face). Subjects in all four groups were told that they had been injected with a vitamin compound: two groups (the *informed* groups) were told about what side-effects they could expect, and two groups were told that there would be no side effects (the *uninformed* groups). After the injection, each subject was left in a waiting room that also contained either a manic, exhilarated person (who was happily flying paper airplanes and playing basketball with crumpled paper and a wastebasket: the *euphoric condition*); or contained an angry young man (whose rage increased until he finally tore up a questionnaire that both he and the subject had been asked to fill out, and stormed out of the room: the *angry condition*). The results: Whether in the euphoric or angry condition, the *informed* subjects remained calm and unaffected by their partners; in the euphoric condition, the *uninformed* subjects became euphoric, whereas in the angry condition, the uninformed subjects tended to display rage. One explanation for these results is that the informed subjects, attributing their bodily symptoms to the injection that they had received, tended to ignore them, whereas the uninformed subjects interpreted their symptoms as signs of emotions, labeled those emotions in accordance with the situation, and then proceeded to further actions appropriate to those emotional labels. This is about as close to William James's frightening bear as we can hope to come in the laboratory.

In the second experiment, Valins (1966) showed pinup pictures of females to male subjects, who heard what they were told were their own amplified heartbeats, while the pictures were being presented. The rate of the heartbeats (which were really not their own, but were independently produced by the experimenter's apparatus) was changed while some of the pinup pictures were shown. On subsequent questioning, subjects reported those pinups to be more attractive than the others. Why? Presumably because the subjects took what they assumed to be the change in their own heartbeat into account when judging their response to the pictures.

These experiments are complex and subject to alternative interpretations. But they make a familiar point: *Helmholtz's rule* can be applied to the perception of our own states and feelings — what we perceive is the answer to the perceptual question, "What event (or thing) is most likely to account for this set of sensory inputs?" (Cf. pp. 82, 131, 155.) You know the food is tempting if your mouth waters and there is nothing else to account for that event (such as the sight of a lemon); to say "I like it (or her or him)" is a self-observation, a summarizing of one's own symptoms and of their probable basis.

But remember also that, although Helmholtz's rule is comforting as a qualitative principle and can be made to fit a very wide variety of facts, it is impossible to predict from it unless we know a great deal about what *is* likely or probable, and unless we also know the size of the unit to which the rule applies. Otherwise, it can lead to mistaken expectations (Chapter 5D). The same problems confront attribution theory, of course, and the difficulties of measuring the likelihood of events in the social environment are, at the very least, as great as those of measuring the ecological frequencies of the physical environment—itself a formidable task (Chapter 4D).

What the person displaying a genuine emotional expression normally experiences, then, is probably a set of bodily symptoms (including the contortion of his facial muscles—a symptom that was missing from the effects produced by epinephrine in the experiment discussed above) and the context that gives them their specific meaning. The facial expression is also a symptom to those who view him, because it is more noticeable to them, of course, than are his pounding heart and trembling knees, and it can be a warning as well.

But a person may voluntarily display an emotional expression (or something more-or-less like one) either to mislead the viewer into believing it to be a genuine symptom, or *as a communicative act, with no pretense that it is an unintentional grimace.* The message is that he finds his present situation to be one that might well produce the genuine emotion. This kind of expression is really a communicative facial *gesture,* an aspect of perception and behavior that is probably much more important to humans than the emotional expressions in which the communicative gestures may originate. We will consider these gestures next, after we discuss the perception of social relationships and events that provide their context and purpose.

C. The Purposes of Communicative Facial Gestures: The Perception of Social Events and Relationships

ENCODING SOCIAL RELATIONSHIPS AND EVENTS

Emotional expressions may help communicate the danger, humor, or surprise in a situation, but they are at best fragmentary, extreme, and relatively uninformative about actual details. Social situations are not perceived merely as strings of emotional situations: Just as we have schemas into which we can organize simple physical sequences and movements (Chapter 6C), we also seem to have ways of summarizing and encoding much more lengthy and complex social events. A remarkable demonstration of this is represented in Figure 83*A*. Heider and Simmel constructed an animated cartoon of geo-

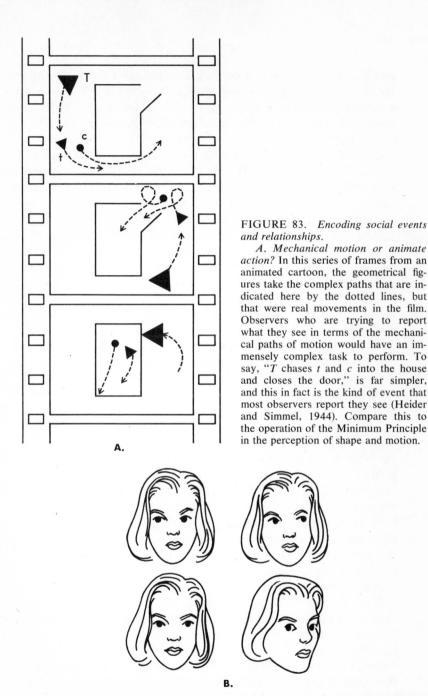

FIGURE 83. *Encoding social events and relationships.*

A. Mechanical motion or animate action? In this series of frames from an animated cartoon, the geometrical figures take the complex paths that are indicated here by the dotted lines, but that were real movements in the film. Observers who are trying to report what they see in terms of the mechanical paths of motion would have an immensely complex task to perform. To say, "T chases t and c into the house and closes the door," is far simpler, and this in fact is the kind of event that most observers report they see (Heider and Simmel, 1944). Compare this to the operation of the Minimum Principle in the perception of shape and motion.

A.

B.

B. Is she looking at me? There is a reciprocal relationship between where the eye must be in its socket, and the direction in which the head is turned, in order that the other person's gaze remains fixed on you. We are remarkably precise in the degree to which we detect that someone is not looking at us; the degree of visual acuity involves detection of differences of about one minute of visual angle, which is about the precision we expect to obtain with such apparently simpler tasks as reading the letters on a chart (Gibson and Pick, 1963).

metrical figures moving about in a succession of different paths. The
film lasted a few minutes and provided too many different paths for
a viewer to encode and remember as a series of geometrical movements; but the movements were simple to perceive as a related series of purposive actions and to remember as a story. In general, no
one could remember the set of movements, but everyone could summarize the relatively simple story. Notice that this is similar to the
way we use schemas to encode the overabundance of stimulus information in reading, in perceiving objects and layouts, and in perceiving sequential views of physical objects and events.

And this, in fact, is how Heider viewed social perception. The abstract schemas by which we encode social events provide the context within which social perception and consequently, social interactions proceed and should be studied. Following Heider and his
students, social psychologists have begun to study what is often
called "naive psychology"—the social assumptions that underlie our
dealings with each other. Naive psychology has converged with attribution theory in its attempt to discover the basic principles of social cause and effect: For example, what do we normally accept as a
satisfactory explanation (or reason, purpose) for someone's actions
or behavior? And if we decide that there is an "internal" (personal)
instead of an "external" (environmental) reason for their behavior do
we then perceive the behavior as, say, a successful achievement
rather than a lucky act, or as a generous rather than self-serving
one? Several recent books, written from different theoretical viewpoints, deal with these questions and some of their research consequences: Bem, 1972; de Charms, 1968; Deci, 1974; Kelley, 1971;
Weiner *et al.*, 1971.

It would strain the definition of perception to discuss these questions here. But the findings could provide a framework for studying
the more directly perceptual elements of social interactions, which—
at least in our culture—depend heavily on one's ability to make reasonably correct inferences about another's purposes and intentions.

Even in formal discourse, like public speaking, individual utter-
ance is often quite ambiguous and depends on the context for its
meaning. Normal conversation is much more syntactically incomplete and ambiguous when heard in isolation, and in order to
comprehend the meaning, the listener must know something about
the speaker's intention (Searle, 1969; Grice, 1968). The speaker
usually conveys his or her intention by nonverbal means—by tone
and intonation (the *prosodic*) factors and by facial and bodily gestures. The comprehension of rapid, incomplete speech (like rapid
reading) places very high demands on a listener's anticipations and

expectations, and a speaker's stances help reduce the listener's uncertainty about the verbal message and about the speaker's intentions (e.g., is he being truculent, attentive, amiable, deferential?)

This should be true not only in anticipating speakers' intentions but in steering the complex, finely tuned "interaction rituals" by which social contacts are conducted and maintained (Goffman, 1967). According to this kind of anthropological-sociological analysis, much of the content of face-to-face interaction, if stated unambiguously, would be too threatening to the participants' pride and would spoil the pleasure they derive from the interaction: most conversations are full of unexpressed questions regarding relative status, what claims one can or cannot make on the other, whether one agrees with another merely to solicit reciprocal agreement, and so on. Facial gestures (and nonverbal communication in general) are useful in communicating this kind of information just because they can be passed over without comment or can even be denied.

There has been some serious study of these *paralinguistic* gestures (also called NVC—nonverbal communication—and *body language*) in recent years, and also a great deal of popular exploitation.

PARALINGUISTIC FACIAL GESTURES, STANCES, AND THEIR PERCEPTUAL EFFECTS

The facial gestures that accompany or replace verbal communication are included in the field of paralinguistics and have been studied and analyzed in much the same way that classical linguists have analyzed phonemes. Researchers have identified many elementary gestures by analyzing motion pictures frame by frame; for example Birdwhistell (1970) has identified some sixty elementary movements, or "kinemes" (such as the single raised eyebrow, the sidewise look, flaring nostrils, pursed lips, protruding chin), but we do not know what their perceptual effects are.

The analysis of speaker and listener behavior during a conversation or a speech shows that *both* speaker and listener accompany the verbal message with facial gestures that are closely synchronized to the utterances; these gestures function to prevent interruptions at inopportune times and to reinforce the speaker (Kendon, 1970). Speakers look toward their listeners at grammatical pauses and at the end of utterances; and listeners respond continuously to what is being said by showing understanding, puzzlement, pleasure, surprise, and so on with their facial expressions (mainly with the eyebrows and mouth). Without these visual displays—as in telephone conversations—interaction is more difficult (Argyle and Cook, 1975). Syn-

chronization to utterances also involves signals that are more difficult to measure than nods, "uh-huhs," and glances. The slight frown
or the "bright" gaze, for example, signal respectively the listener's
reluctance or eagerness to accept the line that the speaker is pursuing. Examination of film records shows that such gestures are displayed by listeners, but what use does the recipient make of them?

The effects of facial gestures. We have seen that *eye contact—*
looking the other person in the eye—is a gesture that is closely synchronized with speech. It also appears to be related to such behavior
as lying, liking, dominance and intimacy. Eye contact declines with
lying (Exline, 1970; Mehrabian, 1972); reflects the degree of liking
or affection (Exline and Winters, 1966; Rubin, 1970); is higher on
the part of a lower status person (Exline and Long, 1971), although
the more dominant person is the last to break a mutual gaze (Strongman and Champness, 1968); and decreases as the intimacy of the
topic of conversation increases (Exline, 1965). How is this aspect of
social situations detected and interpreted? First, we know that we
are remarkably precise in the degree to which we can detect that
someone is *not* looking at us (see Figure 83*B*). Second, subjects consider themselves to be preferred when they are looked at more by
the person who is interviewing them (Mehrabian, 1972), and consider the other person more likeable (up to a point) and more dominant the more he or she looks at them (Argyle *et al.,* 1974).

Eye contact is a facial gesture that is relatively easy to record and
measure objectively. However, other gestures that modify and even
reverse the spoken meaning (such as *ironic* expressions), and that
convey the interactants' stances, are extremely difficult to treat scientifically. Argyle (1975), summarizing a number of studies, finds
that the major dimensions along which attitudes are conveyed are
dominant vs. submissive, and *hostile vs. friendly;* he concludes that,
in a conflict between attitudes conveyed by verbal and nonverbal
means (mostly by voice qualities in the studies that he reviews), it is
the nonverbal attitudes that are communicated most effectively. This
sounds reasonable, and we would expect most people to have
learned to use such cues if they are as available as they seem to be.
However, there is a widespread belief that many people need "sensitivity training" to notice these signals of social interaction; but we
have no very good evidence that such training helps in reading others' expressions (Smith, 1975). More research, using objective measures of facial expression, is badly needed here. Perhaps the FAST
will prove to be a useful tool; see Ekman and Friesen, 1975.

The perception and communication of predispositions and personality. Let us return to the question of why we attribute character traits to people's faces and pictures. To some degree, we arrive at our judgments through subtle indications of social class (such as details of grooming and habitual facial expression) or signs of racial and ethnic affiliation; these carry their own sets of expectations. To some degee our judgments may be based on one person's resemblance to someone else (for example, to some actor who is always cast in some characteristic role). And to some degree they may be based on the habitual, faint expression by which the person chooses to display his characteristic attitude—very few of us hold our faces expressionless, as a general stance. But there is another possibility that bears investigation: Since we are likely to identify the natural or habitual arrangement of a person's features more with one emotion or mood than with another, we may be responding to a purely accidental expression when we perceive character traits; or we may be responding to the incipient emotion, desire, or intention each face seems to signal, however faintly.[2]

For example, flaring nostrils and a downturned mouth may be perceived as a sneer, even though they may be only the natural conformation of the person's face. The rounded cheeks of a chubby face will generally produce lines that suggest a readiness to smile; and the thin lips one is born with may give one's face an habitual expression of decisiveness.

In part, then, the traits and personality characteristics we attribute to people's faces with no basis in fact may be due to expectations arising from accidental expressions. (Compare this explanation with those offered for the Mueller-Lyer, Stroop, and figure-ground phenomena, pp. 80, 177 and 195, respectively.)

These are relatively bland social qualities, however. We look at people because they are interesting or because it is pleasurable to do so, and not just to learn whether they are honest, intelligent, or ready to agree with us. Attractiveness, repulsiveness, and other powerful physiognomic qualities are immediately experienced properties, not mere judgments about character or personality in any simple sense.

[2] We may well learn about facial expressions almost as early as we learn to perceive any other spatial form, and a perfectly neutral curve or line may have some perceived social meaning by virtue of its relationship to some class of expressions. A number of experiments have demonstrated that meaningless curves and jagged lines do in fact communicate "physiognomic" properties (for instance, warmth, happiness, friendliness vs. coldness, sadness, hostility), but we do not know whether they do so in ways that fit this hypothesis.

D. Attractiveness and the Esthetic Qualities
of People and Things

You may look at a picture for information: exactly how should you hold a tennis racket? how decisive or humane does the candidate look? But pictures and other works of art are also looked at *for their own sake*—that is, for their *esthetic quality*. People and commercial products may also have esthetic value as their single most important characteristic.

We may define esthetic value as *disinterested* evaluations—that is, preferences that are not based on the object's usefulness or service for some other purpose. But this is indistinguishable from what attribution theorists call an *endogenous* attribution (Kruglanski, 1975). If I ask why you bought a dog, and your answer is that you want him to frighten burglars, you have given an exogenous reason; if you tell me that he is irresistibly cute, you have given an endogenous reason—merely having him around is an end in itself. So is looking at art, going to the movies, playing backgammon. This does not mean that there really are no deeper bases for endogenous preferences or actions; it means only that one does not have to cite other reasons for liking or enjoying something. To say that esthetic value is an endogenous attribute is a statement about the kinds of explanation people give and accept for their actions and preferences. Before we need worry about a particular definition or theory of esthetics, we must first determine what areas of preference most people agree on. Having found the areas of agreement, we must group together those preferences that have the same bases. If we try to include in one explanation two totally unrelated phenomena, our formulation may really fit neither of them.

Beauty and ugliness may be only skin deep, but they affect our lives in untold ways. Marriage and careers depend heavily on physical attractiveness.[3] Multibillion-dollar cosmetic and fashion industries exist to promote it, and equally large advertising and mass media industries are designed to distribute the sight of skillfully packaged people and products. The automobile industry emphasizes

---

[3] The advantages of being attractive are widespread and deep. The transgressions of attractive children are viewed by adults as being less serious (Dion, 1972), attractive females are less likely to be convicted and their punishments are less severe (in simulated jury trials; see Efron, 1974), and they get better grades than their less attractive classmates with the same IQs (Singer, 1964); and attractive people are liked better both by equally attractive people and less attractive ones (Walster *et al.*, 1966). One is more likely to assume that an attractive person will share one's own attitudes (Schoedel *et al.*, 1975), while people who are perceived as sharing one's own attitudes are thereby rendered more attractive Byrne, 1969, 1971; Secord *et al.*, 1964), which makes the preceding finding doubly important.

the visual attractiveness of its product more than speed, power, or gas economy. People find the sight of other people rewarding, in a wide range of circumstances. Children strive for television and comic books; pornography spans several profitable industries; and even apes will work for the reward of seeing other apes. We know very little about these properties as yet.

Subjects usually agree quite well about what is attractive or unattractive, and therefore we may be able to discover the stimulus bases for these immensely important qualities. Of what use is such information? The simple and precise measurement of the pleasingness of one person or object as compared to another has, of course, immediate commercial application in the "packaging and marketing" of people (in entertainment and in politics). These enterprises are run today by intuition alone, but to the extent that imagination or art can in fact produce consistent results, we may hope to succeed equally by scientific analysis and, perhaps, to eventually understand the basic psychological laws. The latter must, in turn, be important to any understanding of human motivation.

We have touched on one possible contributory factor in our discussion of the accidental expressions that can be associated with particular facial features. There may be stronger mechanisms involved to much the same point, however.

DEMAND CHARACTER AND INNATE RELEASING MECHANISMS

Some of the responses that we make to other people may not be learned at all, but may be examples of what are called *innate releasing mechanisms* when they occur in other animal species. In many species of animals there are characteristic markings that identify members of the same species, identify sex and identify age. And not only do those markings act as triggers to release appropriate behaviors; man-made exaggerations of those markings will elicit those behaviors even more strongly than do the natural markings on the real animals (Figure 84A).

Are there similar innate releasing mechanisms in humans which would explain some of the mysteries of trait attribution and attractiveness mentioned above? So far, there have been few direct inquiries to this point. People do agree about the property of "cuteness" in babies (Figure 84C,1), and exaggerations of babyishness in silhouettes are perceived as being more babyish than those with more realistic proportions (Figure 84C,2). This is similar to the action of innate releasing mechanisms in other species. Perhaps we

(Text continues on page 240)

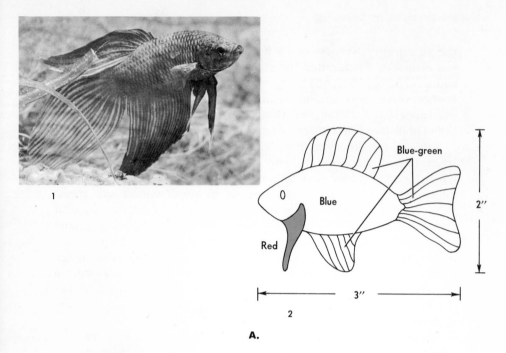

A.

FIGURE 84. *Releasing mechanisms, esthetic qualities, and the attractiveness of social stimuli.*

A. We know that human beings, as well as the lower animals, will do work for food and drink – to gain the necessities of life. Both beast and man will also do work simply to gain the reward of seeing (or hearing, or touching) certain stimuli. The male Siamese fighting fish (*1*), which will fight any male intruding in its territory, can be conditioned to perform some task, such as swimming through a ring, to obtain the reward of seeing the model (*2*) of another male to attack (Thompson, 1963).

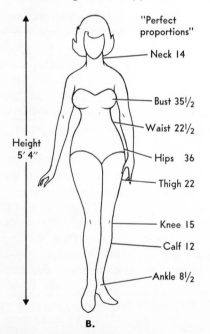

B.

B. With human beings, the list of stimuli that are rewarding to perceive runs from Mozart symphonies to Miss America contests, from Picasso paintings to popular tunes. Except for some arbitrary beauty-contest conventions about "ideal" female dimensions, however, we know less about why certain stimuli are attractive for humans than we do about those for fish.

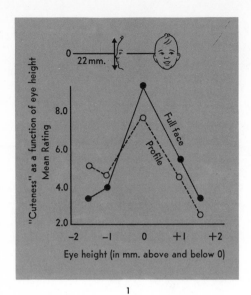

1

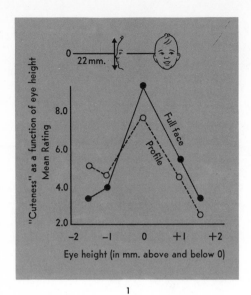

SA, superadult; AD, adult; BB, baby; SB, superbaby; C. control.

2

C. One quality about which we do have a little research, and which might be an innate releasing mechanism for humans (in the way that *A,2* is for male Siamese fighting fish, but in the opposite direction) is "babyishness," or "cuteness". Both males and females agree about the cuteness of simplified pictures of babies (*1*) (Brooks and Hochberg, 1960); exaggerating the ways in which baby silhouette profiles (*BB*) differ from adult profiles (*AD*) results in "superbabies" (*SB–1*): adults judge the exaggerated profiles to be more babyish than the realistic ones, which is much like what happens when we exaggerate the stimuli that are innate releasing mechanisms with animals (Gardner and Wallach, 1965).

(Figure 84 continues)

(Figure 84 continued)

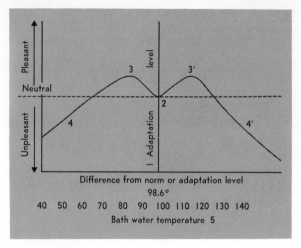

D.

D. There have been many attempts to discover the formulas for esthetic value, to find the laws that will tell us what stimulus pattern will be pleasing or attractive. A very interesting one of recent vintage is the "butterfly curve" shown here, which is intended to apply to various stimuli (McClelland et al., 1953). The vertical line (1) is the adaptation level, or the stimulation we are habituated to (Helson, 1964). According to this curve, a stimulus at adaptation level—say, bath water at body temperature—will be neither pleasing nor unpleasing: It will be neutral (2). As the stimulus departs from the adaptation level slightly—say, by becoming slightly warmer or cooler than 98.6°—it will become pleasant to experience (3, 3′) (Haber, 1958). As the stimulus becomes still more different from the adaptation level, it will become unpleasant and noxious (4, 4′). Although evidence is insufficient to evaluate this theory as yet, think about the cycle of unpopularity, popularity, and neutrality through which popular songs (and other fashion cycles) swing. Many attempts have been made to relate *stimulus complexity* to *esthetic preference* (see Berlyne, 1973; Walker, 1973), and the two explanations may converge if effective complexity changes appropriately with experience (see Figure 51E)—i.e., if with increasing familiarity the viewer or listener learns the principles according to which the work has been produced, anticipates it in larger and larger "chunks," and finally finds it uninterestingly predictable.

have innate "protective responses" that are released by features characteristic of babies; and, of course, certain visual stimuli are sexually arousing (and that may be originally related to the first set of features). We cannot begin to imagine the neural machinery that might underlie the responses to these really complex distal properties. It is therefore difficult to accept the possiblity that we could be prewired to respond to a particular set of forms yet somehow, similar mechanisms do exist in lower animals and probably serve an evolutionary purpose.

On the other hand, what is sexually arousing to the human is also notoriously variable and subject to individual experience and fashion. Within limits, attractiveness probably depends more on grooming, stance, and facial expression than on physiognomic endowment: *Much of fashion is designed to indicate that one is concerned with maintaining the signs of social interest and availability (to the right partner, of course), and one effect of changes in fashion is to permit a person to "drop out of things" by becoming unfashionable.* Attractiveness, therefore, may have more to do with communicating stances than with automatic signals.

Moreover, there are many other ways in which something can be visually interesting, perceptually attractive, and rewarding. While we know scarcely more about them than we do about the possibility of innate releasing mechanisms in humans, we do know somewhat more than you might gather from a course on esthetics, design, or art appreciation.

THE COMPONENTS OF PREFERENCE

As we have seen earlier in research that was incidentally directed to this point (p. 229), "preference" is not an obvious, transparent quality that can be revealed by simple introspection; subjects who rate people or things for their pleasingness, attractiveness or esthetic value must assess their own underlying attitudes in evaluating the objects, on the basis of whatever information they have concerning themselves and how they think they *should* respond to a particular object. Many different sources feed into these indirect evaluations: The function the object is to serve, how other people will regard us when we use the object or are in the person's company, what that object says about our expertise, where the object stands in the set of potential objects from which it was drawn (see Figure 60*B*). We have touched on some additional factors in the caption for Figure 84*D*, but it will be clear to the reader that much rewarding research remains to be done in this area.

E. Perception and Action

The aspects of the perceived world that we discussed in the first six chapters were, in general, preliminary conditions for actions. If you want to get from *here* to *there,* your perception of the intervening space will help you decide what path to take. Occasionally, a much stronger incentive to action arises, as when imminent collision elicits an involuntary wince. Generally, however, the qualities of the physical world do not compel us to act in one way or another. The qualities of social perception, on the other hand, have much more of a *demand character*—that is, they themselves are frequently incentives to action. As we see, so we do. The relationship between perception and behavior is much closer in the case of social qualities.

These hypotheses and scattered patches of research reveal the juncture where the study of perception rejoins the mainstream of psychology and the other social sciences, and promises to become an important tool for understanding and predicting behavior, not merely for analyzing experience.

Bibliography

ANDERSON, B. F. *Cognitive Psychology: The Study of Knowing, Learning, and Thinking.* New York: Academic Press, 1975.

ANDERSON, N. H. Algebraic models in perception. In E. C. Carterette & M. Friedman, eds., *Handbook of Perception, Vol. 2: Psychophysical Judgment and Measurement.* New York: Academic Press, 1974. Pp. 215–291.

ANTES, J. R. The time course of picture viewing. *Journal of Experimental Psychology,* 1974, *103,* 162–170.

ARGYLE, M., and COOK, M. *Gaze and mutual gaze.* London: Cambridge University Press, 1976.

ARGYLE, M. *Bodily Communication.* New York: International Universities Press, 1975.

ARGYLE, M., LEFEBVRE, L., and COOK, M. The meaning of five patterns of gaze. *European Journal of Social Psychology,* 1974, *4,* 125–136.

ARNHEIM, R. *Art and Visual Perception.* Berkeley: University of California Press, 1969.

ARNHEIM, R. *Visual Thinking.* Berkeley: University of California Press, 1964.

ASHER, H. *The Seeing Eye.* London: Duckworth, 1961.

ATTNEAVE, F. Some informational aspects of visual perception. *Psychological Review*, 1954, *61*, 183–193.

ATTNEAVE, F. Transfer of experience with a class-schema to identification-learning of patterns and shapes. *Journal of Experimental Psychology*, 1957, *54*, 81–88.

ATTNEAVE, F. *Applications of Information Theory to Psychology.* New York: Holt, Rinehart, & Winston, 1959.

ATTNEAVE, F., and ARNOULT, M. D. The quantitative study of shape and pattern perception. *Psychological Bulletin*, 1956, *53*, 452–471.

ATTNEAVE, F., and BLOCK, G. Apparent movement in tridimensional space. *Perception and Psychophysics*, 1973, *13*, 301–307.

ATTNEAVE, F., and FROST, R. The discrimination of perceived tridimensional orientation by minimum criteria. *Perception and Psychophysics*, 1969, *6*, 391–396.

BADDELEY, A. D. Immediate memory and the "perception" of letter sequences. *Quarterly Journal of Experimental Psychology*, 1964, *16*, 364–367.

BARLOW, H., BLAKEMORE, C., and PETTIGREW, J. The neural mechanism of binocular depth discrimination. *Journal of Physiology*, 1967, *193*, 327–342.

BECK, J. Apparent spatial position and the perception of lightness. *Journal of Experimental Psychology*, 1965, *69*, 170–179.

BECK, J. *Surface Color Perception.* Ithaca: Cornell University Press, 1972.

BEKESY, G. VON. The variation of phase along the basilar membrane with sinusoidal variation. *Journal of the Acoustical Society of America*, 1947, *19*, 452–460.

BEKESY, G. VON. Neural inhibitory units of eye and skin: Quantitative description of contrast phenomena. *Journal of the Optical Society of America*, 1960, *50*, 1060–1070.

BELLER, H. K. Priming: Effects of advance information on matching. *Journal of Experimental Psychology*, 1971, *87*, 176–182.

BEM, D. J. Self-perception: An alternative interpretation of cognitive dissonance phenomena. *Psychological Review*, 1967, *74*, 188–200.

BEM, D. Self-perception theory. In L. Berkowitz, ed., *Advances in experimental social psychology* (Vol. 6), New York: Academic Press, 1972.

BERLYNE, D. E. *Aesthetics and Psychobiology.* New York: Appleton, 1971.

BERLYNE, D. E. The Vicissitudes of Apopathematic and Thelematoscopic Pneumatology (or The Hydrography of Hedonism.) In D. E. Berlyne and K. B. Madsen, eds., *Pleasure, Reward, Preference,* New York: Academic Press, 1973.

BIEDERMAN, I. Perceiving real-world scenes. *Science,* 1972, 77–80.

BIRDWHISTELL, R. *Kinesics and Content.* Philadelphia: University of Pennsylvania Press, 1970.

BLAKEMORE, C., and CAMPBELL, F.W. On the existence of neurons in the human visual system selectively sensitive to the orientation and size of retinal images. *Journal of Physiology,* 1969, *203*, 237–260.

BLAKEMORE, C., and SUTTON, P. Size adaptation: A new aftereffect. *Science,* 1969, *166,* 245–247.

BORING, E. A new ambiguous figure. *American Journal of Psychology,* 1930, *42,* 444.

BORNSTEIN, M., KESSEN, W., and WEISKOPF, S. Color vision and hue categorization in young human infants. *Journal of Experimental Psychology: Human Perception and Performance,* 1976, *2,* 115–129.

BOSSOM, J., and HELD, R. Shifts in egocentric localization following prolonged displacement of the retinal image. *American Psychologist,* 1957, *12,* 454. (Abstract.)

BOUMA, H., and DE VOOGD, A. H. On the control of eye saccades in reading. *Vision Research,* 1974, *14,* 273–284.

BOWEN, K. F., and SMITH, W. M. The effects of delayed and displaced visual feedback on motor control. Dartmouth College: Department of Psychology, 1977.

BOWER, G. H., KARLIN, M. B., and DUECK, A. Comprehension and memory for pictures. *Memory and Cognition,* 1975, *3,* 216–220.

BOWER, T. G. R. The visual world of infants. *Scientific American,* 1966, *215,* 80–92.

BRADLEY, D. R., DUMAIS, S. T., and PETRY, H. M. Reply to Cavonius. *Nature,* 1976, May 6, *261,* 77–78.

BRANDT, T., WIST, E., and DICHGANS, J. Optisch induzierte Pseudocoriolis-Effekte und Circularvektion. *Arch. Psychiat. Nervekrankh.,* 1971, *214,* 365–389.

BRADSHAW, J., and WALLACE, G. Models for the processing and identification of faces. *Perception and Psychophysics,* 1971, *9,* 443–448.

BREGMAN, A. S., and CAMPBELL, J. Primary auditory stream segregation and perception of order in rapid sequence of tones. *Journal of Experimental Psychology,* 1971, *89,* 244–249.

BREGMAN, A. S., and DANNENBRING, G. L. The effect of continuity on auditory stream segregation. *Perception and Psychophysics,* 1973, *13,* 308–312.

BREGMAN, A. S., and RUDNICKY, A. I. Auditory segregation: Stream or streams? *Journal of Experimental Psychology: Human Perception and Performance,* 1975, *3,* 263–267.

BREITMEYER, B., and GANZ, L. Implications of sustained and transient channels for theories of visual pattern masking, saccadic suppression, and information processing. *Psychological Review,* 1976, *83,* 1–36.

BREITMEYER, B., LOVE, R., and WEPMAN, B. Contour suppression during stroboscopic motion and metacontrast. *Vision Research,* 1974, *14,* 1451–1455.

BRICKER, P. D., and CHAPANIS, H. Do incorrectly perceived stimuli convey some information? *Psychological Review,* 1953, *60,* 181–188.

BROADBENT, D. E. *Perception and Communication.* New York: Pergamon Press, 1958.

BROOKS, V. An exploratory comparison of some measures of attention. MA Thesis, Cornell University, 1961.

BROOKS, V., and HOCHBERG, J. A psychophysical study of "cuteness." *Perceptual and Motor Skills*, 1960, *11*, 205.

BROOKS, V., and HOCHBERG, J. Control of active looking by motion picture cutting rate. *Proceedings of the Eastern Psychological Association 47th Annual Meeting*, New York, 1976. P. 49. (Abstract.)

BROWN, D. R., and OWEN, D. H. Metrics of visual form: Methodological dyspepsia. *Psychological Bulletin*, 1967, *68*, 243–259.

BROWN, R. W., and LENNEBERG, E. H. A study in language and cognition. *Journal of Abnormal and Social Psychology*, 1954, *49*, 454–462.

BRUNSWIK, E. *Perception and the Representative Design of Psychological Experiments*. 2nd ed. Berkeley: University of California Press, 1956.

BRUNSWIK, E., and REITER, L. Eindruchs-charactere schematisierter gesichter. *Zeitschrift fur Psychologie*, 1937, *142*, 67–134.

BUSWELL, G. T. *How People Look at Pictures*. Chicago: University of Chicago Press, 1935.

BYRNE, D. Attitudes and attraction. In L. Berkowitz, ed., *Advances in Experimental Social Psychology*. Vol. 4. New York: Academic Press, 1969.

BYRNE, D., et al. The ubiquitous relationship: Attitude similarity and attraction: A cross-cultural study. *Human relations*, 1971, *24*, 201–207.

CANESTRARI, R. and FARNE, M., Depth cues and apparent oscillatory movement. *Perceptual and Motor Skills*, 1969, *29*, 508–510.

CHASE, W. G., and SIMON, H. A. Perception in chess. *Cognitive Psychology*, 1973, *4*, 55–81.

CHASTAIN, G., and BURNHAM, C. A. The first glimpse determines the perception of an ambiguous figure. *Perception and Psychophysics*, 1975, *17*, 221–224.

CHERRY, E. C. Some experiments on the recognition of speech with one and two ears. *Journal of the Acoustical Society of America*, 1953, *25*, 975–979.

CLOWES, M. Transformational grammar and the systematization of pictures. In A. Grasselli, ed., *Automatic Interpretation and Classification of Images*. New York: Academic Press, 1969.

COHEN, W. Color perception in the chromatic Ganzfeld. *American Journal of Psychology*, 1958, *71*, 390–394.

COHENE, L. and BECHTOLDT, H. Visual recognition of dot-pattern bigrams: An extension and replication. *American Journal of Psychology*, 1975, *88*, 187–199.

COLLINS, A. M., and LOFTUS, E. F. A spreading-activation theory of semantic processing. *Psychological Review*, 1975, *82*, 407–428.

COOPER, L. A. Demonstration of a mental analog of an external rotation. *Perception and Psychophysics*, 1976, *19*, 296–302.

COOPER, L. A., and SHEPARD, R. N. Chronometric studies of the rotation of mental images. In W. G. Chase, ed., *Visual Information Processing*. New York: Academic Press, 1973.

CORBIN, H. H. The perception of grouping and apparent movement in visual depth. *Archives of Psychology*, 1942, No. 273.

COREN, S. C. Subjective contours and apparent depth. *Psychological Review*, 1972, *79*, 359–367.

COREN, S., and HONIG, P. The effect of nontarget stimuli upon the length of voluntary saccades. *Perceptual and Motor Skills*, 1972, *34*, 499–508.

COREN, S. C., and KOMODA, M. K. The effect of cues to illumination on apparent brightness. *American Journal of Psychology*, 1973, *86*, 345–349.

DE CHARMS, R. *Personal Causation*, New York: Academic Press, 1968.

DECI, E. L. Effects of externally mediated rewards on intrinsic motivation. *Journal of Personality and Social Psychology*, 1971, *18*, 105–115.

DE GROOT, A. D. Perception and memory versus thought: Some old ideas and recent findings. In B. Kleinmuntz, ed., *Problem Solving*. New York: Wiley, 1966.

DEUTSCH, J. A., and DEUTSCH, D. Attention: Some theoretical considerations. *Psychological Review*, 1963, *70*, 19–26.

DE VALOIS, R., and JACOBS, G. Primate color vision. *Science*, 1968, *162*, 533–540.

DICHGANS, J., HELD, R., YOUNG, L.R. and BRANDT, T. Moving visual scenes influence the apparent direction of gravity. *Science*, 1972, *178*, 217–218.

DINNERSTEIN, A. J. Image size and instructions in the perception of depth. *Journal of Experimental Psychology*, 1967, *25*, 525–528.

DION, K., BERSHEID, E., and WALSTER, E. What is beautiful is good. *Journal of Personality and Social Psychology*, 1972, *24*, 285–290.

EBENHOLTZ, S. Adaptation to a rotated visual field as a function of degree of optical tilt and exposure. *Journal of Experimental Psychology*, 1966, *72*, 629–634.

EFRON, M. G. The effect of physical appearance on the judgment of guilt, and severity of recommended punishment in a simulated jury task. *Journal of Experimental Research in Personality*, 1974, *8*, 145–54.

EFRON, R. The duration of the present. *Annals of the New York Academy of Science*, 1967, *138*, 713–729.

EGETH, H. Selective attention. *Psychological Bulletin*, 1967, *67*, 41–57.

EGETH, HOWARD, et al. *Conditions for improving visual information processing*. Baltimore, Md: Johns Hopkins University, Department of Psychology, TR No. 69–72, 1972, 59 pp.

EISENSTEIN, S. *Film Form*. New York: Harcourt, Brace & Co., 1949.

EKMAN, P., and FRIESEN, W. V. *Unmasking the Face*. Englewood Cliffs, N. J.: Prentice-Hall, Inc., 1975.

EKMAN, P., FRIESEN, W. V., and ELLSWORTH, P. *Emotions in the Human Face*. Elmsford, N. Y.: Pergamon, 1972.

ELLIS, H. C. Stimulus encoding processes in human learning and memory. In G. H. Bower, ed., *The Psychology of Learning and Motivation*. Vol. 7. New York: Academic Press, 1973.

ENGEN, T. Psychophysics: 1. Discrimination and Detection; 2. Scaling methods. In J. Kling and L. Riggs, eds., *Woodworth and Schlosberg's Experimental Psychology.* New York: Holt, Rinehart & Winston, 1971. Pp. 11–86.

EPSTEIN, A., PARK, J., and CASEY, A. The current status of the size-distance hypothesis. *Psychological Bulletin,* 1961, *58,* 491–514.

EPSTEIN, W. The known-size apparent-distance hypothesis. *American Journal of Psychology,* 1961, *74,* 333–346.

EPSTEIN, W. Phenomenal orientation and perceived achromatic color. *Journal of Psychology,* 1961, *52,* 51–53.

EPSTEIN, W. Nonrelational judgment of size and distance. *American Journal of Psychology,* 1965, *78,* 120–123.

EPSTEIN, W. and LANDAUER, A. Size and distance judgments under reduced conditions of viewing. *Perception and Psychophysics,* 1969, *6* (5), 269–272.

ERDELYI, M. H. A new look at the new look: Perceptual defense and vigilance. *Psychological Review,* 1974, *81,* 1–25.

ERIKSEN, C. W., and COLLINS, J. F. Some temporal characteristics of visual pattern perception. *Journal of Experimental Psychology,* 1967, *74,* 476–484.

ERIKSEN, C. W., and SPENCER, T. Rate of information processing in visual perception: Some results and methodological considerations. *Journal of Experimental Psychology Monographs,* 1969, No. 79.

ERIKSSON, E. S. Movement parallax during locomotion. *Perception and Psychophysics,* 1974, *16,* 197–200.

ERIKSSON, S., and ZETTERBERG, P. *Experience and veridical space perception.* Report 169. Sweden: University of Uppsala, Department of Psychology, 1975.

ERLEBACHER, A., and SEKULER, R. Explanation of the Muller-Lyer illusion: Confusion theory examined. *Journal of Experimental Psychology,* 1969, *80,* 462–467.

ESCHER, M. L. *The Graphic Work of M. C. Escher.* New York: Duell, Sloan and Pearce, 1960.

ESTES, W. K. The locus of inferential and perceptual processes in letter identification. *Journal of Experimental Psychology: General,* 1975, *104,* 122–145.

ESTES, W. Memory, perception, and decision in letter identification. In R. Solso, ed., *Information Processing and Cognition: The Loyola Symposium,* Hillsdale, N. J.: Erlbaum Assoc., 1975.

EVANS, R. M. Psychological aspects of color and illumination. *Illuminating Engineering,* 1951, *46,* 176–184.

EXLINE, R. Visual interaction: The glances of power and preferences. *Nebraska Symposium on Motivation,* 1971, 163–206.

EXLINE, R. and LONG, B. Unpublished study reported in R. V. Exline (1971).

EXLINE, R., THIBAUT, J., HICKEY, C., GUMPERT, P. Visual interaction in relation to Machiavellianism and an unethical act. In R. Christie and F. L. Geis eds., *Studies in Machiavellianism.* New York: Academic Press, 1970.

EXLINE, R., and WINTERS, L. Affective relations and mutual gaze in dyads. In S. Tomkins & C. Izzard, eds., *Affect, Cognition, and Personality.* New York: Springer, 1975.

FARBER, J., and MCCONKIE, A. Linkages between apparent depth and motion in linear flow fields. *Bulletin of the Psychonomic Society,* 1977, *10,* 250 (abstract).

FAVREAU, O., EMERSON, D., and CORBALLIS, M. Movement aftereffects contingent on color. *Science,* 1972, *76,* 78–79.

FESTINGER, L., ONO, H., BURNHAM, C., and BAMBER, D. Efference and the conscious experience of perception. *Journal of Experimental Psychological Monographs,* 1967, No. 637 (whole issue).

FESTINGER, L., and HOLTZMAN, J. D. Retinal smear as a source of information about magnitude of eye movement. New York: New School for Social Research, Department of Psychology, 1977.

FESTINGER, L., WHITE, C., and ALLYN, M. Eye movements and decrement in the Müller-Lyer illusion. *Perception and Psychophysics,* 1968, *3,* 376–382.

FISHER, D. F. Reading and visual research. *Memory and Cognition,* 1975, *3,* 188–196.

FISHER, D. F. Spatial factors in reading and search: The case for space. In R. Monty and J. Senders, eds., *Eye Movements and Psychological Processes.* Hillsdale, New Jersey: Erlbaum, 1976.

FISHER, D.F., and LEFTON, L. A. Peripheral information extraction: A developmental examination of reading processes. *Journal of Experimental Child Psychology,* 1976, *21,* 77–93.

FLOCK, H., and FREEDBERG, E. Perceived angle of incidence and achromatic surface color. *Perception and Psychophysics,* 1970, *8,* 251–256.

FLOCK, H., WILSON, A., and POIZNER, S. Lightness matching for different routes through a compound scene. *Perception and Psychophysics,* 1966, *1,* 382–384.

FRIJDA, N., and VAN DER GEER, J. Codability and recognition: An experiment with facial expressions. *Acta Psychologica,* 1961, *18,* 360–368.

GALANTER, E. Contemporary psychophysics. In *New Directions in Psychology.* New York: Holt, Rinehart & Winston, 1962.

GALPER, R. E. Recognition of faces in photographic negative. *Psychonomic Science,* 1970, *19,* 207–208.

GALPER, R. E., and HOCHBERG, J. Recognition memory for photographs of faces. *American Journal of Psychology,* 1971, *84,* 351–354.

GANZ, L. The mechanism of figural aftereffect. *Psychological Review*, 1966, *73*, 128–150.

GARDNER, B. T., and WALLACH, L. Shapes of figures identified as a baby's head. *Perceptual and Motor Skills*, 1965, *20*, 135–142.

GARNER, W. *Uncertainty and Structure of Psychological Concepts*. New York: Wiley, 1962.

GARNER, W. Good patterns have few alternatives. *American Scientist*, 1970, *58*, 34–42.

GARNER, W., and CLEMENT, D. Goodness of pattern and pattern uncertainty. *Journal of Verbal Learning and Verbal Behavior*, 1963, *2*, 446–452.

GAZZANIGA, M. *The Bisected Brain*, New York: Appleton, 1970.

GEYER, J. Perceptual systems in reading: The prediction of a temporal eye-voice span constant. In H. K. Smith, ed., *Perception and Reading*. Newark, Del.: International Reading Association, 1968.

GIBSON, E. *Principles of Perceptual Learning and Development*. Englewood Cliffs, N. J.: Prentice-Hall, Inc., 1969.

GIBSON, E., and LEVIN, H. *The Psychology of Reading*. Cambridge, Mass: M.I.T. Press, 1975.

GIBSON, E., and WALK, R. The "visual cliff." *Scientific American*, 1960, *202*, 64–71.

GIBSON, E. J., OSSER, H., SCHIFF, W., and SMITH, J. An analysis of critical features of letters, tested by a confusion matrix. In *Final Report on a Basic Research Program on Reading* (Cooperative Research Project No. 639). Cornell University and U. S. Office of Education, 1963.

GIBSON, J. Adaptation, aftereffect, and contrast in the perception of curved lines. *Journal of Experimental Psychology*, 1933, *16*, 1–31.

GIBSON, J. J. *The Perception of the Visual World*. Boston: Houghton Mifflin, 1950.

GIBSON, J. J. Perception as a function of stimulation. In S. Koch, ed., *Psychology: A Study of Science*. Vol. 1. New York: McGraw-Hill, 1959.

GIBSON, J. J. Observations on active touch. *Psychological Review*, 1962, *69*, 477–491.

GIBSON, J. J. *The Senses Considered as Perceptual Systems*. Boston: Houghton Mifflin, 1966.

GIBSON, J., and BACKLUND, F. An aftereffect in haptic space perception. *Quarterly Journal of Experimental Psychology*, 1963, *15*, 145–153.

GIBSON, J., OLUM, P., and ROSENBLATT, F. Parallax and perspective during aircraft landings. *American Journal of Psychology*, 1955, *68*, 372–385.

GIBSON, J., and PICK, A. Perception of another person's looking behavior. *American Journal of Psychology*, 1963, *76*, 386–394.

GIBSON, J. J., and GIBSON, E. J. Perceptual learning: Differentiation or enrichment? *Psychological Review*, 1955, *62*, 32–41.

GILCHRIST, A. Perceived lightness depends on perceived spatial arrangement. *Science*, 1977, *195*, 185–187.

GILLAM, B. A depth processing theory of the Poggendorff illusion. *Perception and Psychophysics,* 1971, *10,* 211–216.

GILLAM, B. New evidence of "closure" in perception. *Perception and Psychophysics,* 1975, *17,* 521–524.

GILLAM, B. Perceived common rotary motion of ambiguous stimuli as a criterion for perceptual grouping. *Perception and Psychophysics,* 1972, *11,* 99–101.

GIRGUS, J. A developmental approach to the study of shape processing. *Journal of Experimental Child Psychology,* 1973, *16,* 363–374.

GIRGUS, J. A developmental study of the effect of eye movement on shape perception in a sequential viewing situation. *Journal of Experimental Child Psychology,* 1976, *22,* 386–399.

GIRGUS, J., and HOCHBERG, J. Age differences in shape recognition through an aperture in a free-viewing situation. *Psychonomic Science,* 1972, *28,* 237–238.

GLANZER, M., and CLARK, W. The verbal loop hypothesis: Conventional figures. *American Journal of Psychology,* 1964, *77,* 621–626.

GOFFMAN, E. *Interaction Ritual.* Garden City: Anchor Books, 1967.

GOGEL, W., HARTMAN, B., and HARKER, G. The retinal size of a familiar object as a determiner of apparent distance. *Psychological Monographs,* 1957, *71* (No. 442), 1–16.

GOGEL, W., and MERSHON, D. H. Depth adjacency in simultaneous contrast. *Perception & Psychophysics,* 1969, *5,* 13–17.

GOGEL, W., and TEITZ, J. The effect of perceived distance on perceived movement. *Perception and Psychophysics,* 1974, *16,* 70–78.

GOLDIAMOND, I., and HAWKINS, W. F. Vexierversuch: The log relationship between word frequency and recognition obtained in the absence of stimulus words. *Journal of Experimental Psychology,* 1958, *56,* 457–463.

GOLDSTEIN, A. G., and CHANCE, J. E. Recognition of children's faces. *Child Development,* 1964, *35,* 129–136.

GOLDSTEIN, A. G., and MACKENBERG, E. Recognition of human faces from isolated facial feature: A developmental study. *Psychonomic Science,* 1966, *6,* 149–150.

GOMBRICH, E. *Art and illusion:* Princeton: Princeton University Press, 1956.

GOMBRICH, E. The mask and the face. In E. H. Gombrich, J. Hochberg, and M. Black, *Art, Perception, and Reality.* Baltimore: Johns Hopkins University Press, 1972.

GOODALL, J. V. L. The behavior of free-living chimpanzees in the Gomb stream reserve. *Animal Behavior Monographs,* 1968, *1,* 161–311.

GOUGH, P. One second of reading. In J. Kavanaugh and I. Mattingly, eds., *Language by Ear and by Eye.* Cambridge: M.I.T. Press, 1972.

GRAHAM, N. Spatial frequency channels in human vision: Detecting edges without edge detectors. In C. Harris, ed., *Visual Coding and Adaptability.* Hillsdale, N. J.: Erlbaum, 1978.

GREGORY, R. *The Intelligent Eye*. New York: McGraw-Hill, 1970.

GREGORY, R. Cognitive contours. *Nature*, 1972, *238*, 51–52.

GREGORY, R. Visual illusions. In B. M. Foss, ed., *New Horizons in Psychology*. Harmondsworth, Eng.: Penguin Books, 1966.

GRICE, H. Utterer's meaning, sentence-meaning and word-meaning. *Foundations of Language*, 1968, *4*, 225–242.

GRUBER, H. The relation of perceived size to perceived distance. *American Journal of Psychology*, 1954, *67*, 411–426.

GUZMAN, A. Decomposition of a visual scene into three-dimensional bodies. In A. Graselli, ed., *Automatic Interpretation and Classification of Images*. New York: Academic Press, 1969.

HABER, R. N. Discrepancy from adaptation level as a source of affect. *Journal of Experimental Psychology*, 1958, *56*, 370–384.

HABER, R. N. The effects of coding strategy on perceptual memory. *Journal of Experimental Psychology*, 1964, *68*, 257–262.

HABER, R. N. Nature of the effect of set on perception. *Psychological Review*, 1966, *73*, 335–351.

HABER, R. N. Information processing. In E. Carterette and M. Friedman, eds., *Handbook of Perception*. Vol. 1, New York: Academic Press, 1974.

HABER, R. N., and HABER, L. R. Word length and word shape as sources of information in reading. *Bulletin of the Psychonomic Society*, 1977, *10*, 251, (abstract).

HABER, R. N., and HERSHENSON, M. *The psychology of visual perception*. New York: Holt, Rinehart and Winston, 1973.

HAGEN, M. A., and ELLIOTT, H. B. An investigation of the relationship between viewing condition and preference for true and modified linear perspective. *Journal of Experimental Psychology: Human Perception and Performance*, 1976, *2*, 479–490.

HANDEL, S., and GARNER, W. R. The structure of visual pattern associates and pattern goodness. *Perception and Psychophysics*, 1965, *1*, 33–38.

HARMON, L., and JULESZ, B. Masking in visual recognition: Effects of two-dimensional filtered noise. *Science*, 1973, *180*, 1194–1197.

HARRIS, C. Adaptation to displaced vision: Visual, motor, or proprioceptive change? *Science*, 1963, *140*, 812–813.

HARRIS C. Perceptual adaptation to inverted, reversed, and displaced vision. *Psychological Review*, 1965, *72*, 419–44.

HARRIS, C., and GIBSON, A. Is orientation-specific color adaptation in human vision due to edge detectors, afterimages, or "dipoles"? *Science*, 1968, *162*, 1056–1057.

HARRIS, C., and HABER, R. N. Selective attention and coding in visual perception. *Journal of Experimental Psychology*, 1963, *65*, 328–333.

HAY, J., and PICK, H. Visual and proprioceptive adaptation to optical displacement of the visual stimulus. *Journal of Experimental Psychology*, 1966, *71*, 150–158.

HAY, J., and SAWYER, S. Position constancy and binocular convergence. *Perception and Psychophysics*, 1969, *5*, 310–312.

HAYES, W., ROBINSON, J., and BROWN, L. An effect of past experience on perception: An artifact. *American Psychologist*, 1961, *16*, 420.

HEBB, D. *The Organization of Behavior*. New York: Wiley, 1949.

HEBB, D. *A Textbook of Psychology*. Philadelphia: Saunders, 1958.

HEIDER, F., and SIMMEL, M. An experimental study of apparent behavior. *American Journal of Psychology*, 1944, *57*, 243–259.

HEINEMANN, E., TULVING, E., and NACHMIAS, J. I. The effects of oculomotor adjustments on apparent size. *American Journal of Psychology*, 1959, *72*, 32–45.

HELD, R., DICHGANS, J., and BAUER, J. Characteristics of moving visual scenes influencing spatial orientation. *Vision Research*, 1975, *15*, 357–365.

HELD, R., and HEIN, A. Adaptation of disarranged hand-eye coordination contingent upon re-afferent stimulation. *Perceptual and Motor Skills*, 1958, *8*, 87–90.

HELD, R., and HEIN, A. Movement produced stimulation in the development of visually guided behavior. *Journal of Comparative Psychology*, 1963, *56*, 872–876.

HELD, R., and REKOSH, J. Motor-sensory feedback and the geometry of visual space. *Science*, 1963, *141*, 722–723.

HELD, R., and SHATTUCK, S. Color and edge-sensitive channels in the human visual system: Tuning for orientations. *Science*, 1971, *174*, 314–316.

HELMHOLTZ, H. VON. *Treatise on physiological optics. Vol. III* (trans. from the 3rd German ed., J. P. C. Southall), New York: Dover, 1962.

HELSON, H. *Adaptation Level Theory*. New York: Harper & Row, 1964.

HELSON, H. A common model for affectivity and perception: An Adaptation-Level approach. In D. E. Berlyne and K. B. Madsen, eds., *Pleasure, reward, preference*. New York: Academic Press, 1973.

HENLE, M. An experimental investigation of past experiences as a determinant of visual form perception. *Journal of Experimental Psychology*, 1942, *30*, 1–22.

HERSHBERGER, W. Attached-shadow orientation perceived as depth by chickens reared in an environment illuminated from below. *Journal of Comparative and Physiological Psychology*, 1970, *73*, 407–411.

HESS, C., and PRETORI, H. Messende Untersuchungen über die Gesetzmäsigkeit des simultanen Helligkeits-Contrastes. *Archiv. f. Ophthalmol.*, 1894, *40*, 1–27. Translated by H. R. Flock and J. H. Tenney. *Technical Report FLP-1*. York University, 1969.

HOCHBERG, C. B., and HOCHBERG, J. Familiar size and the perception of depth. *Journal of Psychology*, 1952, *34*, 107–114.

HOCHBERG, J. Perception: Toward the recovery of a definition. *Psychological Review*, 1956, *63*, 400–405.

HOCHBERG, J. Nativism and empiricism in perception. In L. Postman, ed., *Psychology in the Making*. New York: Knopf, 1962.

HOCHBERG, J. The psychophysics of pictorial perception. *Audio-Visual Communication Review*, 1962, *10*, 22–54.

HOCHBERG, J. In the mind's eye. In R. N. Haber, ed., *Contemporary theory and research in visual perception*. New York: Holt, Rinehart and Winston, 1968.

HOCHBERG, J. Attention, organization, and consciousness. In D. I. Mostofsky, ed., *Attention: Contemporary Theory and Analysis*. New York: Appleton-Century-Crofts, 1970a.

HOCHBERG, J. Components of literacy: Speculations and exploratory research. In H. Levin and J. Williams, eds., *Basic Studies in Reading*. New York: Basic Books, 1970b.

HOCHBERG, J. The representation of things and people. In E. H. Gombrich, J. Hochberg, and M. Black, *Art, Perception, and Reality*. Baltimore: Johns Hopkins University Press, 1972a.

HOCHBERG, J. Perception, I. Color and shape. II. Space and movement. In J. W. Kling and L. A. Riggs, eds., *Woodworth & Schlosberg's Experimental Psychology*. Third Ed. N.Y.: Holt, Rinehart and Winston, 1972b.

HOCHBERG, J. Higher-order stimuli and interresponse coupling in the perception of the visual world. In R. B. Macleod and H. L. Pick, eds., *Perception: Essays in Honor of James J. Gibson*. Ithaca: Cornell University Press, 1974, 17–39.

HOCHBERG, J. Organization and the Gestalt tradition. In E. C. Carterette and M. Friedman, eds., *Handbook of Perception*. Vol. 1. New York: Academic Press, 1974.

HOCHBERG, J. Toward a speech-plan eye-movement model of reading. In R. A. Monty and J. W. Senders, eds., *Eye movements and psychological processes*. Hillsdale, N. J.: Erlbaum, 1976.

HOCHBERG, J., and BECK, J. Apparent spatial arrangement and perceived brightness. *Journal of Experimental Psychology,*1954, *47*, 263–266.

HOCHBERG, J., and BROOKS, V. The psychophysics of form: Reversible-perspective drawings of spatial objects. *American Journal of Psychology*, 1960, *73*, 337–354.

HOCHBERG, J., and BROOKS, V. Pictorial recognition as an unlearned ability: A study of one child's performance. *American Journal of Psychology*, 1962, *75*, 624–628.

HOCHBERG, J., and BROOKS, V. Reading as intentional behavior. In H. Singer, ed., *Theoretical Models and Processes of Reading*. Newark, Del.: International Reading Association, 1970.

HOCHBERG, J., and BROOKS, V. The integration of successive cinematic views of simple scenes. *Bulletin of the Psychonomic Society*, 1974, *4*, 263.

HOCHBERG, J., and BROOKS, V. Psychological aspects of the cinema. In E. C. Carterette and M. P. Friedman, eds., *Handbook of Perception*, Vol. X. New York: Academic Press. (In press, a.)

HOCHBERG, J., and BROOKS, V. Film cutting and visual momentum. In R. A.

Monty and J. W. Senders, eds., *Eye Movements and Psychological Processes, II.* Hillsdale, N.J.: Erlbaum. (In press, b.)

HOCHBERG, J., and GALPER, R. E. Recognition of faces: I. An exploratory study. *Psychonomic Science,* 1967, *9,* 619–620.

HOCHBERG, J., and GALPER, R. E. Attribution of intention as a function of physiognomy. *Memory and Cognition,* 1974, *2,* 39–42.

HOCHBERG, J., and GELLMAN, L. The effect of landmark features on mental rotation times. *Memory and Cognition,* 1977, *5,* 23–26.

HOCHBERG, J., and MCALISTER, E. A quantitative approach to figural "goodness" *Journal of Experimental Psychology,* 1953, *46,* 361–364.

HOCHBERG, J., TRIEBEL, W., and SEAMAN, G. Color adaptation under conditions of homogeneous stimulation (Ganzfeld). *Journal of Experimental Psychology,* 1951, *41,* 153–159.

HOLWAY, A., and BORING, E. The moon illusion and the angle of regard. *American Journal of Psychology,* 1940, *53,* 109–116.

HOOD, D., and WHITESIDE, J. Brightness of ramp stimuli as a function of plateau and gradient widths. *Journal of the Optical Society of America,* 1968, *58,* 1310–1311.

HOTOPF, W. H. N. The size-constancy theory of visual illusions. *British Journal of Psychology,* 1966, *57,* 307–318.

HOWARD, I. Orientation and motion in space. In E. Carterette and M. Friedman, eds., *Handbook of Perception.* Vol. 3. New York: Academic Press, 1973. Pp. 291–315.

HUBEL, D., and WIESEL, T. Receptive fields, binocular interaction, and functional architecture in the cat's visual cortex. *Journal of Physiology,* 1962, *160,* 106–154.

HUBEL, D., and WIESEL, T. Receptive fields and functional architecture of monkey striate cortex. *Journal of Physiology,* 1968, *195,* 215–243.

HUBEL, D., and WIESEL, T. Stereoscopic vision in the macaque monkey. *Nature,* 1970, *225,* 41–42.

HURVICH, L., and JAMESON, D. An opponent-process theory of color vision. *Psychological Review,* 1957, *64,* 384–404.

HURVICH, L., and JAMESON, D. Opponent processes as a model of neural organization. *American Psychologist,* 1974, *29,* 88–102.

ITTELSON, W. H. Size as a cue to distance: Static localization. *American Journal of Psychology,* 1951a, *64,* 54–67.

ITTELSON, W. H. Size as a cue to distance: Radial motion. *American Journal of Psychology,* 1951b, *64,* 188–202.

ITTELSON, W. H., and KILPATRICK, F. Experiments in Perception. *Scientific American,* 1952, *185,* 50–55.

IZARD, C. E. *The Face of Emotion.* New York: Appleton-Century-Crofts, 1971.

IZARD, C. E. The emotions and emotion constructs in personality and culture research. In R. B. Cattell, ed., *Handbook of Modern Personality Theory.* Chicago: Aldine, 1969.

JAHODA, G. Geometric illusions and environment: A study in Ghana. *British Journal of Psychology*, 1966, *57*, 193–199.

JAMESON, D., and HURVICH, L. Theory of brightness and color contrast in human vision. *Vision Research*, 1964, *4*, 135–154.

JAMESON, D., and HURVICH, L. From contrast to assimilation: In art and in the eye. *Leonardo*, 1975, *8*, 125–131.

JOHANSSON, G. *Configurations in Event Perception*. Uppsala: Almquist and Wiksells Boktryschkeri AB., 1950.

JOHANSSON, G. Visual perception of biological motion and a model for its analysis. *Perception and Psychophysics*, 1973, *14*, (2), 201–211.

JOHANSSON, G. *Spatio-temporal Differentiation and Integration in Visual Motion Perception. Report No. 160.* Uppsala, Sweden: Department of Psychology, 1974.

JONGMAN, R. W. *Het oog van de Maester*. Amsterdam: Van Gorcum, 1968. (Cited in Chase and Simon, 1973.)

JONIDES, J., and GLEITMAN, H. A conceptual category effect in visual search: O as letter or as digit. *Perception and Psychophysics*, 1972, *12 (b)*, 457–460.

JULESZ, B. Binocular depth perception of computer-generated patterns. *Bell System Technical Journal*, 1960, *39*, 1125–1162.

JULESZ, B. Binocular depth perception without familiarity cues. *Science*, 1964, *45*, 356–362.

JULESZ, B. *Foundations of Cyclopean Perception*. Chicago: University of Chicago Press, 1971.

KAHNEMAN, D. *Attention and Effort*. Englewood Cliffs, N. J.: Prentice-Hall, Inc., 1973.

KANIZSA, G. Marzini quasi-percettivi in campi con stimolazione homogenea. *Rivista di Psicologia*, 1955, *49*, 7–30.

KAUFMAN, L. Some new stereoscopic phenomena and their implications for theories of stereopsis. *American Journal of Psychology*, 1965, *78*, 1–20.

KAUFMAN, L., and PITTBLADO, C. B. Further observations on the nature of effective binocular disparities. *American Journal of Psychology*, 1965, *78*, 379–391.

KAUFMAN, L. *Sight and Mind*. New York: Oxford University Press, 1974.

KAUFMAN, L., and ROCK, I. The moon illusion. *Scientific American*, 1962, *207*, 120–130.

KAUFMAN, L., and ROCK, I. The moon illusion: I. *Science*, 1962, *136*, 953–961.

KAVANAGH, J. F., and MATTINGLY, I. eds., *Language by Ear and by Eye*. Cambridge, Mass.: The M.I.T. Press, 1972.

KELLEY, H. Attribution theory in social psychology. In D. Levine, ed., *Nebraska Symposium of Motivation*. Lincoln: University of Nebraska Press, 1967. Pp. 192–238.

KELLEY, H. *Causal schemata and the attribution process*. Morristown N. J.: General Learning Press, 1971.

KENDON, A. Some relationships between body motion and speech: An analysis of an example. In A. Siegman and B. Pope, eds., *Studies in Dyadic Communication,* Elmsford, N. Y.: Pergamon, 1970.

KENNEDY, J. M. *A Psychology of Picture Perception,* San Francisco: Jossey-Bass, 1974.

KILPATRICK, F., and ITTELSON, W. The size-distance invariance hypothesis. *Psychological Review,* 1953, *60,* 223–231.

KING, W., and GRUBER, H. Moon illusion and Emmert's law. *Science,* 1962, *135,* 1125–1126.

KOFFKA, K. *Principles of Gestalt Psychology.* New York: Harcourt, Brace, 1935.

KOHLER, I. Experiments with goggles. *Scientific American,* 1962, *206,* 62–72.

KOHLER, W. *Gestalt Psychology.* New York: Liveright, 1929.

KOHLER, W., and WALLACH, H. Figural aftereffects: An investigation of visual processes. *Proceedings of the American Philosophical Society,* 1944, *88,* 269–357.

KOLERS, P. A. Experiments in reading. *Scientific American,* 1972, *227,* 84–91.

KOLERS, P. A. Some differences between real and apparent movement. *Vision Research,* 1963, *3,* 191–206.

KOLERS, P. A. The recognition of geometrically transformed text. *Perception and Psychophysics,* 1968, *3,* 57–64.

KOLERS, P. A. *Aspects of Motion Perception.* Oxford, Eng. Pergamon Press, 1972.

KOLERS, P. A., and POMERANTZ, J. R. Figural change in apparent motion. *Journal of Experimental Psychology,* 1971, *87,* 99–108.

KOLERS, P. A., and VON GRÜNAU, M. Shape and color in apparent motion. *Vision Research,* 1976, *16,* 329–335.

KOPFERMANN, H. Psychologische Untersuchungen uber die Wirkung Zweidimensionalar Darstellunger körperlicher Gebilde. *Psychologische Forschung,* 1930, *13,* 293–364.

KOSSLYN, S. M. Information representation in visual images. *Cognitive Psychology,* 1975, *7,* 341–370.

KRAUSKOPF, J. Figural aftereffects with a stabilized retinal image. *American Journal of Psychology,* 1960, *73,* 294–297.

KRAUSKOPF, J. Effect of retinal image stabilization on the appearance of heterochromatic targets. *Journal of the Optical Society of America,* 1963, *53,* 741–744.

KRUEGER, L. E. Effect of frequency of display on speed of visual search. *Journal of Experimental Psychology,* 1970, *84,* 495–498.

KRUEGER, L. E. Familiarity effects in visual information processing. *Psychological Bulletin,* 1975, *82,* 949–974.

KRUGLANSKI A. W. The endogenous-exogenous partition in attribution theory. *Psychological Review,* 1975, *82,* 387–406.

LAND, E. Color vision and the natural image. *Proceedings of the National Academy of Science,* 1959, *45,* 115–129.

LASHLEY, K. S. The problem of serial order in behavior. In L. A. Jeffress, ed., *Cerebral Mechanisms in Behavior.* New York: Wiley, 1951.

LEEPER, R. A study of a neglected portion of the field of learning: The development of sensory organization. *Journal of Genetic Psychology,* 1935, *46,* 41–75.

LEFTON, L. Guessing and the order of approximation effect. *Journal of Experimental Psychology,* 1973, *101,* 401–403.

LEIBOWITZ, H. W. Effect of reference lines on the discrimination of movement. *Journal of the Optical Society of America,* 1955a, *45,* 829–830.

LEIBOWITZ, H. W. The relation between the rate threshold for the perception of movement and luminance for various durations of exposure. *Journal of Experimental Psychology,* 1955b, *49,* 209–214.

LEIBOWITZ, H. W., BESSEY, T., and MCGUIRE, P. Shape and size constancy in photographic reproductions. *Journal of the Optical Society of America,* 1957, *47,* 658–661.

LEIBOWITZ, H. W., and BOURNE, L. Time and intensity as determiners of perceived shape. *Journal of Experimental Psychology,* 1956, *51,* 227–281.

LEIBOWITZ, H. W., and CHINETTI, P. Effect of reduced exposure duration on brightness constancy. *Journal of Experimental Psychology,* 1957, *54,* 49–53.

LEIBOWITZ, H. W., and PICK, H. Cross-cultural and educational aspects of the Ponzo illusion. *Perception and Psychophysics,* 1972, *12,* 403–432.

LEVIN, H., and KAPLAN, E. L. Eye-voice span (EVS) within active and passive sentences. *Language and Speech,* 1968, *11,* 251–258.

LEVIN, H., and TURNER, A. Sentence structure and the eye-voice span. In H. Levin, E. J. Gibson and J. J. Gibson, eds., *The Analysis of Reading Skill. (Final Report Project No. 5–1213,* from Cornell University to U. S. Office of Education.) December, 1968.

LEVINE, M., and JANKOVIC, I. N. Introduction to spatial problem solving. *Bulletin of the Psychonomic Society,* 1977, *10,* 263 (abstract).

LIBERMAN, A., COOPER, F. S., SHANKWEILER, D. P., and STUDDERT-KENNEDY, M. Perception of the speech code. *Psychological Review,* 1967, *74,* 431–461.

LIBERMAN, A. The grammars of speech and language. *Cognitive Psychology,* 1970, *1* (4), 301–323.

LINDSAY, P. H., and NORMAN, D. A. *Human information processing:* An introduction to psychology. New York: Academic Press, 1972.

LIT, A. The magnitude of the Pulfrich stereo phenomenon as a function of binocular differences of retinal illuminance at scotopic and photopic levels. *American Journal of Psychology,* 1949, *62,* 159–181.

LOFTUS, G. R. A framework for a theory of picture recognition. In R. A. Monty and J. W. Senders, eds., *Eye Movements and Psychological Processes*. Hillsdale, N. J.: Erlbaum, 1976.

LOMBROSO, C., and FERRERO, G. *La Femme Criminelle et la Prostitue'e*. Paris: Germer Bailliere, 1896.

LYNCH, K. *The Image of the City*. Cambridge, Mass.: M.I.T. Press, 1960.

MACKWORTH, N. H., and MORANDI, A. J. The gaze selects informative details within pictures. *Perception and Psychophysics*, 1967, *2*, 547–552.

MALPASS, R. S., and KRAVITZ, J. Recognition for faces of own and other "race." *Journal of Personality and Social Psychology*, 1969, *13*, 330–335.

MALPASS, R. S., LAVIGUEUR, H., and WELDON, D. E. Verbal and visual training in face recognition. *Perception and Psychophysics*, 1973, *14*, 285–292.

MARKS, W. B., DOBELLE, W. H., and MACNICHOL, E. F. Visual pigments of single primate cones. *Science*, 1964, *143*, 1181–1183.

MASSARO, D. W. Perception of letters, words, and nonwords. *Journal of Experimental Psychology*, 1973, *100*, 349–353.

MCCLELLAND, D., and ATKINSON J. The projective expression of needs, I: The effect of different intensities of the hunger drive on perception. *Journal of Psychology*, 1948, *25*, 205–222.

MCCLELLAND, D., ATKINSON, J., CLARK, R., and LOWELL, E. *The Achievement Motive*. New York: Appleton-Century-Crofts, 1953.

MCCONKIE, G. W., and RAYNER, K. The span of the effective stimulus during a fixation in reading. *Perception and Psychophysics*, 1975, *17*, 578–586.

MCCONKIE, G. W., and RAYNER, K. Identifying the span of the effective stimulus in reading: Literature review and theories of reading. In Singer, H., and Ruddell, R. B., eds., *Theoretical Models and Processes of Reading*, 2nd Ed. Newark, Delaware: International Reading Association, 1976.

MCCULLOUGH, C. Color adaptation of edge-detectors in the human visual system. *Science*, 1965, *149*, 1115–1116.

MEFFERD, R. B., and WIELAND, B. A. Apparent size-apparent distance relationship in flat stimuli. *Perceptual and Motor Skills*, 1968, *26*, 959–966.

MEHRABIAN, A. *Nonverbal Communication*. Chicago: Aldine-Atherton, 1972.

MERSHON, D. H., and GOGEL, W. C. Failure of familiar size to determine a metric for visually perceived distance. *Perception and Psychophysics*, 1975, *17*, 101–106.

METZGER, W. *Gesetze des Sehens*. Frankfurt-am-Main: Kramer, 1953.

METZLER, J., and SHEPARD, R. N. Transformational studies of the internal representation of three-dimensional objects. In R. Solso, ed., *Theories of Cognitive Psychology: The Loyola Symposium*. Potomac, Md.: Lawrence Erlbaum, 1974.

MIKAELIAN, H., and HELD, R. Two types of adaptation to an optically rotated visual field. *American Journal of Psychology*, 1964, *77*, 257–263.

MILLER, G. A., GALANTER, E., and PRIBRAM, K. *Plans and the Structure of Behavior.* New York: Holt, Rinehart and Winston, 1960.

MINSKY, M., and PAPERT, S. *Perceptrons.* Cambridge, Mass.: M.I.T. Press, 1969.

MORAY, N. Attention in dichotic listening: Affective cues and the influence of instructions. *Quarterly Journal of Experimental Psychology*, 1959, *11*, 56–60.

MORAY, N., FITTER, M., OSTRY, D., FAVREAU, D., NAGY, V. Attention to pure tones. *Quarterly Journal of Experimental Psychology*, 1976, *28*, 271–283.

MURCH, G. M., and HIRSCH, J. The McCollough effect created by complimentary afterimages. *American Journal of Psychology*, 1972, *85*, 241–247.

MURPHY, R. Recognition memory for sequentially presented pictorial and verbal spatial information. *Journal of Experimental Psychology*, 1973, *100*, 327–334.

NAVON, D. Irrelevance of figural identity for resolving ambiguities in apparent motion. *Journal of Experimental Psychology: Human Perception and Performance*, 1976, *2*, 130–138.

NEISSER, U. Visual search. *Scientific American*, 1964, *210*, 94–102.

NEISSER, U. *Cognitive Psychology.* New York: Appleton-Century-Crofts, 1967.

NEISSER, U., and BECKLEN, R. Selective looking: Attending to visually specified events. *Cognitive Psychology*, 1975, *7*, 480–494.

ONO, H. Apparent distance as a function of familiar size. *Journal of Experimental Psychology*, 1969, *79*, 109–115.

ORLANSKY, J. The effect of similarity and difference in form on apparent visual movement. *Archives of Psychology*, 1940, *246*, 85.

OYAMA, T. Perceived size and perceived distance in stereoscopic vision and an analysis of their causal relations. *Perception and Psychophysics*, 1974, *16*, 175–181.

PALMER, S. E. Visual perception and world knowledge: Notes on a model of sensory-cognitive interaction. In D. A. Norman and D. E. Rumelhart, eds., *Explorations in Cognition.* San Francisco: W. H. Freeman, 1975.

PANTLE, A., and SEKULER, R. Size-detecting mechanisms in human vision. *Science*, 1968, *162*, 1146–1148.

PENROSE, L., and PENROSE, R. Impossible objects: A special type of visual illusion. *British Journal of Psychology*, 1958, *49*, 31–33.

PERKY, C. An experimental study of imagination. *American Journal of Psychology*, 1910, *23*, 422–452.

PETERSIK, J. T., and PANTLE, A. J. Contrast response of antagonistic movement-analysing mechanisms. *Bulletin of the Psychonomic Society*, Oct. 1976, 240 (Abstr).

PEW, R. W. Human perceptual-motor performance. In B. H. Kantowitz, ed., *Human Information Processing: Tutorials in Performance and Cognition.* New York: Erlbaum, 1974.

PIRENNE, M. *Optics, Painting, and Photography.* Cambridge, Eng.: Cambridge University Press, 1970.

POLLACK, I., and SPENCE, D. Subjective pictorial information and visual search. *Perception and Psychophysics,* 1968, *3,* 41–44.

POMERANTZ, J. R., SAGER, L. C., and STOEVER, R. J. Perception of wholes and of their component parts: some configural superiority effects. *Journal of Experimental Psychology: Human Perception and Performance.* (In press).

POSNER, M., and MITCHELL, R. Chronometric analysis of classification. *Psychological Review,* 1967, *74,* 392–409.

POSNER, M. I. Abstraction and the process of recognition. In G. H. Bower and J. T. Spence, eds., *The Psychology of Learning and Motivation.* Vol. 3. New York: Academic Press, 1969. Pp. 44–96.

POSNER, M. I. *Cognition: An introduction.* Glenview, Ill.: Scott, Foresman and Company, 1973.

POSNER, M. I., BOIES, S. J., EICHELMAN, W. H., and TAYLOR, L. Retention of visual and name codes of single letters. *Journal of Experimental Psychology,* 1969, *7*(No. 1, Pt. 2), 1–16.

POSNER, M. I., and KEELE, S. W. On the genesis of abstract ideas. *Journal of Experimental Psychology,* 1968, *77,* 353–363.

POSNER, M. I., and KEELE, S. W. Retention of abstract ideas. *Journal of Experimental Psychology,* 1970, *83,* 305–308.

POSNER, M. I., NISSEN, M., and KLEIN, R. Visual dominance: an information-processing account of its origins and significance. *Psychological Review,* 1976, *83(2),* 157–171.

PUDOVKIN, V. I. *Film Technique and Film Acting.* Memorial Edition. London: Vision Press, 1958.

PYLYSHYN, Z. W. What the mind's eye tells the mind's brain: A critique of mental imagery. *Psychological Bulletin,* 1973, *80,* 1–24.

RAYNER, K. The perceptual span and peripheral cues in reading. *Cognitive Psychology,* 1975, *7,* 65–81.

REED, S. K. Pattern recognition and categorization. *Cognitive Psychology,* 1972, *3,* 382–407.

REED, S. K. *Psychological Processes in Pattern Recognition.* New York: Academic Press, 1973.

REED, S. K., and JOHNSEN, J. A. Detection of parts in patterns and images. *Memory and Cognition,* 1975, *3,* 569–575.

REICHER, G. M. Perceptual recognition as a function of meaningfulness of stimulus material. *Journal of Experimental Psychology,* 1969, *81,* 275–280.

REISZ, K., and MILLAR, G. *The Technique of Film Editing.* New York: Hasting House, 1968.

RESTLE, F. Moon illusion explained on the basis of relative size. *Science,* 1970, *167,* 1092–1096.

RIGGS, L. Curvature as a feature of pattern vision. *Science,* 1973, *181,* 1070–1072.

RIGGS, L., RATLIFF, F., CORNSWEET, J., and CORNSWEET, T. The disappearance of steadily fixated visual test objects. *Journal of the Optical Society of America,* 1953, *43,* 493–501.

ROCK, I., and EBENHOLTZ, S. The relational determination of perceived size. *Psychological Review,* 1959, *66,* 387.

ROCK, I., and EBENHOLTZ, S. Stroboscopic movement based on change of phenomenal rather than retinal location. *American Journal of Psychology,* 1962, *75,* 193–207.

ROCK, I., HILL, A., and FINEMAN, M. Speed constancy as a function of size constancy. *Perception and Psychophysics,* 1968, *4,* 37–40.

ROSCH, E. Cognitive representations of semantic categories. *Journal of Experimental Psychology: General,* 1975, *104,* 192–233.

ROSENBLATT, F. *Principles of neurodynamics.* New York: Spartan Books, 1962.

RUBIN, E. *Visuell wahrgenommene Figuren.* Copenhagen: Glydendalske, 1921.

RUBIN, Z. Measurement of romantic love. *Journal of Personality and Social Psychology,* 1970, *16,* 265–273.

RYAN, T. A., and SCHWARTZ, C. B. Speed of perception as a function of mode of representation. *American Journal of Psychology,* 1956, *69,* 60–69.

SANFORD, E. C. *A course in Experimental Psychology. Part 1: Sensation and Perception.* London: Heath, 1897.

SAUCER, R. Processes of motion perception. *Science,* 1954, *120,* 806–807.

SCHACHTER, S. The interaction of cognition and physiological determinants of emotional state. *Advances in Experimental Social Psychology,* 1964, *1,* 49–80.

SCHACHTER, S., and SINGER, J. E. Cognitive, social, and physiological determinants of emotional state. *Psychological Review,* 1962, *69,* 379–399.

SCHIFFMAN, H. R., and LORE, R. Depth perception in the rat *(Rattus Norvegicus):* prepotency of three-dimensional over two-dimensional surfaces. *Perception,* 1975, *4,* 73–77.

SCHLOSBERG, H. The description of facial expressions in terms of two dimensions. *Journal of Experimental Psychology,* 1952, *44,* 235.

SCHMIDT, R. A. A schema theory of discrete motor skill learning. *Psychological Review,* 1975, *82,* 225–260.

SCHOEDEL, J., FREDERICKSON, W. A., and KNIGHT, J. M. An extrapolation of the physical attractiveness and sex variables within the Byrne attraction paradigm. *Memory and Cognition,* 1975, *3,* 527–530.

SEARLE, J. R. *Speech acts: an essay in the philosophy of language.* Cambridge: Cambridge University Press, 1969.

SECORD, P. Facial features and interference processes in interpersonal perception. In R. Tagiuri and L. Petrillo eds., *Person Perception and Interpersonal Behavior*. Stanford: Stanford University Press, 1958. Pp. 310–315.

SECORD, P., BACKMAN, C. W., and EACHUS, H. T. Effects of imbalance in the self-concept on perception of persons. *Journal of Abnormal and Social Psychology*, 1964, *68*, 442–446.

SECORD, P., and MUTHARD, J. Personalities in faces, IV: A descriptive analysis of the perception of women's faces and the identification of some physiognomic determinants. *Journal of Psychology*, 1955, *39*, 269–278.

SEGAL, S., and FUSELLA, V. Influences of imaged pictures and sounds on detection of visual auditory signals. *Journal of Experimental Psychology*, 1970, *83*(3), 458–464.

SEGALL, M., CAMPBELL, D., and HERSKOVITZ, M. *The Influence of Culture on Visual Perceptions*. Indiana: Bobbs-Merrill, 1966.

SEKULER, R., and GANZ, L. Aftereffect of seen motion with a stabilized retinal image. *Science*, 1963, *139*, 419–420.

SEKULER, R., and LEVINSON, E. The perception of moving targets. *Scientific American*, 1977, *236* (1), 60–73.

SEKULER, R., and NASH, D. Speed of size scaling in human vision. *Psychonomic Science*, 1972, *27*, 93–94.

SEKULER, R., and PANTLE, A. A model for aftereffects of seen movement. *Vision Research*, 1967, *7*, 427–439.

SHELDON, W. H., and TUCKER, W. B. *The Varieties of Human Physique*. New York: Harper, 1940.

SHEPARD, R. N., and JUDD, S. A. Perceptual illusion of rotation of three-dimensional objects. *Science*, 1976, *191*, 952–954.

SHEPARD, R. N., and METZLER, J. Mental rotation of three-dimensional objects. *Science*, 1971, 701–703.

SHIFFRIN, R. M. The locus and role of attention in memory systems. In P. M. A. Rabbitt and S. Dornic, eds., *Attention and Performance*. Vol. V. London: Academic Press, 1975.

SHIFFRIN, R. M., MCKAY, D. P., and SHAFFER, W. O. Attending to forty-nine spatial positions at once. *Journal of Experimental Psychology: Human Perception and Performance*, 1976, *2*, 14–22.

SIMON, H. An information processing explanation of some perceptual phenomena. *British Journal of Psychology*, 1967, *58*, 1–12.

SIMON, H. What is a chunk? *Science*, 1974, *183*, 482–488.

SINGER, J. The use of manipulative strategies: Machiavellianism and attractiveness. *Sociometry*, 1964, *27*, 128–150.

SINGER, H., and RUDDELL, R. G. *Theoretical models and processes of reading*, 2nd Ed. Newark, Delaware: International Reading Association, 1976.

SMITH, F., LOTT, D., and CRONNELL, B. The effect of type size and case alternation on word identification. *American Journal of Psychology*, 1969, *8*, 215–218.

SMITH, K., and SMITH, W. *Perception and Motion.* Philadelphia: Saunders, 1962.

SMITH, O. W., and SMITH, P. C. An illusion of parallelism. *Perceptual and Motor Skills,* 1962, *15,* 455–461.

SMITH, O. W., and SMITH, P. C. Developmental studies of spatial judgments by children and adults. *Perceptual and Motor Skills,* 1966, *22,* 3–73.

SMITH, P. B. Controlled studies of the outcome of sensitivity training. *Psychological Bulletin,* 1975, *82,* 597–602.

SNODGRASS, J. G. Psychophysics. In *Experimental Sensory Psychology.* Bertram Scharf, ed., Glenview, Illinois: Scott, Foresman & Co., 1975, 17–67.

SONODA, G. Perceptual constancies observed in plane pictures. *Bulletin of the faculty of literature of Kyushu University,* 1961, *7,* 199–228.

SORCE, J. F., and CAMPOS, J. J. The role of expression in the recognition of a face. *American Journal of Psychology,* 1974, *87,* 71–82.

SPERLING, G. The information available in brief visual presentations. *Psychological Monographs,* 1960, *74,*(11, Whole No. 498).

SPERLING, G. A model for visual memory tasks. *Human Factors,* 1963, *5,* 19–31.

SPOTTISWOODE, R. *A Grammar of the Film.* Berkeley: University of California Press, 1962.

STERNBERG, S. Memory-scanning: Mental processes revealed by reaction-time experiments. *American Scientist,* 1969, *57,* 421–457.

STEVENS, S. S. To honor Fechner and repeal his law. *Science,* 1961, *133,* 80–86.

STROMEYER, C. and JULESZ, B. Spatial-frequency masking in vision: Critical bands and spread of masking. *Journal of the Optical Society of America,* 1972, *62,* 1221–1232.

STRONGMAN, K. T., and CHAMPNESS, B. G. Dominance hierarchies and conflict in eye contact. *Acta Psychologica,* 1968, *28,* 376–386.

STROOP, J. R. Studies of interference in serial verbal reactions. *Journal of Experimental Psychology,* 1935, *18,* 643–662.

TAUSCH, R. Optische Taüschungen als artifizielle Effekte der Gestaltungsprozesse von grossen und Formenkonstanz in der naturlichen Raumwahrnehmung. *Psychologische Forschung,* 1954, *24,* 299–348.

THOMPSON, M. C., and MASSARO, D. W. Visual information and redundancy in reading. *Journal of Experimental Psychology,* 1973, *98,* 49–54.

THOMPSON, T. Visual reinforcement in Siamese Fighting Fish. *Science,* 1963, *141,* 55–57.

THORNDIKE, E. The instinctive reactions of young chicks. *Psychological Review,* 1899, *6,* 282–291.

TINKER, M. A. *Legibility of print.* Ames: Iowa State University Press, 1963.

TOLMAN, E. C. *Purposive Behavior in Animals and Men.* New York: Century, 1932.

TOLMAN, E. C. Cognitive maps in rats and men. *Psychological Review*, 1948, *53*, 189–208.

TOWNSEND, J. T. Some results concerning the identifiability of parallel and serial processes. *British Journal of Mathematical and Statistical Psychology*, 1972, *25*, 168–199.

TRAVERS, J. R. Word recognition with forced serial processing: Effects of segment size and temporal order variation. *Perception and Psychophysics*, 1974, *16*, 35–42.

TRIESMAN, A. M. Contextual cues in selective listening. *Quarterly Journal of Experimental Psychology*, 1960, *12*, 242–248.

TRIESMAN, A. M. Monitoring and storage of irrelevant messages and selective attention. *Journal of Verbal Learning and Verbal Behavior*, 1964, *3*, 449–459.

TRIESMAN, A. M., and GEFFEN, G. Selective attention: Perception or response? *Quarterly Journal of Experimental Psychology*, 1967, *19*, 1–18.

TRIESMAN, A. M. Strategies and models of selective attention. *Psychological Review*, 1969, 76(3) 282–299.

UTTAL, W. R. *An Autocorrelation Theory of Form Detection*. Hillsdale, N. J.: Erlbaum, 1975.

VALINS, S. Cognitive effects of false heart-rate feedback. *Journal of Personality and Social Psychology*, 1966, *4*, 400–408.

VANDERPLAS, J. M., SANDERSON, W. R., and VANDERPLAS, J. N. Statistical and associational characteristics of 1,100 random shapes. *Perceptual and Motor Skills*, 1965, *21*, 339–348.

VORKAPICH, S. A fresh look at the dynamics of filmmaking. *American Cinematographer*, February 1972.

WALD, G. The receptors for human color vision. *Science*, 1964, *145*, 1007–1017.

WALK, R., and DODGE S. Visual depth perception of a ten-month-old monocular human infant. *Science*, 1962, (134, 1692)

WALKER, E. L. Psychological complexity and preference: A hedgehog theory of behavior. In D. E. Berlyne and K. B. Madsen, eds., *Pleasure, Reward, Preference*. New York: Academic Press, 1973, 65–97.

WALLACH, H. On constancy of visual speed. *Psychological Review*, 1939, *46*, 547–552.

WALLACH, H. Brightness constancy and the nature of achromatic colors. *Journal of Experimental Psychology*, 1948, *38*, 310–324.

WALLACH, H. Perception of motion. *Scientific American*, 1959, *201*, 56–60.

WALLACH, H., O'CONNELL, D. N., and NEISSER, U. The memory effect of visual perception of three-dimensional form. *Journal of Experimental Psychology*, 1953, *45*, 360–368.

WALLACH, H., YEBLICH, G., and SMITH, A. Target distance and adaptation in distance perception in the constancy of visual direction. *Perception and Psychophysics*, 1972, *11*, 3–34.

WALSTER, E., ARONSON, V., ABRAHAMS, D., and NOTTMAN, L. Importance of physical attractiveness in dating behavior. *Journal of Personality and Social Psychology,* 1966, *4,* 508–516.

WARREN, R. E. Stimulus encoding and memory. *Journal of Experimental Psychology,* 1972, *94,* 90–100.

WARREN, R. E. and HESS, M. On the representation of certain digit sequences in memory. *Bulletin of the Psychonomic Society,* 1975, *6,* 213–215.

WARREN, R.M., OBUSEK, C. J., FARMER, R. M., and WARREN, R. P. Auditory sequence: Confusion of patterns other than speech or music. *Science,* 1969, *164,* 585–587.

WARREN, R. M., and WARREN, R. P. A critique of Stevens' "new psychophysics." *Perceptual and Motor Skills,* 1963, *16,* 797–810.

WARREN, R. M. and WARREN R. P. Auditory illusions and confusions. *Scientific American,* 1970, *223,* 30–36.

WEINER, B. *Theories of Motivation: From Mechanism to Cognition.* Chicago: Markham, 1972.

WEINER, B., FRIEZE, I., KUKLA, A., REED, F., REST, S., and ROSENBAUM, R. *Perceiving the causes of success and failure.* Morristown, N.J.: General Learning Press, 1971.

WEISSTEIN, N., and BISAHA, J. Gratings mask bars and bars mask gratings: Visual frequency response to aperiodic stimuli. *Science,* 1972, *176,* 1047–1049.

WERTHEIMER, MAX Principles of perceptual organization. In D. Beardslee and M. Wertheimer, eds., *Readings in Perception.* Princeton: Van Nostrand, 1958. Pp. 115–135.

WERTHEIMER, MICHAL Psychomotor co-ordination of auditory and visual space at birth. *Science,* 1961, *134,* 1692.

WHEELER, D. Processes in word recognition. *Cognitive Psychology,* 1970, *1,* 59–85.

WIST, E., DIENES, H., DICHGANS, J., and BRANDT, T. Perceived distance and the perceived speed of self-motion: Linear vs. angular velocity? *Perception and Psychophysics,* 1975, *17,* 549–554.

WITKIN, H., LEWIS, H., HERTZMAN, M., MACHOVER, K., MEISSNER, P., and WAPNER, S. *Personality Through Perception.* New York: Harper, 1954.

WOHLGEMUTH, A. On the aftereffect of seen movement. *British Journal of Psychological Monographs,* 1911, Supplement 1.

WOOD, R. W. The "haunted-swing" illusion. *Psychological Review,* 1895, *2,* 277–278.

WOODWORTH, R. *Experimental Psychology.* New York: Holt, Rinehart and Winston, 1938.

YIN, R. Looking at upside-down faces. *Journal of Experimental Psychology,* 1969, *81,* 141–145.

YONAS, A., and HAGEN, M. Effects of static and kinetic depth information on the perception of size in children and adults. *Journal of Experimental Child Psychology,* 1973, *15,* 254–265.

ZANFORLIN, M. Some observations on Gregory's theory of perceptual illusions. *Quarterly Journal of Experimental Psychology,* 1967, *29,* 193–197.

ZUSNE, L. *Visual Perception of Form.* New York: Academic Press, 1970.

Illustration Credits
and References

2A: This figure by W. E, Hill was first published in *Puck — The Comic Weekly* in 1915.

2C: Photo by H. H. Pittman from the National Audubon Society Collection. By permission of Photo Researchers, Inc.

2D: By permission of Wide World Photos, Inc.

11: Modified from illustrations on p. 24 of *Color As Seen and Photographed*, 2nd ed., 1971. By permission of Eastman Kodak Company.

14: Modified from illustrations on p. 24 of *Color As Seen and Photographed*, 2nd ed., 1971. By permission of Eastman Kodak Company.

15: Adapted from L. Hurvich and D. Jameson, An Opponent-Process Theory of Color Vision, *Psychological Review,* Vol. 64 (1957), 384–404. Copyright 1957 by the American Psychological Association. Reprinted by permission.

17: Adapted from *The Seeing Eye* by H. Asher (London: Gerald Duckworth & Co. Ltd.). Used by permission.

36B: "The 'Visual Cliff'" by Eleanor J. Gibson and Richard D. Walk, *Scientific American,* April 1960. Photo by William Vandivert. Used with permission of the *Scientific American* and William Vandivert.

40: Courtesy Institute for International Social Research, Princeton, N.J.

45A: Based on Lloyd Kaufman and Irvin Rock, The Moon Illusion, *Scientific American,* July 1962. Used with permission.

46D: Courtesy of the American Museum of Natural History.

51A-1: W. Kohler and H. Wallach, Figural After-Effects, an Investigation of Visual Process, *Proceedings* of the American Philosophical Society, Vol. 88, No. 4 (1944), 269–357. Reprinted by permission.

51B: Based on, Experiments with Goggles, by Ivo Kohler, *Scientific American,* May 1962. Used with permission.

51C: This figure by W. E. Hill was first published in *Puck — The Comic Weekly* in 1915.

54B: Redrawn from J. E. Hochberg and J. Beck, Apparent Spatial Arrangement and Perceived Brightness, *Journal of Experimental Psychology,* Vol. 47 (1954). 263–66.

59A: From *The Perception of the Visual World* by James J. Gibson. Copyright © 1950 by James J. Gibson. Used by permission of Houghton Mifflin Company.

59B: J. Gibson, P. Olum, and F. Rosenblatt, Parallax and Perspective during Aircraft Landings, *American Journal of Psychology,* Vol. 68 (1955), 372–85. Copyright 1955 by the University of Illinois Press. Used with permission.

59C: From *The Perception of the Visual World* by James J. Gibson. Copyright © 1950 by James J. Gibson. Used by permission of Houghton Mifflin Company.

59D-1&2: General Electric Project *Contact Analog.*

59E: Bowen, K. F. and Smith, W. M. The effects of delayed and displaced visual feedback on motor control. Dartmouth College: Department of Psychology, 1977.

65B: J. E. Hochberg and V. Brooks, The Psychophysics of Form: Reversible-Perspective Drawings of Spatial Objects, *American Journal of Psychology,* Vol. 73 (1960), 337–54. Copyright © 1960 by the University of Illinois Press. Used with permission.

65C: F. Attneave, Some Informational Aspects of Visual Perception, *Psychological Review,* Vol. 61 (1954), Figs. 1 and 2. Copyright 1954 by the American Psychological Association. Reprinted by permission.

69: Adapted from L. Penrose and R. Penrose. Impossible objects: a special type of visual illusion. *British Journal of Psychology,* 1958, *49,* 31–33.

70: Adapted from E. H. Gombrich, J. E. Hochberg, and M. Black, *Art, Perception, and Reality* (Baltimore: The Johns Hopkins University Press, 1972). Reprinted by permission.

72A,B: Adapted from Shepard, R. N. and Judd, S. H. Perceptual illusion of rotation of three-dimensional objects. *Science,* 1976, *191,* 952–954.

74B-1: Bradley, D. R., Dumais, S. T., and Petry, H. M. Reply to Cavonius, *Nature,* 1976, May 6, *261,* 77–78.

74B-3: Coren, S. C. Subjective contours and apparent depth. *Psychological Review,* 1972, *79,* 359–367.

76: Eriksen, C. W., and Spencer, T. Rate of information processing in visual pattern perception. *Journal of Experimental Psychology,* 1967, *74,* 476–484.

82: Harold Schlosberg, The Description of Facial Expressions in Terms of Two Dimensions, *Journal of Experimental Psychology,* Vol. 44 (1952), 235. Copyright 1952 by the American Psychological Association. Photographs reprinted by permission.

84A-1: By permission of the New York Zoological Society.

84A-2: Travis I. Thompson, Visual Reinforcement in Siamese Fighting Fish, *Science,* Vol. 141 (1963), 55–57. Copyright 1963 by the American Association for the Advancement of Science. Used with permission.

84C-2: Reprinted with permission of author and publisher from: Gardner, Beatrice T., and Wallach, Lise. Shapes of Figures Identified As a Baby's Head. *Perceptual and Motor Skills,* 1965, 20, 135–142.

Name Index

Subject Index

Page numbers set in bold face indicate where definitions or examples are given.